D0712801

Help at Any Cost

Help at Any Cost

HOW THE TROUBLED-TEEN INDUSTRY CONS PARENTS AND HURTS KIDS

MAIA SZALAVITZ

RIVERHEAD BOOKS

New York

2006

RIVERHEAD BOOKS
Published by the Penguin Group
Penguin Group (USA) Inc., 375 Hudson Street, New York, New York 10014, USA ·
Penguin Group (Canada), 90 Eglinton Avenue East, Suite 700, Ontario M4P 2Y3,
Canada (a division of Pearson Penguin Canada Inc.) · Penguin Books Ltd, 80 Strand,
London WC2R 0RL, England · Penguin Ireland, 25 St Stephen's Green, Dublin 2,
Ireland (a division of Penguin Books Ltd) · Penguin Group (Australia), 250 Camberwell Road,
Camberwell, Victoria 3124, Australia (a division of Pearson Australia Group Pty Ltd) ·
Penguin Books India Pvt Ltd, 11 Community Centre, Panchsheel Park,
New Delhi–110 017, India · Penguin Group (NZ), Cnr Airborne and Rosedale Roads,
Albany, Auckland 1310, New Zealand (a division of Pearson New Zealand Ltd) ·
Penguin Books (South Africa) (Pty) Ltd, 24 Sturdee Avenue, Rosebank,
Johannesburg 2196, South Africa

Penguin Books Ltd, Registered Offices: 80 Strand, London WC2R 0RL, England

Library of Congress Cataloging-in-Publication Data

Szalavitz, Maia.
Help at any cost : how the troubled-teen industry cons parents and hurts kids / Maia Szalavitz.
p. cm.
Includes bibliographical references.
ISBN 1-59448-910-6
1. Youth—Services for—United States. 2. Behavior modification—United States.
3. Juvenile detention homes—United States. I. Title.
HV1431.S97 2006 2005044957
362.74'8'0830973—dc22

Printed in the United States of America
1 3 5 7 9 10 8 6 4 2

BOOK DESIGN BY AMANDA DEWEY

Some names and identifying characteristics of individuals have been changed;
an asterisk at first mention indicates that a person's actual name is not used.

While the author has made every effort to provide accurate telephone numbers and Internet
addresses at the time of publication, neither the publisher nor the author assumes any responsibility for errors, or for changes that occur after publication. Further, the publisher does
not have any control over and does not assume any responsibility for author or third-party
websites or their content.

For my father, Miklos Szalavitz, whom I miss terribly, and for "troubled teens," who need to be heard, not harmed

Contents

What we do to our children,
they will do to society.

—PLINY THE ELDER

Introduction

ADOLESCENCE STRIKES FEAR in the hearts of even the best parents—and raising a teenager, even in ideal circumstances, involves many conflicts and constant worry. But what should you do if your son becomes so out-of-control, so defiant, so irresponsible and impulsive that you know he's not just a typical rebellious teen? What can you do if your daughter refuses to "just say no," runs away, risks pregnancy? Where should you turn when the archetypal "troubled teen" is your child?

Over the last four decades, a multibillion-dollar industry[1] has arisen that claims to answer these questions and promises peace to parents who send their children to residential facilities for "tough love." These "behavior modification" programs offer hope to parents who have become desperate, who feel the need for drastic solutions, who have lost faith in the mental health system and perhaps in their own ability to provide effective discipline. For parents whose teens are not yet in deep trouble, the programs claim preventive powers—which amounts to promising an all-purpose answer for any type of adolescent difficulty from depression or minor drug use to out-of-control aggression and defiance. With draconian discipline, they promise to whip difficult kids into shape.

Andrea Bradbury* was one obvious candidate for a tough love program. Her parents, a Florida postal worker and a school lunchroom manager, grew increasingly frustrated by their adopted daughter's mood swings and disobedient behavior, which intensified during her teen years. Her apparent promiscuity was troubling—especially when she began running away from home to be with her various boyfriends. The Bradburys spent many late nights waiting for word about her whereabouts, desperately wanting the phone to ring but also frightened about what news it might bring. They suspected, too, that Andrea's problems were negatively affecting her younger brother, Richard. Andrea just wouldn't follow the rules, wouldn't listen, and wouldn't respond to discipline. Why wasn't their daughter getting the message? What would it take to get through to her?

Bob and Sally Bacon were also deeply concerned about their sixteen-year-old son, Aaron. Bob, an architect, and Sally, who worked various jobs, lived in an upscale neighborhood in Phoenix. Aaron had been a brilliant student and was a popular boy with a sunny personality. But when he hit his sophomore year of high school, his disposition turned darker. His grades sank. He became sullen, taciturn, and dishonest. The Bacons tried family therapy, but nothing seemed to reach him. Bob and Sally had always believed in explaining their values, in talking things out, reasoning everything through. But they worried they had been too soft. Did Aaron need them to put their foot down?

THE PROBLEM OF DIFFICULT, misbehaving teens is one that affects all kinds of families. No matter how ignorant or educated a parent you are, when it's your child at risk, when your beloved baby has grown into someone you desperately want to protect but can no longer understand,

---

*Throughout this book, an asterisk at first mention of a name indicates that the person's real name is not used.

you can become vulnerable to someone who offers answers, especially answers that don't imply mental illness, since there is still such tremendous stigma attached to psychiatric disorders. And adding to parents' quite understandable reluctance to expose themselves to judgment and shame is the fact that treatments for mental and behavioral problems are underfunded, misunderstood, and underresearched. Consequently, it's difficult even to know what type of help to seek, more challenging to find providers who utilize the best practices if you do manage to learn about them, and difficult to afford help if quality treatment can be located.

This is where tough love programs come in. Their main message is this: Today's teens are so out-of-control and so morally compromised that only extremely harsh, perhaps even brutal tactics can keep them in line. A bit of cruelty is necessary, even kind—signifying good parenting, the opposite of abuse. Whether you have been a lenient parent or a strict one doesn't matter, it's not your fault: even the best parenting can be overcome by outside pressures. Awash in America's cultural morass, parents have become too swamped to discipline effectively. And the answer, according to tough love proponents, is that troubled children need to be removed from this toxic environment, isolated, infantilized, and reparented, returned only when they are fully prepared to comply with family rules. To prevent backsliding after treatment, parents are instructed on how to lay down and enforce the law, to make family membership itself contingent on total cooperation.

Tough love residential programs guarantee results—to turn rebellion into happy obedience, defiance into self-discipline—to parents who take their advice. They offer parental absolution: it's the child, inevitably influenced by a decadent and invasive culture, who is at fault, the child who must be sent off to be treated, although, of course, the parents must participate fully in the solution.

Parents who choose such treatment are rarely aware that there's no scientific evidence that favors it, nor do they tend to know about its troubled history marked by abuse and family disruption. They are also unlikely to be informed about how tough love programs almost invariably exaggerate the risks troubled teens face and inflate the severity of their children's particular problems in order to make the sale. They rarely even know, in fact, just who benefits from referring them to a particular program. In this industry, many programs quietly pay "satisfied" parents and seemingly objective "educational consultants" for recommendations, online endorsements, and enrollments.

And because of the shame that surrounds seeking help for teen behavioral problems, parents often don't activate the social networks that they would normally use to seek the best care if, for example, a child had cancer. Worse, the media has been complicit in keeping them in the dark. It has accepted programs' unsubstantiated claims of widespread success as evidence for efficacy instead of demanding scientific proof. Consequently, for the past four decades, the troubled-teen industry, pushing the philosophy of "tough love," has profited from parental shame, media complacency, and government antidrug hyperbole, exploiting families' desperation, fear, and ignorance.

The scope of the problem is difficult to document. It is hard to know exactly how prevalent the tough love philosophy is and how common its most extreme forms are—but University of California sociologist Elliott Currie, who has studied teen residential programs, says the view is so pervasive that he cannot "confidently" say that he knows of any programs which are not influenced by it. At the very least, several hundred facilities that openly advocate the tough love approach are currently in operation in the U.S. or outside the country, but almost exclusively serving American citizens.

Some use Nature as a way of inflicting harsh consequences on noncompliant teens and call themselves wilderness programs; others advertise as military-style "boot camps." Some use military tactics in the wilderness. Some label themselves "specialty," "emotional growth," "behavior modification," or "therapeutic" boarding schools and pitch themselves as an alternative to psychiatry. Some call themselves "residential treatment centers." Still others offer explicitly religious tough love. The proportion of existing teen residential programs that use the most extreme tactics is not known, but it is clear that the idea that tough treatment is necessary dominates the industry.

These programs have enrolled tens of thousands of teens over the years—it is impossible to know how many because no one keeps statistics. Because much of the business is unregulated, it's difficult to know what actually goes on inside many of these facilities. Since almost all claim that all teens' stories of maltreatment or abuse are simply the lies of troublemakers, most complaints are dismissed without investigation. After all, if these kids told the truth, they wouldn't need to be in the program, would they?

All tough love programs share the belief that difficult teens are always acting deliberately, even those who have been diagnosed with mental illnesses—and that through harsh confrontation and deprivation of privileges, they can be broken and resocialized to better conform with parental and societal expectations. Listening to the complaints of such teens would only "enable" further bad behavior; believing their stories would allow them to "manipulate" authorities into serving their selfish ends.

Tough love programs package punishments once seen fit only for juvenile delinquents who had been convicted of serious crimes—and sell them to worried middle- and upper-class parents as "rehabilitation." The programs are pitched as alternatives not just to incarceration, but also to regular schooling and traditional therapies for conditions ranging from attention deficit disorder and other learning disabilities to just plain difficult behavior. Since neither public nor private insurance tends to cover such care, the upper and middle classes are the primary customers. These programs are also sold to parents of children with serious mental illnesses such as bipolar disorder—parents who have often been disappointed by the mental health system and lack of access to long-term residential psychiatric treatment.

The cost of the tough love treatment is comparable to the tuition at an Ivy League university. The programs are not regulated by the federal government, and the states often have little or no oversight. They do not require diagnosis or outside evaluation—they rely simply on parents' accounts of their children's troubles (and their bank accounts) to determine admission. Under case law that allows parents near-absolute discretion over medical and educational decisions for their children, teens can be locked down without appeal until they reach age eighteen—and sometimes even longer.

The stories you'll read here detail treatment programs that utilize punishments banned for use on criminals and by the Geneva Conventions. Beatings, extended isolation and restraint, public humiliation, food deprivation, sleep deprivation, forced exercise to the point of exhaustion, sensory deprivation, and lengthy maintenance of stress positions are common. And even in those programs where physical abuse is absent, incessant verbal attacks are a core component. Program operators typically recommend that children be brought to the facility by surprise: either dropped off by parents without knowing in advance where they are going or taken from their beds in the middle of the night by "escort services," who tend to be large men with handcuffs.

The history of these adolescent residential programs is, in essence, a story of how abusive, dehumanizing practices that reformers of mental hospitals and prisons have attempted to stamp out for centuries have been repackaged and are currently being sold by a booming industry as essential and beneficial for kids. It is also a story of how thousands of well-meaning, caring, and intelligent parents have been taken in by a business that uses exaggerated claims of risk to teens to sell its services. It's a story of splintered families; of parents convinced by program operators that extreme, even traumatically stressful treatments are their children's only hope.

THE IDEA of using "tough love" to reform troubled kids goes back at least as far as the Bible. Modern tough love, however, has two distinct origins. In both, it began as a philosophy for dealing with drug problems and spread outward to other behaviors. It can be summed up as the notion that love and freedom must be made contingent on good behavior.

This concept was first practiced in residential treatment for heroin addicts, beginning with a program called Synanon in 1958. Synanon's basic treatment philosophy was that addicts, by living together and brutally confronting one another about their flaws, could help one another re-cover. Here "tough love" was a way of breaking people down with attack therapy, isolation, and rigid restrictions, and gradually restoring limited freedom and positive affirmation to those who complied.

Counselors Phyllis and David York popularized the idea that families, not just treatment programs, should practice tough love, with their 1982 bestseller, *ToughLove*. According to the Yorks, if a child refuses to stop taking drugs, the rest of the family should withdraw from him com-pletely and expel him from home until he quits. The Yorks' *ToughLove* spawned hundreds of eponymous support groups around the country (including some that carry on today) for parents who wanted help in practicing it.

The Yorks' solution was quite similar to ideas prevalent in support groups for families of alcoholics and addicts, most notably the twelve-step Al-Anon program. Al-Anon members often suggest the tough ap-proach of withdrawing support from an addicted person as a way of preserving the sanity and health of the rest of the family. Al-Anon, how-ever, stresses repeatedly that the effect this has on the alcoholic or addict himself is unpredictable. He might recover, Al-Anon members say—but they also note that he might just leave and get worse. The family, as an Al-Anon slogan puts it, "cannot create, control or cure" addiction.

ToughLove's twist was to claim that harsh measures actually helped end teen problems, rather than just improve life for other family mem-bers. But neither *ToughLove* nor the tough residential programs that took up its philosophy have ever proved that their methods are actually ef-fective in the long run. They let testimonials tell the story, a method that's fine for advertising, but that medical history has shown to be a poor way to sort out helpful treatments from fraudulent ones.

BY EXAMINING four major examples—Straight Incorporated, the North Star wilderness boot camp, the World Wide Association of Specialty Pro-grams, and the KIDS program—this book will demonstrate how both parents and kids can be harmed by these treatments and will reveal the complete lack of evidence for their effectiveness in treating any of the problems they claim to help parents and teens conquer.

The first section looks at Straight Incorporated, the first large-scale tough love program aimed exclusively at teenagers. Straight was born as Ronald Reagan declared war on drugs; Nancy Reagan even called the program her "favorite." But its roots are in two earlier programs with decidedly abusive histories. The first was Synanon, mentioned previously. The second predecessor, The Seed, was a government-funded experimental behavior-modification program based on Synanon and soon found to be similarly abusive. Through the experience of one of Straight's victims, who was at first a strong supporter, then a driven opponent of its methods, the inner workings and widespread influence of the program are made clear.

As the Straight network began to decline in the early '90s, a new form of tough love was rising to prominence: the boot-camp wilderness program, which is covered in the second section of *Help at Any Cost*. Boot camps and wilderness programs had developed separately, but they were brought together as a profitable treatment for teen dysfunction by a Utah entrepreneur in the late '80s. Here, too, Synanon-style attack therapy was used. Concerns about both the safety and the management of these programs became a public issue as teenagers began to die in them. The story of one such death—that of Aaron Bacon, whose story was briefly highlighted previously—and the failure of the system to provide justice for his family illustrate both the potentially fatal flaws in the tough love method and the lack of oversight that still makes such programs dangerous.

The history of tough love repeatedly finds one version becoming "controversial" and contracting while another, superficially different but essentially the same, expands to replace it. The third section of this book looks at the biggest and most successful network of tough love programs now operating, the World Wide Association of Specialty Programs (WWASP). This network currently includes at least six programs in four states and two foreign countries—which are pitched to parents variously as "behavior modification," "boot camp," and "specialty" boarding schools.

WWASP centers on highly confrontational "seminars" and groups, which also owe much to Synanon and to large group trainings like the '70s self-improvement seminars epitomized by Werner Erhard's est.

Three stories here show how the toxic methods of the past still thrive in today's tough love programs: the story of Laurie Berg, a woman who adopted a boy whose parents disowned him when he refused to continue the WWASP program; the story of Karen Lile and Kendall Bean, whose experience with a WWASP parent seminar so frightened them that they removed their daughter from the program; and that of Amberly Knight, who ran a WWASP program but later rejected its tactics when she discovered that they were abusive and couldn't be reformed.

The final section of the book will look at the long-term effects of tough love programs through the lens of a lawsuit brought by one victim, Lulu Corter. She was held for thirteen years in a Straight-copycat program called KIDS. Testimony in the Corter case shows how tough love programs fail the tests for safety and efficacy required of medical treatments and how they can split previously intact families for decades. The story of this trial also shows how civil suits are one way to bring these programs to account.

The book's conclusion will offer solutions for policymakers and analyze why tough love has been so popular for so long despite its evident abuses and failure to produce scientific evidence of efficacy. An appendix to help parents find genuine help for troubled teens is also included.

IN RESEARCHING THIS BOOK, I've found that not only is the notion that tough love is effective incorrect, but even the need for treatment for most of the teens who currently receive it is suspect. Despite the fact that government statistics show that levels of youth violence, suicide, drug use, pregnancy, and overall mortality have all decreased drastically in recent years, the media constantly reiterates the idea that each generation's challenges are worse than the last's. This continuous fearmongering alienates parents from their children. Telling parents that kids today face qualitatively and quantitatively different problems prevents them from considering their own stupid, reckless, youthful behavior and how they lived through and outgrew it. Instead of reassurance related to their own histories, they hear instead from the government, the media and tough-love-promoting "experts" that "it's different now."

When the media presents today's teens as worse than any have been before, when it focuses on "warning signs" that are actually normal behavior for youth, when it pathologizes things like underage drinking, which 82 percent of Americans do,[2] parents are terrorized and consequently very vulnerable to the programs' sales pitch. And this is especially true in today's climate of hyper-parenting, where every physical activity requires safety padding, headgear, and minute supervision and every hiccup leads to a medical exam. In this context, tough love treatments appear to be an obvious choice for kids in trouble—or even a preventive measure for those who seem to be headed that way.

For parents whose children are already using drugs heavily, having risky sex, failing school, running away, and causing constant conflict, the lure is even more irresistible. Don't tens of thousands of teens die each year because of drugs and alcohol? Isn't early intervention needed to break a cycle that could lead to a life of crime? Isn't tough therapy the only thing that gets through to out-of-control teens?

In fact, the answer to each of those three questions is no. Death in one's teens—no matter what the cause—is extremely rare in the United States today. For example, 17,944 youths between ages ten and twenty died in 2002[3] (the latest figure available from the CDC's National Center for Health Statistics): that's from all causes and out of a population of some 40 million people that age. Mortality among teens and young adults dropped nearly 40 percent between 1950 and 2000,[4] and that downward trend has only continued. Even if all of the risky-behavior-related deaths occurred only among the highest-risk kids—the 4 million estimated by the Surgeon General to have serious behavioral and psychological problems[5]—this would still only put their risk of death at four in 1,000 per year.

The need for treatment to solve teen problems has been exaggerated.

For instance, there's no evidence that residential care is better than care given at home—in fact, some studies find that kids in residential treatment do worse than those treated in the community. One study compared kids with depression, anxiety, and attention deficit/hyperactivity disorder randomly assigned to either residential or at-home treatment. It found that 63 percent of those treated at home had fewer symptoms—but that the majority of those in residential care got worse. Only 11 percent of those in live-in treatment improved.[6]

For those involved with alcohol or other drugs, research finds that with parental discipline and no professional help, the majority of teens, even the most troubled, end their heavy drinking and/or out-of-control drug use by their mid-twenties. According to the government-funded Monitoring the Future survey, 6.5 percent of nineteen- and twenty-year-olds smoked marijuana daily in 2003. But just 3.5 percent of twenty-five- and twenty-six-year-olds did so—46 percent fewer.[7] Similar statistics apply when you follow a group over time, rather than look at just one year. The older people get, the less they drink to excess, take drugs, or commit crimes.[8] The dramatic reduction in binge drinking that occurs when people start regular full-time employment (and particularly when they start work after college or get married) is well documented.[9]

The sheer numbers of people who end excessive drug use and drinking in their mid-twenties or sooner cannot possibly be accounted for by self-help group attendance or treatment utilization. There are just too many people and too few groups and treatment centers. Most of these people, often with their parents' guidance and nothing more, just grow up and get their acts together. If you think about your own circle of friends and your own high school and college years, you'll find it probably supports what the research here shows. Many people have a period of being, as George W. Bush notably put it, "young and irresponsible," but most grow up to be normal, productive adults (and they usually do so long before he did, which was in his forties).[10] Tolerating unwanted behavior until their children's early adulthood may not be the solution parents want, but considering the huge risks of available treatments, it is comforting to know that in most cases, the problems do correct themselves over time.

WHAT ALL THIS boils down to is that tough love programs are sold on false premises, exaggerating both the risks to untreated teens and the benefits of residential treatment. It also means that any claim that a program "saved" a kid needs to be taken with a grain of salt—unless there was a control group followed who had the same level of initial problems and who received no treatment or different treatment.

In addition, it signifies that because there's a strong maturational tendency toward health, any treatments for troubled kids need to ensure that they don't block this natural progress and make things worse. That may seem easy, but there's significant evidence that simply grouping problem kids together for treatment and labeling them as deviant enhances, rather than reduces, antisocial behavior.[11] Using such treatment "just in case" is risky. Thinking that "it can't hurt" is erroneous.

AND JUST AS they distort the evidence that kids will die without their help, so too do tough love promoters make claims for their programs' effectiveness that they simply cannot substantiate. Few parents are aware that while there is little evidence that tough love programs help rehabilitate (and none that finds them superior to other methods—boot camps don't even do better than juvenile prison, for example!),[12] there's a great deal of data that suggests the possibility of serious harm. This will be amply demonstrated in the pages ahead. As I write this, the National Institutes of Health have just released a "state of the science" consensus statement on dealing with juvenile delinquency and youth violence. Such statements are not released until the leading experts in a field concur that there is enough evidence and that it leans strongly enough in one direction to allow key conclusions to be drawn.

The NIH draft consensus report on treatment for teens reads in part, "Programs that seek to prevent violence [and other "health-risking" behaviors] through fear and tough treatment do not work[13] . . . and there is some evidence that they may make the problem worse rather than simply not working. . . . Such evidence as there is offers no reason to believe that group detention centers, boot camps, and other "get tough" programs do anything more than provide an opportunity for delinquent youth to amplify negative effects on each other."[14]

Because tough love has become part of American culture, because it has been advocated by some mainstream psychologists and psychiatrists (and because the majority of experts who do oppose it haven't realized the need to publicly denounce it), however, few parents have thought to ask for evidence of its effectiveness. The assumption is that because it's widely recommended, because it's a thriving industry, because the concept is so well known, it works.

But there is no "FDA" that approves behavioral programs that are safe and effective and rejects those that do harm or don't work. There is no requirement that psychotherapies—even for children—be proven safe and effective before they are marketed. The media has always seen parents' stories of tough love success as sufficient evidence of efficacy. When accounts of abuse come out, the media "balances" these complaints with testimonials from supporters. But they rarely ask the larger questions: Which stories are more common? What happens to teens who don't get tough love, despite behavior that might otherwise have prompted it? Who does better?

Much as we'd like to think otherwise, we really can't know if any therapies—even talk therapies that rely on creating narratives about our lives—are helpful just from personal stories, even our own. Without controlled research, it's impossible to know if cure, harm, or lack of response is more likely for a particular group of people. No matter how powerful and plentiful individual accounts are, the plural of "anecdote" is not "scientific data." In fact, what has allowed modern medicine and technology to advance beyond the wildest dreams of our ancestors has been the skeptical and demanding scientific method. But unfortunately, we're not using it here.

This book tells the true story of tough love: how it has been aggressively marketed to unsuspecting parents by people who manipulate their fears and make false promises. It shows how such programs have alienated parents from their own children, telling them in advance to disbelieve complaints of maltreatment and, in fact, advising them to view such complaints as evidence that the child is still "manipulative" and in need of lengthier "therapy." It also demonstrates how tough love reemerges in a new guise every decade or so, each time ending in abuse scandals and lawsuits. It calls for massive reform in the teen-treatment industry to make its practices transparent and provide greater oversight— and it suggests effective alternatives for parents who need help now.

As family life becomes ever more constricted and scheduled, as competition for places in prestigious colleges is heightened, teens have less room for error. Standardized testing has produced standardized teaching, with less and less latitude for teachers to inspire joy in learning. The gifted, the attention-impaired, and the learning-disabled suffer and may consequently "act out," a leading risk for placement in tough love programs. Zero tolerance policies—which expel or suspend kids from regular schools for just one alcohol or drug incident—have spread across the country and can also result in mandated tough love treatment. Post-Columbine incidents that would once have been dismissed as youthful hijinks are now seen as signs of incipient sociopathy. And many caring, intelligent, desperate-to-do-the-right-thing parents are sucked in.

Creative, difficult, challenging teenagers—the ones most likely to become our artists, our writers, our social critics, and our scientists—are at risk in this climate. Tough love programs, no matter how well intended, often wind up destroying these kids in their attempts to save them. If there were good research that showed that such programs are effective, there might be an ethical dilemma over their use. But in the absence of such data—and the presence of much that suggests they produce damage, not improvement—we should stick with the first principle of medical ethics: "First, do no harm."[15]

The stories you are about to read show what happens when that principle is ignored.

ONE

Getting Straight
in the 1980s

THERE WAS SOMETHING very odd about the burglars who broke into the Straight Incorporated facility in early 1988. They had left a nine-step written plan for the crime in their car. One had been caught red-handed on the roof, carrying two pairs of gloves and two ski masks. When the police arrived, a ladder was propped against one of the building's walls; a rope was dangling from an open skylight.

But Richard Bradbury and his accomplice were not stupid. They were committing a desperate act of civil disobedience. They were willing to go to prison, if necessary, to expose the abuses they said they had witnessed at Straight. They hadn't tried to steal valuables—only records that they had legal permission to obtain. Straight had repeatedly—and illegally—refused to surrender them.

It was unusually cold in Pinellas Park, Florida (near St. Petersburg), on the night of the burglary, January 26. Bradbury had chosen the frigid day deliberately, figuring that few Floridians would loiter after the program's board meeting in sub-freezing temperatures. These meetings usually lasted until at least midnight. Bradbury and his friend had watched from their car as the program's cofounder, Mel Sembler, who served as the Republican Party's finance chair for George W. Bush's 2000 presidential campaign, and between 2001 and 2005 as U.S. ambassador to Italy, drove off in his Mercedes. They waited until about one A.M. to strike.

As a former Straight participant as well as an ex-employee, Bradbury knew the warehouselike space intimately. Using tools strapped to his belt, he worked open a skylight. Then, he secured a rope to an air-conditioning unit. He grabbed it and moved down until he was able to grasp the building's rafters, which were roughly two stories above its hard concrete floor. Then he froze. Below, he could see the program's notorious blue plastic chairs, hundreds of them lined up in neat rows. As a Straight participant, Bradbury had spent twelve or more hours a day sitting in one of those hard-backed chairs, ramrod-straight with his hands on his knees, his eyes glued to the person who was speaking.

Those were the rules: teenagers who didn't sit in this precise posture while a counselor or fellow teen in the group was speaking would be dragged to the floor and restrained by their fellow participants. The "misbehaver," as Straight labeled such people, would be placed on his back, while other participants literally sat on his abdomen and legs. A participant would be assigned to control each limb and a fifth person would often hold the misbehaver's head, sometimes slamming the teen's mouth closed and restricting breathing to force compliance. Of course, this happened a lot less frequently and a lot more gently when parents were there for weekly "open meetings." But otherwise, and even sometimes with parents present, the restraints were brutal and could last for hours.

While he worked for Straight, Bradbury thought that young people like him needed such harsh, uncompromising treatment to save their lives. By 1988, however, he had come to see the program as ill conceived. He was spending nearly every waking moment strategizing about how to shut it down. He had masterminded the burglary.

Bradbury worked his way along the rafters, and then forced himself to let go when he was no longer over the chairs. He landed hard but on his feet, then ran to the front office. He had been trying to build a case against the Straight program in order to have state regulators shut it down. In two years, he hadn't gotten far. The burglary plan was part of his growing frustration.

Knowing that a silent alarm would have alerted the police as soon as he and his partner hit the roof, he yelled up to his accomplice to tell him to leave and grabbed some papers. Realizing that they weren't the right documents, he dropped them. Then he heard sirens and ran out the back door. There was no point in going to jail if he didn't have the evidence he needed, he decided.

Behind the facility was a canal, roughly twelve feet deep and sixty feet across. Seeing no other option, Bradbury jumped into the freezing water, but instantly sank because he was still wearing his tools. Fighting his way up, he left them on the stream's bank, swam across the canal and hid in some palmetto branches. For hours, he sat shivering in the brush, listening to police radios, helicopters, and dogs.

RICHARD BRADBURY is an unlikely activist: at thirty-eight, he lives in North Tampa with his parents and has spent only a year and a half of his life living on his own. Adopted by a school lunchroom manager and a postal worker when he was about a year old, Bradbury has lived in the same neighborhood since 1969. His early childhood wasn't particularly remarkable. He recalls it as happy, saying he enjoyed playing baseball, participating in Cub Scouts, and trading Star Wars cards.

His life changed dramatically, however, when he was about eleven. A fireman who lived nearby began to sexually molest him. Like many victims of sexual abuse, Richard didn't feel he could discuss the problem with his parents, so he didn't tell—even when the abuse began to involve several other men. It continued for three or four years. And throughout, Richard kept quiet.

He eventually began to believe that other kids in the neighborhood had heard about his shameful secret. Other boys—either because they, too, had been victimized or because they sensed his shame, he believes—

began to taunt him with homosexual slurs. "Fagbury," they called him, with the acute cruelty of children. Demoralized, Bradbury stopped attending school, missing three or four months of seventh grade and almost all of eighth. He found a job almost as soon as he quit for good. Since both of his parents were high school dropouts themselves, they didn't question his decision. As long as he pulled his weight in the family, high school attendance—let alone college—wasn't expected.

The year he should have been in ninth grade, however, Bradbury decided for himself that he wanted more education. "I decided, 'Well, they can call me what they want, but I'm going to go back,'" he said. The school placed him in a work experience program and he thrived. At fourteen, he was the local Burger King's employee of the year.

By age seventeen, he had his own car—a white 1979 Plymouth Champ—and he even made interest payments on it to his father. He had his own bank account. He wanted to join the Marines. At the time, they required at least a tenth-grade education, so he took the credits he needed. His ultimate goal was to become a sheriff. In short, Richard became the kind of son who would make most American parents extremely proud: sure, he'd tried marijuana and cigarettes once or twice, and he drank sometimes, but he'd never been in trouble with the law and generally behaved well.

His little sister, however, was another story. She had been adopted as a baby when Richard was three and they had clashed from the start. Bradbury now believes that Andrea suffers from mental illness—and she was completely out of control as a teenager. Constantly running away, behaving erratically, cutting school, arguing with her family—in contrast to her brother, she was the wild child every parent fears a teenager might become.

And in the early 1980s, when President Reagan had swept into office with his vision of "Morning in America," parents were especially worried about their teenagers. First Lady Nancy Reagan had begun her public crusade against drugs with a 1982 trip that included a lengthy visit to Straight Incorporated. In fact, Mel Sembler claims that he was the first to suggest that Nancy make drugs her cause.[1] And Straight seemed to inspire her passion for it. After speaking with the youth in the program, Mrs. Reagan told a reporter that America "was in danger of losing a whole generation" to drugs.[2]

Spurred on by her crusade, growing concerns about adolescent drug use spawned a series of checklists for parents, claiming to distinguish between ordinary adolescent angst and teen drug addiction or its "warning signs." Such lists were published in the media and distributed by antidrug groups, like Straight itself, which developed its own version. These lists contained items that could indict nearly every teen at some time, like "living in filthy bedrooms and saying it is their room and they can do what they want,"[3] "leaving dirty dishes around and claiming they did not do it"[4] "sullen, uncaring attitudes and behavior"[5] and "staying out late."[6] They have never been scientifically verified as effective in identifying addicts—but virtually identical lists, including signs like "defiance" and "all black dress" are still distributed by today's tough love programs.[7]

Parents panicked. They worried that any unruly behavior could signify great trouble. While the '70s had been the age of "Let it all hang out," by the beginning of the '80s, the conservative backlash was under way. Money was tight, the Soviet Union threatened nuclear apocalypse, and there was no time for "searching" or "seeking." To stay competitive, America had to be tough and, well, straight.

The parent-led antidrug movement that Nancy Reagan would so enthusiastically sign on to was a big factor in the success of programs like Straight. It had started in the South. In 1976, a woman named Keith Schuchard (who also goes by the name Marsha), an English professor in Atlanta, discovered her daughter's friends smoking marijuana at the girl's thirteenth birthday party. She'd smoked pot herself in college—but seventh-graders doing it? Why weren't people outraged? She organized a meeting to find out and soon found that, indeed, many other parents were worried. By 1979, she had created the Parents' Resource Institute for Drug Education (PRIDE). The group decided that marijuana's dangers, particularly to very young teens, had been underplayed—and that the best way to raise parents' concern about them was to highlight this and link marijuana use to inevitable progression to harder drugs.[8] Thousands of parents joined her in a heavily marijuana-focused antidrug campaign. The average age for trying marijuana in the peak years for marijuana use in the U.S. (the late '70s and early '80s) was eighteen, however;[9] unlike Schuchard's daughter, the vast majority of seventh-graders, then and now, were not getting stoned. Even fewer would ever try hard drugs.

Phyllis and David York's book *ToughLove* became parents' antidrug manifesto. Both Yorks were licensed therapists who labeled their own children "rotten." Phyllis herself had experimented with heroin in her youth and had moved on without outside help, but she, like Schuchard, dismissed her own experience as irrelevant to today's drug problem. It was "exploring higher consciousness"[10] she wrote. These kids today, in contrast, were just "getting high" for "no other effect than the pleasure."[11] Their hedonistic and impulsive desires put them "at risk." "Like clones stamped out in some satanic laboratory, they share an underlying selfishness,"[12] Phyllis York claimed.

The only answer was to crack down hard, *ToughLove* proclaimed. There was no room for "touchy-feely" stuff and understanding why kids seek escape. These kids had to be stopped. The Yorks had inadvertently discovered the ToughLove method when, infuriated by their daughter's drug arrest, they refused to bail her out. Their other daughter offered to help her sister instead, but Phyllis shrieked, "I'll kill you! You will not make her bail."[13] The couple even refused to visit their daughter in treatment—and they believed that their own firm stance, not treatment, sparked her recovery.

Dismissing their own profession, the Yorks claimed that counseling "only prolonged the problems by looking for the cause in the family's behavior." The fault lay entirely with the children. Parents had to take back control. Their only failure was lack of discipline—and this, not mental distress or any other psychological, social, or biological cause— was the root of their children's troubles. Parents were urged to set firm limits, not post bail if a child had legal trouble and require treatment completion as a condition of any continued family support. The Yorks had no evidence other than their own limited experience with their daughter to support these prescriptions. But they were incredibly popular. *ToughLove* support groups sprung up around the country, and soon many parents in it recommended Straight Incorporated.

The Bradburys were referred to Straight by a friend who had a son enrolled and believed it had saved his life. Richard's sister was signed up. The Bradburys had been told that Straight could turn even the worst teenager around, and their daughter certainly seemed to qualify. And Straight officials said that Andrea would be dead or in prison within a year if they didn't enroll her.

Since Richard found his sister's antics irritating and embarrassing, he wasn't especially upset when she was sent away. Nor was he surprised that it had happened: his parents had been trying to figure out what to do with her for years. The proceedings had been very secretive, however—one day, Andrea was just gone. Richard continued to work diligently toward his goal of being a sheriff, completing the high school credits he needed to join the Marines. He was ready to make a life for himself. He had no idea what Straight would soon mean to him.

On April 16, 1983, his world would be shattered forever.

IN NOVEMBER 1974, Senator Sam Ervin (D–North Carolina) presented a report to Congress entitled "Individual Rights and the Federal Role in Behavior Modification." Ervin is best known for heading the Senate committee that investigated Watergate and helped bring down President Nixon, and when this report was issued, he led the Senate's Subcommittee on Constitutional Rights. Ervin saw attempts to psychologically change people's behavior without their consent as a potential threat to American self-determination. Serving with him on the committee that wrote the report were such diverse politicians as Senator Edward Kennedy (D–Massachusetts) and Strom Thurmond (R–South Carolina).

The report was spurred by disturbing accounts of federal funding for human experiments on prisoners, mental patients, juvenile delinquents, and others, which, Ervin wrote in its preface, attempted to "develop new methods of behavior control capable of altering not just an individual's actions but his very personality and his manner of thinking."[14] Ervin noted that this research was being conducted "in the absence of strict controls"[15] and questioned whether the federal government had any business carrying out experiments that could "pose substantial threats to our basic freedoms."[16]

The report noted that behavior modification was not like ordinary learning because it "is not based on the reasoned exchange of information."[17] Ervin conceded that such therapies could be useful in certain circumstances, but he did not think the threat that they posed to personal liberty should be dismissed lightly.

Ervin's investigators discovered that the federal government was funding a great deal of diverse research in the area. Experiments were even being conducted on children and teenagers, often without the knowledge or consent of their parents. One of the programs that came under scrutiny was a federally funded Florida program for teens known as "The Seed." The investigators described the methods of such treatment this way:

> Individuals are required to participate in group therapy discussions where intensive pressure is often placed on the individuals to accept the attitudes of the group. More intensive forms of encounter groups begin first by subjecting the individual to isolation and humiliation in a conscious effort to break down his psychological defenses. Once the individual is submissive, his personality can begin to be reformed around attitudes determined by the program director to be acceptable. *[It is] similar to the highly refined brainwashing techniques employed by the North Koreans in the early 1950's* [emphasis added].[18]

Neither the teens enrolled in The Seed nor their parents were told that these methods were experimental. Nor were they informed that by 1973, research had been published suggesting that such encounter groups could cause lasting emotional damage. One major study of these groups found that 9.1 percent of those who completed more than half of the sessions had long-term psychological difficulties that lasted at least six months following the end of their time in the group.[19] These difficulties included depressions severe enough to require hospitalization, suicidal thoughts, manic and psychotic episodes, and reductions in self-esteem. There was even one suicide, but researchers thought it was caused by other factors. The 200-plus subjects in this study were normal college students interested in self-exploration who could drop out at any time[20]—not troubled teens with no choice in the matter like those sent to The Seed.

Worse, the most damaging types of encounter groups, according to the authors of the study, were those with a highly aggressive leader who harshly berated participants and had group members attack one another to produce conformity. One of the groups that had the highest level of casualties was Synanon, which was the model for The Seed's program.[21]

The program that the Bradbury kids attended, the one that Nancy Reagan would later call her "favorite," Straight Incorporated, had sprung directly from The Seed. It was founded, in fact, by Seed parent participants after bad publicity related to the Ervin report and other media and regulatory attacks made recruiting new patients to The Seed difficult. But Straight's methods—from its extreme confrontation to its rigid structure—were virtually identical to those of The Seed and quite similar to Synanon. At first, Straight was staffed nearly entirely by former "Seedlings" and their parents. And similar techniques—in some cases, identical "therapies" and structures and in some cases even the same blue plastic chairs (!)—are still used in hundreds of programs holding thousands of American teenagers today.

WHEN HE WAS SEVENTEEN, Richard Bradbury was told by his parents that he had to be "checked out" by Straight Incorporated or he had to leave home. The vehemence of their threat startled him. "I thought, 'What is all this?' I was just completely taken aback," he said.

His sister, however, was advancing in Straight. "Newcomers"—those just starting the program's "first phase"—lived with families of participants who were further along, called "oldcomers." In order for Andrea to be allowed to return home for her "second phase," the Bradburys had to set up their house as a "host home" for newer patients, just as other parents had previously housed their daughter.

The rationale for requiring Richard to be "checked out" by Straight was that because he was living in a home that would soon host "newcomers," the program had to be sure he wasn't a "druggie" and bad influence. Of course, discovering that siblings of participants also needed treatment could be a lucrative source of additional customers, but parents who'd come to see the program as a savior didn't look for such conflicts of interest. Straight was a nonprofit, so it didn't occur to them that it could have expansionary motives or seek to enrich its top employees.

Host homes were specially prepared to incarcerate often unwilling teens. They were inspected to ensure that this was done properly. Motion detectors were placed on the doors of the bedrooms in which the teens would sleep. The oldcomer who lived there would place his or her bed against the bedroom door at night to further prevent escape. Windows were locked. Fire safety wasn't a consideration. As one father later told 60 Minutes, "One of the questions I asked in the early training sessions we were going through [was], 'What if my home were to catch on fire during the night?' and they said, the standard answer was, if your child was on the street, your child would die, in case of a fire, your child would die, so you're not any worse off."[22]

Also for security, anytime a newcomer wanted to walk, he or she would have to ask permission of the oldcomer and be guided to the destination—even into the bathroom—with the oldcomer's hand on the belt loop at the back of the newcomer's pants. Even on the toilet or in the shower, newcomers were to be closely observed.

This setup allowed Straight to provide what was essentially inpatient treatment at low cost and without regulation of the conditions of the young people's confinement. True, new participants didn't sleep at the facility—but they didn't sleep in their own homes, either, for months and sometimes years. The "host" homes where they stayed were essentially locked-down foster care—but of a peculiar type, where neither the home nor the family had been vetted for safety the way ordinary foster families are. For regulatory purposes, of course, the program could present itself as "outpatient" because it could honestly claim that the teens didn't live at its facility. But this wasn't how it felt to the kids, who stayed with strangers for months or more, locked in at night.

And parents didn't learn the restrictive particulars of host home arrangements—or the peculiar logic for neglecting fire safety—until they'd already been involved with the program for several months and been impressed by its results on their child. Their formerly slovenly, defiant, foul-mouthed teenagers were now neatly dressed and begging forgiveness. The girl who'd said how much she hated you was now expressing deep love and apologizing for the heartache she'd caused; she seemed finally to understand that you'd only restricted her out of love. The sullen boy who'd cussed you out was now calmly saying how much he respected your opinions and that he, too, wanted only to rejoin the family he'd so often angrily dismissed. These transformations eased any doubts that parents had about the rigid rules of confinement. The fact that they could see hundreds of other parents following the same strictures and getting the same good results quelled any lingering concern when they had to set up their own "host home."

Sure, some of what the program recommended did appear awfully harsh. But it was powerful stuff they were dealing with at Straight— powerful stuff that could be misunderstood if you didn't realize the dangers that drugs posed. You could see a kid who'd come in looking like the absolute scowling stereotype of a rebellious long-haired druggie on the road to death, and a month later, there he was with a crew cut and a sweet smile and a hug for Mom and Dad. Any doubts you had about the way the kids led each other around by the belt loop, the way some were restrained on the floor, faded away. If that's what was necessary to get your kid back, then that's what a good parent had to do. No one wanted to be seen as the parent who wouldn't go that last mile for their child.

So, because they had absolutely no reason to believe he was involved with drugs and no reason to question the program, Richard's parents told him that his interview at Straight would be a formality. Five minutes, that's it. And since Richard knew he didn't have a drug problem, he didn't think being screened for one would pose problems. He had no idea how Straight's intake process really worked. He wouldn't be going home for months and wouldn't leave the Straight program for over two years. He says, in fact, that in his mind he's never been able to leave.

SYNANON BEGAN as a clique of Alcoholics Anonymous members who gathered around a man named Chuck Dederich in Santa Monica, California in the late 1950s. Dederich had been born in 1913 in Toledo, Ohio. Because of his heavy drinking and subsequent failure in his sales career, his second wife introduced him to the twelve-step fellowship of AA. He became a fanatical convert—but was also convinced that he could improve on the system.

AA's name is familiar to most Americans. The content of its twelve steps—and the emphasis the program places on being a volunteer organization, rather than something that should be forced on people—is not as well known. AA began when two alcoholics met in Akron, Ohio, in 1935 and recognized that although on their own they couldn't stay sober, by helping each other, they could. Its steps involve admitting one's "powerlessness" over alcohol (step one), then surrendering to "a power greater than ourselves" or "God as we understood Him" in order to be "restored to sanity" (steps two and three). The process also involves taking "moral inventory" and "admitting to God, to ourselves and another human being the exact nature of our wrongs" (steps four and five), as well as asking Him to "remove these defects of character" (steps six and seven). Finally, members are expected to make amends to those they have harmed (steps nine and ten), practice prayer and meditation (eleven), and spread the message about AA's effectiveness to others (the twelfth step).

AA's own literature stresses repeatedly that the program is "for people who want it, not people who need it." In other words, the process of surrender, confession, and helping others should be entered into by choice, not because family members or the criminal justice system demand it.

But many who adapted AA's ideas to treatment programs, as Synanon, The Seed, and Straight would do, ignored this. They decided, instead, that coercion was essential. Over time, this authoritarian position would become firmly ensconced in American addiction treatment, especially for young people.

Synanon won national and international acclaim following Dederich's "discovery" that his small group of alcoholics had managed to "cure" a heroin addict, a feat that in the '50s was believed impossible. The heroin addict had attended Dederich's weekly meetings, which were brutally direct, no-holds-barred encounter groups aimed at attacking people's AA-confessed "character defects" and speeding their "return to sanity." These sessions were called "the game," while addicts became known as "character disorders."

Synanon took its name from an addict's attempt to pronounce seminar and symposium at the same time, according to most accounts. Others say the name was its founder's play on "Sinners Anonymous." The group started out by pooling its resources and beginning to live communally.

Life in the program was challenging—addicts, who began showing up as Dederich publicized his "cure," kicked heroin with no chemical assistance. Even before they'd recovered from withdrawal sickness, they were confronted by the community's demands. Newcomers were given the least desirable work assignments and the least private rooms. They also had to participate in "the game," which at times would run for days without pauses for food and sleep. "Verbal humiliation" was the essence of Synanon's "game," according to former member David Gerstel.[23] Nonetheless, as the media spread the word about its addiction cure, it was inundated with potential members.

Synanon would be fraught with paradoxes from start to finish: its "game" used angry, hate-filled emotional attacks in an attempt, it said, to help people love more. It imposed an authoritarian, totalistic regime more extreme than those in most psychiatric hospitals to (it claimed) promote enhanced freedom from drugs and other psychological problems. It enforced complete conformity and a very rigid hierarchy while being viewed, at least at first, as an idealistic, hippie-style, antiauthoritarian utopia.

By the late 1960s, Dederich had been glowingly profiled in *Life* magazine. *Time* magazine and TV newscasts praised Synanon; a Hollywood movie glamorized it. Soon numerous politicians and law enforcement officials were visiting this strange community that promised to solve one of the country's most pressing social problems and trying to replicate it elsewhere.

Before they copied it, however, few thought to look at Synanon's dropout rate. It turned out that 90 percent of those who started left within one year, the majority leaving within weeks. In one of the few statistical analyses of Synanon ever done, the New Jersey Drug Study Commission found that of 1,180 addicts who had entered Synanon, 717 left within 41 days. Only 26 graduated successfully, with 50 staying on as staff and 387 still in treatment at the time of the research. Which meant that only 10 percent of those who started treatment had demonstrated any kind of long-term abstinence and if another 10 percent of those still in treatment succeeded at the same rate, the total would still be just 15 percent.[24] This was at least as pathetic as the success rate reported by earlier government-run hospital programs to which Synanon had claimed to be superior.

But as with ToughLove, as with Alcoholics Anonymous itself, as with many other widely accepted talk therapies, anecdote was enough to generate huge participation and hundreds of copycat programs.

RICHARD BRADBURY drove with his father to an unmarked building for his "five-minute" evaluation interview with Straight Incorporated at ten A.M. on April 16, 1983. While he waited to be seen, Richard saw something that made him extremely anxious. "In the lobby they've got this boy," he said, "and another boy is holding on to him by the belt loop. This boy is white as a ghost, he looks like somebody has beaten the hell out of him, and he's mopping the floor. And the boy holding him doesn't look a whole lot better."

Richard noticed a cuckoo clock on the wall and fought an impulse to flee. A teenager, Paul*, appeared and identified himself as a trainee staff member. He took Richard into a small room, which Richard noted was made of rough, stucco-like concrete with a solid wooden door and no windows. Paul sat near the door in a blue plastic chair, a position Richard eventually figured out was taken in order to prevent escape attempts.

Richard sat in his own blue chair facing him. "He starts asking me, 'Have you ever stuck things in your butt? Have you ever had sex with a dog? Have you masturbated, have you engaged in sexual contact with guys?'" Richard says. He could see that Paul was using a written questionnaire and recording his responses, but was shocked by the personal questions. Because of his history of sexual abuse, he felt especially uncomfortable, but he didn't disclose it.

After filling out the forms, Paul took Richard back to the lobby, saying he should wait there for his "results." Richard looked out the window at his car, glancing again at the cuckoo clock. Something told him to run. But before he could act, Paul returned with three other teenage boys. They took him back into the small concrete room and told him he'd be staying at Straight.

Richard could see that his father hadn't even been consulted yet. He also knew that he had no sort of problem that warranted a lockdown behavior-modification treatment. He refused to stay, but the boys physically kept him from leaving. Soon Miller Newton, the national clinical director of the Straight program, walked in. Newton would play a key role in Straight's history and that of its tough love descendants. He'd become involved when his own son developed a drug problem in the late '70s. By 1982, he had been named national clinical director. He would develop the Straight model for replication, setting up Straight programs and training staff, some of whom would ultimately set up copycat centers themselves. In 1984, Newton would found his own treatment network, called KIDS, using the Straight model. It would operate until 1998, with sites open at various times in New Jersey, California, and Utah.

Newton told Richard's father to call his wife and have her bring $2,500 to the center, saying that their son had "failed" his screening and they needed to pay a deposit and admit him right away. Straight cost around $14,000 total per child—this covered a typical stay of eighteen months. Richard recalls his mother arriving and saying to Newton repeatedly, "There's nothing wrong with that boy." He also remembers Newton's reply, which was something like, "You have a choice. If you don't put him in the program, we're going to terminate your daughter Andrea from the program. And when she goes out in the street and dies from drugs, it's going to be your fault."

Richard's parents felt trapped. They did believe that Andrea was getting better—for one thing, she was no longer running away and giving them grief. They also knew the kinds of risks she had been taking on the street. By then, they'd heard her discuss her shocking sexual and drug-taking behavior in great detail at open meetings. They believed they had no choice but to admit Richard.

AS THE '60S morphed into the '70s, Synanon seemed like it would grow forever. By the mid-'70s, it had six facilities in California alone. Around 1,000 people lived at its three main sites. Synanon also operated programs in Detroit, New York, Seattle, Washington, D.C., Chicago, Puerto Rico, Berlin, and Malaysia. It ran a business that sold advertising and promotional items, which was grossing roughly $10 million in annual sales by 1978.

For most of Synanon's early life, its media coverage was positive, even worshipful. But by the '70s, negative coverage had increased dramatically. *Time* magazine, which said that Synanon was "a once respected drug program," called it "a kooky cult" in 1977. In early 1978, KGO-TV in San Francisco revealed that the group had purchased more than $60,000 worth of weapons and ammunition. Local newspapers told of friction with neighbors and claims of abuse by teenage runaways, who had often been mandated into Synanon for treatment as an alternative to incarceration by states that included California, Nevada, and Michigan.

Synanon fought back hard. It established an all-star team of more than forty lawyers. It threatened lawsuits against anyone who published a story that was less than glowing. Its lawyers also fought off all attempts to regulate the program. Synanon sued *Time* for $76 million, KGO for $42 million, and Hearst's *San Francisco Examiner* for $40 million. The Hearst suit was related to two 1972 exposés that called the group "the racket of the century." Hearst had to pay $600,000 to Synanon in an out-of-court settlement in 1976 for the first of these articles, when it turned out that the lead reporter had fabricated another story and had a criminal record. Synanon proudly contacted the Guinness Book of World Records, claiming that it had won the largest U.S. libel settlement ever.[25] Two years later, Hearst settled another Synanon suit, this one for conspiracy against it, for $2 million.[26]

Not surprisingly, the media backed off—except, primarily, for one tiny local paper, the *Point Reyes Light*, which would ultimately win a Pulitzer Prize for its doggedness in exposing Synanon's crimes. Over the years, the horrifying story came out as the *Light*'s owners, Dave and Cathy Mitchell, guided by University of California sociologist Richard Ofshe, began to unravel what had gone wrong.

Synanon had been investigated several times over the years by local grand juries. A 1976 investigation, prompted by reports of runaways, cleared the group and went so far as to chide the county probation department for not mandating local delinquents into it. By 1977, however, there was another investigation. Synanon had developed a "boot camp" program for its youth, the first of its kind. It involved rigorous physical training and severe punishment for noncompliance. Synanon had originally billed itself as an opponent of all violence—even verbal violence was supposed to be limited to the confrontations of "the game"—but now it created the "Imperial Marines," who were supposed to defend the group from an increasingly hostile outside world.

The grand jury cited this testimony from a fifteen-year-old girl who had twice run away: "When I returned, [for punishment, I was] made to eat standing up and given only three hours' sleep. I was not allowed showers and I was made to work cleaning up pig feces with carrot sticks, putting the feces in cups."[27]

Though the grand jury report didn't have an immediate effect because

Synanon still had massive popular and political support, it was the beginning of a series of devastating revelations that would ultimately shut it down. Synanon stopped graduating people: now, if an addict or teenager sentenced to it were to truly recover, he would be required to live in the Synanon facility for life. Members were told, in fact, that they would return to addiction, become prostitutes, be institutionalized for insanity, or die if they left.

Then, starting in 1977, Synanon began to require that all male residents who lived there for more than five years have vasectomies or be expelled. Leaving meant facing the threatened risks of relapse and death—as well as starting a financial life and career from scratch. Men as young as eighteen were operated on by Synanon-member doctors after being bullied into it during lengthy "game" sessions. Women were coerced into having abortions. Chuck Dederich had declared that children of members were a financial drain on the community, because they didn't bring in money the way the juvenile delinquents it was paid to "treat" did.

Shortly thereafter, Dederich (who, of course, wasn't sterilized himself) began to require that established couples swap partners. He coordinated the new matches. And all the while, Synanon continued to portray itself as a tough rehabilitation program for juvenile delinquents and addicts, who continued to be court-mandated into the now-kinky program to be "straightened out."

As these bizarre facts became public, however, Synanon finally started losing support. It also began losing in court. Members who had left were fighting for custody of children with those who'd stayed; others were suing for having been forcibly returned and beaten.

When Synanon began to lose cases to Los Angeles attorney Paul Morantz, it publicly threatened him. And three weeks after the group lost a $300,000 judgment to one of his clients in 1978, some members, under the direction of Dederich, cut the rattles off a four-and-a-half-foot rattlesnake and left the snake in his mailbox. Morantz reached in and was bitten as the snake sprang out. He screamed and a neighbor called an ambulance, saving his life.

The snake ultimately killed Synanon, however. Morantz's neighbors had reported a suspicious car driving aimlessly through their neighborhood before the attack—and it turned out to be registered to Synanon. For the organization, the timing couldn't have been worse: the Jonestown cult massacre in Guyana occurred just a month after they'd placed the snake in the mailbox. The media was suddenly focused on how seemingly benign communal groups could turn deadly. More than 900 people had died at Jonestown.

Fortunately, as is not the case with other cult investigations, Dederich was arrested without incident for his participation in the snake incident. The rehab pioneer was dead drunk when police found him. By 1980, when he and two other members pled no contest to conspiracy to commit murder, the organization began to fall apart. It took more than ten years, though, before a 1989 IRS action seeking $17 million in back taxes bankrupted it. Synanon formally dissolved in 1991.[28]

RICHARD BRADBURY would later recall his shock at hearing that he'd been "diagnosed" and essentially imprisoned on the basis of a five-minute grilling about his sex and drug habits, conducted by a teenager. His interrogator had no professional training—and in fact, what the staff had been taught were techniques professionals are instructed to avoid. Such methods allowed them to find nothing but what they already thought was there.

Counselors at Straight were told that all drug users are "druggies" (addicts) who suffer from "denial." Therefore, any refusal by a prospective participant to admit drug involvement was seen as a sure sign that the child was heavily addicted—while any admission of use was an indication that more serious drug-taking must be occurring. This catch-22 meant that nearly every teen interviewed would be admitted because both denying and admitting drug involvement got a child labeled a "druggie."

The coercive nature of the intake interview and the length of time participants spent facing invasive questioning in a tiny room with few breaks also made the process prone to inducing false confessions. Based on the research on false confessions, in fact, it would be hard to design a situation more prone to producing them than the Straight program.

After his parents were essentially blackmailed into admitting him, Richard Bradbury was told that if he didn't "sign himself in" for two weeks "voluntarily," his parents would have him court-ordered to stay for two years. He refused, but was then forcibly kept in the interview room and attacked over and over about the fact that he must be a "druggie." From ten A.M. till six P.M., Richard faced hostile questions and threats aimed at having him accept that he needed to be a "newcomer" at Straight Incorporated.

Again and again, he was told he must be a drug addict, and that if he admitted it, it would be the first step to recovery. He was ridiculed, taunted, and humiliated for not "owning up" to his problem. He was confronted about being a liar and a manipulator. In response, he argued that he didn't need to be there and wasn't going to sign in. But by six P.M., he had had it, and he agreed to stay for two weeks simply to stop the harassment.

Immediately, the teens brought Richard out to say good-bye to his parents. They had warned him not to say anything other than "I love you" to them, implying that the consequences for doing otherwise would be severe. He complied in exhausted resignation, and was taken to another room where he was forcibly strip-searched by his teenage interrogators. They searched every body cavity—a search that would be humiliating for anyone, but that was particularly awful for Richard.

Then he was dragged by his belt loop into the big room with the blue chairs, which was filled with at least 300 other teenagers. He was introduced to the huge group, who roared, "Love you, Richard," in response. Every time someone finished speaking, the teens would wave their arms and heads in a frenzy. Then someone would be called on by one of the two counselors who sat on tall stools up front. Once the speaker had been selected, the room settled into a chilling stillness, as every eye turned as if drawn magnetically in his direction.

Within three days, Richard began to question his sanity. Everyone else seemed to be behaving crazily, but they acted as though it was perfectly normal while he, who acted normally, was treated as though he was nuts. He was given little food, and sleep was hard to come by in the few hours he was given to do so, locked in a stranger's bedroom.

And all the while, he was repeatedly confronted about his "problems," told he wasn't "owning up," attacked by literally dozens of other teenagers in front of hundreds, who seemed absolutely certain that they were right. What if what they were saying was true? Was it possible he'd been hiding things from himself?

LIKE SYNANON, Straight's second predecessor, The Seed, had been started by a charismatic former alcoholic and failed stand-up comic. Art Barker seems to have been exposed to the Synanon method during a visit to New York, where he'd observed those who were setting up similar programs. By 1971, he had somehow managed to get a grant from the federal government to study whether the method could prevent and treat teen drug use. The Seed's first site was in Fort Lauderdale, Florida. There, teens spent twelve hours a day sitting on blue chairs, waving with great intensity. As in Synanon, counselors who lead these "rap groups" were former participants, not professionals. The Seed was also just as brutally confrontational as Synanon. And just like Synanon, it became violent: kids who didn't comply would be aggressively thrown to the floor and "restrained" by other participants.

The Seed also used concepts from AA's twelve steps, like confession of one's past bad behavior and surrender to a "higher power." But Barker added several unique twists. Unlike AA, The Seed didn't let its participants choose their own "higher power"—it declared itself their master. And, unlike Synanon, it wasn't a commune. While teens who had advanced to a certain "phase" in the program lived at home, when they first entered, for at least several months, they stayed at "host homes."

By the mid-'70s, The Seed had already developed a love-hate relationship with the press that followed a similar curve to that of Synanon. Early articles shone with praise and promise, earning the program endorsements from politicians like Representative Claude Pepper (D–Florida).

Later stories focused on "controversy," pitting supporters against those who increasingly believed that the program was dangerous. In 1974, a Florida alternative weekly ran an article with this subhead: "Former comic Art Barker says he will turn your drug-crazed kid into a dream teen. Others say his program, the Seed, practices the brainwashing of the future." The article included the usual glowing anecdotes from proud parents and reformed teens. But it also contained claims by a local psychiatrist that the program had led to suicide attempts and institutionalization, as well as the story of a teen who'd never really been a drug user, but was beaten by his father at a Seed open meeting, at the urging of the crowd, because he'd refused to admit his problem.

Barker, for his part, called his critics "fools," "druggies," and mentally ill.[29] And at first—just as with Synanon—the criminal justice system, politicians, and the media sided with the man whom some parents claimed to be "the savior" of their kids.

But even that far back, there were warning signs. In 1973, Stanford psychology professor Philip Zimbardo had published an account of the horrifying results of his "Stanford Prison Experiment" in the *New York Times Magazine*. In the experiment, he had randomly assigned college student volunteers (who had been prescreened to exclude people with mental problems) to play the roles of prisoners and guards in a mock prison in the basement of the university's psychology department. Prisoners were locked into barred "cells" which had been constructed for the study. They had to wear numbered uniforms; the guards wore police-style dress. Within days, the "prisoners" rebelled. The "guards" had started out using dehumanizing tactics like strip searches and arbitrary "head counts"—and now they really began to abuse the prisoners. For example, they denied bathroom privileges and refused to replace the filthy buckets the prisoners had to use instead of toilets. They made the prisoners do hundreds of push-ups. At one point, they even made prisoners clean up feces with their bare hands.

After three days, one prisoner broke down, "suffering from acute emotional disturbance, disorganized thinking, uncontrollable crying, and rage." But Zimbardo, who became allied with the guards because he was running the experiment, was reluctant to release him: what if he was just trying to "con" them? Already, he had begun to think like a corrections officer, not a psychological researcher concerned for his subjects.

Five days in, Zimbardo decided to stop the experiment, believing that if the participants continued to play their roles, they could incur serious damage. About one-third of the guards had become sadistic and seemed to enjoy abusing their power—but personality tests given in advance hadn't predicted who would respond this way. Many of the prisoners were seriously distressed. And this was after less than a week, with a group of college students who knew they were just participants in an experiment which they could quit at any time.[30]

The "roles" played by Seed participants were enforced for far longer—and it was younger teens, not college students, who were being given the power to physically discipline and control the lives of the newer "Seedlings."

FOR HIS FIRST THREE DAYS in Straight, Richard Bradbury wasn't allowed to talk. In his lengthy days at the facility, he witnessed incredibly emotional and bizarre events. Teenagers would confess drug-related bad behavior and sexual experiences, would weep and wail with guilt, and then get praised for their honesty. Richard found their tales of sex with animals and massive drug use far-fetched, but no one else seemed to question them. In fact, the more extreme and humiliating the story, the greater praise the teller seemed to receive.

Bradbury rapidly recognized that unless he came up with something to confess, he would never be able to progress through the program and be free. He watched as kids who refused to do so were attacked. The attackers would "motivate" as hard as possible; that is, they would flap their arms and heads and flail about so vigorously that the counselor would deem them "motivated" enough to be called upon. One by one, those selected would run up to the person who had "misbehaved."

An attacker would often literally spit on the "misbehaver," hurling vicious abuse, shouting at him while inches from his face. Then the next

kid would do the same. If the victim dared talk or fight back, or if someone sat in the wrong position on his blue chair, he would be restrained
by other kids. Sometimes, participants who confronted misbehavers
seemed to deliberately provoke them so they could initiate a restraint.
The constant threat of violence and the continual verbal attacks convinced Richard that the only way out was to comply.

Without being able to communicate with his parents or anyone else
"outside," he had no reality checks. He was pretty sure he was not really
a "druggie," but after days of being told that he was, and knowing that admitting it was the only way to change his extremely distressing circumstances, he became ready to do so.

On his third day at Straight, Richard "motivated" energetically. He got
called on. He stood up in front of several hundred "peers" and admitted
to being a "druggie." With tears in his eyes, he confessed that he belonged
there and had smoked pot and gotten drunk. And of course, as he "came
clean" he was applauded and told "Love you" in a stentorian, massed
shout. It was a powerful experience, much more powerful and overwhelming than he'd expected.

But then Richard told the story of his sexual abuse. He already felt
great pressure to open up, and he had developed an almost paranoid
sense that people in the program might already be aware of his devastating secret. He wanted to explain to them that the sexual abuse, not
his substance problems, was why he had dropped out of school. He told
the group that he'd been too embarrassed by the abuse and the cruel
taunts of his peers to return to classes.

To his shock, however, this disclosure yielded attack, not applause. He
said he was told immediately that "I was a cocksucker and a faggot, and
that's what I liked doing." His revelation was greeted as an excuse, a denial of the effects of his drug use, not as the awful truth it was.

Further, this disclosure really allowed Straight to get its hooks into
him. Richard had inadvertently showed the program his weak spot. He
had told them what made him most ashamed; in essence, what buttons
to press. From that day forward, his sex-abuse history was used to belit-
tle him. Counselors and peers told him, in graphic language, that he

must have wanted or even asked for it from the fireman and his friends. They spat the details back at him in coarse terms to increase his humiliation. They told him that if he didn't graduate Straight, he would undoubtedly grow up homosexual. They implied that this was a fate worse than death.

Straight participants continually taunted Richard. His counselors and peers played on his anxieties about his masculinity and went so far as to tell him that masturbating or wanting to do so meant that he preferred male partners. Over and over he was told that if he didn't finish the program, didn't participate fully, didn't confess any thoughts he had about drugs or sex, he'd soon be out begging to do what he'd been made to do as a child. Straight was the only thing, they said, that could save him.

Within weeks, Richard went from being a young man who had goals and a life plan to one who was desperately confused and dependent. And in the climate of vicious homophobia that was Straight Incorporated (the name, clearly, didn't refer just to drugs), the atmosphere of suffocating social pressure, and with a natural desire just to get back home, he gave in. Richard was terrified by the staff of Straight; he says it was fear more than anything else that made him comply. If Straight said it could make him good and make him feel better, well then, he was going to do everything it said, do everything right, and become, as he put it "the best Straight-lover in the world."

Every night, when even more confession was required in the form of a written "moral inventory," based on AA's fourth step, Richard opened up further. As required, he reported on the day's events, his feelings about them, and what he'd done wrong. He "turned himself in" when he had thoughts about masturbating. Not doing so would have meant he didn't love Straight, and if he didn't love Straight, he would never get better. He made up stories about how his drinking and pot-smoking had put him at great risk. He complied with every rule and rapidly advanced in the program, moving from "first phase" (in which he lived in a foster home and had no outside contacts) to "second phase" (in which he brought "newcomers" to his own home) to "third phase" (a little more freedom) and "fourth phase" (return to school or work).

Within months, Richard was a Straight counselor trainee, leading attacks on others. Soon, he became a paid staffer. He now genuinely believed that the program had saved his life and that its tough tactics were necessary, helpful, and productive. With all his heart, he threw himself into the work of rescuing others, many of whom, as in his own case, apparently couldn't see at first that they desperately needed such help. A little violence might be necessary—but the joyous reunions of families and the freedom from drugs and from what Straight had repeatedly stressed was deviant sexuality were worth it. Richard could no longer see that Straight was inducing false confessions of sexual and drug-related misbehavior, could no longer distinguish the truth about his past from the story he'd constructed for the program about it.[31]

TWO

Richard's Reversal

RICHARD BRADBURY might have worked at Straight for years without questioning his allegiance. But one day, he ran into John Foley, a neighbor, whom he'd known since childhood. When Richard was in his teens and John in his twenties, they'd discovered that they both loved biking and began to ride together. And then, in 1983, Richard had just disappeared.

For at least a year, John didn't see his friend and wondered what had become of him. So when he noticed Richard's car pulling into his driveway, he went over to catch up. Richard told him self-importantly that he was now "saving lives." John was shocked at the change in the young man he'd known as a "fun-loving" and "down-to-earth" kid. He noted that his friend seemed to have lost his sparkle and spontaneity. "All of a sudden he's this really straitlaced guy. And that wasn't his natural personality at all," he said. His first thought was that Richard must have joined some crazy cult. He arranged to meet him a few days later for iced tea, to try to help him.

For his part, Richard had become uncomfortable around outsiders because of his immersion in Straight. He was not supposed to have contact with people from his "druggie past." But Richard did recall that John was a Jehovah's Witness, and that this meant he avoided drink and drugs. He couldn't see why there would be any problem with talking to someone like that. When they met, John asked Richard about Straight. Richard blithely described just the mildest outlines of the program. Even this shocked his friend, especially since Richard seemed to consider it all completely appropriate. Richard says John told him, "'You're crazy. You can't treat those kids that way.'" Richard said in response, "John, you just don't understand."

But Foley came to believe that he understood much better than Bradbury did. He was studying psychology at the University of South Florida and began meeting Richard daily, then recounting Richard's Straight stories to his professors and classmates. One social worker immediately recoiled, having previously heard horror stories about Straight. Even with his limited knowledge of psychology, John recognized rapidly that an organization in which untrained kids, unsupervised by professionals, treated each other made no therapeutic sense. Fearful both for Richard and for the others, John tried to dissuade him from continuing to participate.

At first, Richard brushed off John's concerns. According to John, he would justify the violence by saying, "You have to do that because these people are manipulative. They'll do anything they can get away with, so you have to use authority on them and you have to get them into submission, and then you can start making progress." It was tough, but everything was done out of love and a sincere desire to help. Besides, Richard would argue, "spare the rod and spoil the child" is legitimate as a child-rearing technique—and schools also have a long history of using corporal punishment. He couldn't see why this was wrong when applied to troubled adolescents—especially when the alternatives were sexual perversion and drug abuse.

The program's sexual humiliation, on the other hand, couldn't be justified as easily. What Richard had learned about how Straight used it made him increasingly uncomfortable. He says he kept hearing that some of the female counselors had moved beyond verbal taunts and into physical sexual molestation. The verbal stuff alone was pretty horrifying: boys were constantly called "cocksuckers" and "faggots" while girls were labeled "sluts" and "whores." Boys were told that premarital sex was "masturbating inside girls."

After talking with Foley for weeks, Bradbury decided that the sexual abuse among the girls was just wrong. He said he'd heard counselors say they did it to "break" them. He figured that if Straight's top executives knew what was really going on, they would come to the same conclusion and put a stop to it. After all, they shared the common goal of helping kids. So, in the fall of 1985, he calmly approached a staff supervisor. He told her what he knew, said that he thought it was not appropriate, and suggested that it be stopped. He said he supported Straight with all his heart, but didn't believe that such practices could possibly help kids.

But just as had happened when he first disclosed his own history of sexual abuse, Richard was blindsided. The supervisor didn't take in a word of his critique. Rather than saying she'd investigate, she verbally blasted Richard and threatened that he'd be "started over" in first phase if he continued to question Straight. Counselors weren't immune from such "setbacks" if they didn't stay in line—someone could actually go from being a paid counselor to being a "patient" again.

Richard tried several more times to convince the staff that the sexual abuse should stop. Every time, he was threatened with being set back. "I thought, man, this is awful weird," Richard said. "I'd been the best Straight-lover in the world." But the staff would brook no criticism. What was being done was what had to be done. If Straight did it, it was right—and if someone questioned Straight, he was wrong. Period.

By late 1985, Richard had decided to quit. He wrote a six-page resignation letter, complete with the names of those he believed to be the perpetrators of sexual abuse. He distributed it to the entire staff and left. A few days later, Richard says, he received a phone call from one of

Straight's top executives, who asked him to come in for a talk. He says that when he arrived, he was baited and attacked. The leadership didn't want to change the program, Richard learned—but they did very much want to keep him quiet. When he noticed that the program's consultant psychiatrist was lurking in the hallway, he began to think that Straight staffers were trying deliberately to anger him, in hopes that he would get physical and give them a reason to have him committed.

And, this time, he says, "Instead of standing out there looking at the cuckoo clock thinking I should leave, I did leave." He felt confused, angry, and lost—almost as if he'd gone crazy. "I still think this is the most wonderful place in the world," he said, explaining that at the time, he continued to believe that if Straight eliminated the sexual abuse, it would be perfect. Not sure what to do, and anxious about going home, he called a friend and asked to stay with him for a few days until the situation cooled off.

That friend suggested something that would change Richard's life. He said that once he regained his equilibrium, Richard should stand outside the Straight building with a picket sign, demonstrating against the group until the media, the politicians, the regulators, the parents themselves, or anyone else who could help decided to do something about it. And that is exactly what Richard would do, on and off, for most of the next seven years.

AT FIRST, because of his ambivalence, Richard emblazoned very moderate demands on the signs he carried as he picketed alone outside Straight's building. STRAIGHT NEEDS TO MAKE SOME CHANGES, his first sign read. He marched around the parking lot, holding it high and talking to the few Straight people who dared to stop and ask him what he was doing. Sometimes he paid friends to march with him to bolster his resolve. But over time, the program lost its hold on him, and his protests became angrier. Ultimately, he wound up carrying signs bearing slogans like CLOSE STRAIGHT IN '88 and STRAIGHT IS CHILD ABUSE.

Doubts continued to torment him, however. "Could you imagine holding a picket sign that says STOP CHILD ABUSE, CLOSE STRAIGHT, and you're thinking that you deserved [the abuse] and that the place that you're picketing is good? And the only reason why you're standing there is because you know you should be because it's the right thing to do? That is very hard to do," he said, adding that even now, "Every blue moon I'll have a voice pop in my head that'll say, 'Well, didn't it do some good?' And I'll just laugh: that's a joke. Anybody that believes it did some good still believes in their mind, in their heart, that they deserved to be treated that way."

When he started picketing in 1985, Richard had no idea what he was up against. He knew nothing about Straight's history and little about Straight's political clout. He didn't realize just how many leading citizens in the St. Petersburg area, both Republicans and Democrats—from top law enforcement officials to leaders in the trial lawyers' association to dozens of respected physicians and business owners—had placed their own children in the program. He didn't even know that by the time he'd quit, Straight had already been successfully sued for false imprisonment by a young man named Fred Collins, whose experiences with the program were eerily similar to his own. Collins's story had been featured on *60 Minutes* in 1984—but Straight's news blackout for many of its participants meant that few of those to whom it was most relevant had seen the show.

One day, sometime in 1986, a longhaired man approached Richard as he picketed. He carried a thick file folder. He didn't give his name, but said he worked for a nearby psychiatric center and had seen many kids admitted after being at Straight. They'd been in terrible shape. He told Richard, "If you can close them, you can have it," handed him the folder, and left.

By this point, Richard had recognized that Straight couldn't be reformed. He'd heard that there had been legal and regulatory actions against the program but had little knowledge of them. He'd read some about Fred Collins, but didn't know much. The file from the longhaired stranger contained news clippings going back years. What he ultimately learned blew him away.

FRED COLLINS had grown up in Alexandria, Virginia, in an upper-middle-class home. He was highly intelligent and had participated in gifted programs. While he had gone through a pot-smoking rebellious period during his teens in which he let his grades slide, he'd quickly outgrown it and was accepted to Virginia Tech for engineering. Just like Richard, however, Fred had a troubled younger sibling, in his case a brother. George used drugs and got drunk frequently, neglecting school in favor of chasing girls. He angered his achievement-focused parents by constantly threatening to quit school. The Collinses attended ToughLove meetings, where they met parents who claimed that Straight Incorporated worked wonders. Saying they were going to Disney World, Mr. and Mrs. Collins lured George into vacationing with them in January of 1982. They dropped him off at Straight instead.

By this time, Fred had completed his first semester of college. He'd adjusted well, getting top grades. But he agreed to visit his brother at Straight after finals, not knowing that he was to be screened for admission himself. Just like Richard, he was horrified by the intrusive sexual questions he was asked by his teenage interrogators. He told author Arnold Trebach, who was the first to write about Straight's role in the drug war, that he'd openly admitted to his questioners that he'd used marijuana and alcohol occasionally, but had also said that it had not led to problems for him.[1] To Straight, of course, this meant he was "in denial"—and he was soon forcibly enrolled, despite being a legal adult of nineteen at the time.

Fred recalled the humiliating strip search, the endless rap groups, and the constant pressure to confess. And just like Richard Bradbury, he too ultimately capitulated and began to believe that he did have a drug problem. He didn't accept, however, that he needed Straight's help. After four and a half months, he was transferred from the Florida program to a new facility near his home in Virginia. He thought he might escape from there—and managed to do so on Halloween, 1982, despite his parents' multiple locks and alarm systems.

Fred fled back to college. His fraternity brothers fed and sheltered him. For weeks, Collins stayed underground, at one point hiding in an industrial clothes dryer when his father and some Straightlings showed up at the frat house. He steered clear of alcohol and pot, still half afraid that he was an addict. He spent part of this time living at the home of a friend, who had a high-powered rifle. When a man wearing a white coat came to pick up some furniture one day, Fred panicked. He leveled the gun at the intruder, accusing him of having been sent by Straight. If his friend hadn't arrived just then to reassure Fred that the poor guy was who he said he was, Fred says he might have killed him. He told Trebach, "I was going to blow him away. That's how nuts I was."[2]

Shortly thereafter, Fred decided to seek legal advice, hoping to put an end to his fears about being kidnapped back into the program. And so began the case that first widely exposed Straight's true nature.

FRED COLLINS told his incredible story to a jury in the federal court for the Eastern District of Virginia. The case was covered extensively in the *Washington Post*, in Florida newspapers, and ultimately on *60 Minutes*.[3] Collins sued for false imprisonment, intentional infliction of emotional distress, and assault and battery. He sought both compensatory and punitive damages.

For its part, Straight sought to prove that Fred was a drug addict, which they claimed to have discovered during his sibling interview, and that he'd entered treatment voluntarily when he'd been diagnosed. In his opening statement, one of the attorneys for Straight boasted confidently, "The evidence will show you that Straight is the most successful drug rehabilitation program in the country."

Fred's lawyer, Phil Hirschkop, argued that Fred had been abused, imprisoned, and attacked by Straight. He said that Fred was a good kid, who had smoked some pot and drunk some beer, but that by no means did he have a substance-abuse problem. Besides, Fred was legally an adult. Even "if Fred Collins was a heroin addict, they had no right to kidnap him," he contended.

Straight chose Chris Yarnold, who then supervised admissions, to testify about how the program made diagnoses—a huge mistake. Yarnold said he'd diagnosed Fred as a marijuana addict because his eyes were red. Hirschkop pounced. "Mr. Yarnold, are you telling these seven good people you can look in someone's eyes and tell that they've been smoking marijuana?" he asked.[4]

Yarnold said yes, not seeming to understand the glaringly obvious problems with his approach. By having Yarnold examine Fred's eyes again, Hirschkop demonstrated that Yarnold didn't notice either in court or during his intake that Fred wore contact lenses, which could account for the redness.

Not surprisingly, the jury didn't find Yarnold's testimony convincing. Straight had clearly allowed a rank amateur to make life-changing decisions. But its expert witness, the founding director of the government's National Institute on Drug Abuse, wasn't much more successful when he tried to use science to justify Collins's treatment. Dr. Robert DuPont, then a paid consultant to Straight, testified that Fred was a "pathological user" who'd "voluntarily" entered the program.[5]

DuPont claimed that Fred used drugs in a way that "recklessly disregarded" his "real interests." He said he'd concluded this because Fred had drunk alcohol while being prescribed a medication that should not be taken in combination with it and because Fred's father claimed his son had defied a parental ultimatum to stop smoking pot. DuPont said he considered these incidents "sick, pathological, and evidence of drug dependence."[6]

What he didn't say at first, but was forced to admit by Hirschkop, however, was that Fred didn't meet the criteria for the American Psychiatric Association's definition of drug dependence, the standard tool for diagnosing addiction. The APA's *Diagnostic and Statistical Manual of Mental Disorders* (*DSM*) requires that drug use significantly interfere with social and occupational functioning in order to be considered problematic. Straight saw all illegal drug use as pathological and requiring treatment, so it didn't use genuine medical criteria for diagnosis. Admissions like those of Fred Collins and Richard Bradbury were the inevitable result.

The plaintiff's expert, James Egan, chair of psychiatry at Washington, D.C.'s Children's Hospital National Medical Center, testified that Fred was not addicted. Egan said that Fred did have some serious problems—but these resulted entirely, he believed, from his family's involvement with Straight. He testified that Fred was depressed and suffered significant anxiety. He reported Fred's frequent, terrifying nightmares about Straight. Egan also said that Straight had adversely affected Fred's romantic relationships, producing guilt and anxiety.

But worst of all was what Straight had done to the Collins family. Fred's greatest pain, he testified, was caused by "the serious estrangement from his family, the sense that he was in essence on his own, that he has been abandoned emotionally, interpersonally, financially, that each time he sees a father and son on the street, for example, he is emotionally overcome."[7] Fred's brother and father had testified against him in the case. On the advice of Straight, his parents had cut him off, hoping that the loss of funds and support would force him to do as they wanted and return to the program.

In order to drive home his case for pain and suffering, Hirschkop called another Straight participant to the stand, a girl who had attended Straight with Collins. Leigh Bright testified about a series of events that began with her punishment for refusing to participate in exercise. She was thrown face-first to the floor repeatedly by girls making her do "push ups." Toe-touches were simulated by grabbing her by the hair, yanking her head back violently, and then forcing her forward. "They did that so many times that my head went numb," Leigh said.

Then, she was carried "like a pig on a skewer," into the open meeting room. Soon thereafter, angered by her continued defiance, Straight's national clinical director, Miller Newton, grabbed Bright by the hair, dragged her to the floor, and cursed at her, ordering that she be kept awake and "marathoned" for three days. For over seventy hours at her "host home" and in the Straight building, Leigh was shouted at and doused with water: anything to keep her eyes open. She was even slammed into a concrete wall. At one point, she was dragged off the toilet while having a bowel movement and made to clean feces from the toilet bowl with her bare hands and a paper towel—just as had happened in Zimbardo's Stanford prison experiment. Eventually, she began to hallucinate.

Newton did not deny "marathoning" Straight participants like Leigh. In a letter he'd sent in response to Florida regulators' concerns, he even tried to justify it. He said "marathoning" was "a therapeutic technique," not punishment. He admitted making teens crawl between each other's legs and be hit in a "spanking machine" but said this "was intended to be humiliating, rather than physical punishment." He also admitted putting kids on a peanut-butter-sandwich-only diet for days. He told regulators he'd stop all of this, not because it was wrong, but because it could be "misinterpreted" and the program could not "police" it properly.[8]

THE JURY TOOK just under three hours to make its decision in the first part of the Collins case, rapidly concluding that Fred Collins had been falsely imprisoned by Straight Incorporated and that he was not a drug addict. But, curiously, they didn't find that Straight had intentionally inflicted emotional distress. They said that they believed Straight's rough tactics might have been necessary for real addicts. According to Trebach, who interviewed most of the jurors, deliberations centered on convincing one holdout, the only female juror, who agreed with Straight. She wanted to give Collins a judgment of one dollar, so that he'd stop denying his addiction.

The rest of the jury stood strongly with Collins. Robert Hartzell, an administrator in the federal courts, explained his reasoning to Trebach. At first, he thought that society should do "whatever it takes" to stop drugs, he said, "but then you hear about locking them up without authority to do so and then you hear about at least questionable practices from the standpoint of mental and physical abuse and you get a little scared because if you want to be honest about it, you know that that self-righteous organization can be convinced that . . . there can't be anything wrong with scooping you up off the street and the first thing you know, you're scooped up because you're a Lutheran."[9] The jury ultimately agreed that Collins should be paid $40,000 to compensate for being illegally confined and $180,000 in punitive damages to let Straight know that what it did was wrong.

But the message didn't get through. After the verdict, Miller Newton told a reporter that what he'd learned from the case was that "it certainly will open the door for people with twenty-five bucks and an unemployed attorney to come after us."[10] Mel Riddile, director of the Virginia Straight, lamented, "Every time someone over eighteen wants to leave, we'll have to let them walk out instead of trying to convince them that it's in their own best interest to stay."[11] And Straight soon prevailed over Collins in another case, this one attempting to ban the Straight treatment method.

AFTER HE'D BEEN GIVEN the news clips about Straight by his anonymous source, Richard Bradbury began to do more research. With persistence, he gradually pieced together a history of the organization. He found reports, for example, that detailed the same complaints that both he and Collins had made, going back to the early '70s. Beatings. Unlawful detention. Bizarre sex-related incidents. There was even a report by a state agency in 1972 that comprehensively debunked The Seed's claims of extraordinary success. The state found that only 41 percent of youth who entered completed The Seed, and that of these, only 10 percent were followed up, so there was no way of knowing if most were drug-free. The Seed's claim of a "90 percent success" rate—which had led to Straight's making similar boasts—had been objectively falsified as early as 1972.[12]

The same report found that nearly one-fifth of the teens in the program had never used drugs at all and contrary to its claims that three-fourths of them were heroin junkies, 75 percent had not even tried heroin.[13] From Bradbury's research, it also became clear that the press had compounded the public's ignorance by reporting the 41 percent program-completion rate as a "41 percent success rate," and falsely claiming that this meant The Seed was superior to other treatment. By the time the Congressional Report on Behavior Modification was issued in 1974, The Seed had reportedly "treated" some 5,000 teens in three Florida cities.[14] Unbelievably, at the time, in more than one Florida high school, a significant proportion of each grade had become "Seedlings," the recruitment fueled by false accusations of drug use leading to false confessions. In some schools, the percentage was as high as 30 percent, according to former students and school officials. And the program had global expansion plans. One psychiatrist told a journalist, "If Barker goes according to schedule, The Seed should be in full command of the world's children sometime in the summer of 1984."[15]

The Ervin report put a kibosh on those plans, or at least on Barker's participation. The government wanted to know what The Seed had done with its money and why it had never published the "research" for which that money had been earmarked. Rather than deal with what Barker called "the excessive demands, harassment, and bureaucracy" that came with extending its grants, The Seed withdrew.

The abusive nature of the program's therapy was noted in both the *New York Times* and the *Washington Post*, as well as in local newspapers. Even parents who had been strong supporters began to have second thoughts, both about Barker and about expanding a program that Congressional investigators and the press had strongly opposed.

Many still passionately believed in The Seed's treatment model, however. Some decided that if they created a new program with the same structure, with greater professional supervision and a different name, they could provide the benefits of The Seed, while removing the rough edges and the controversial Barker. And so, in 1976 shopping mall magnate Mel Sembler, who was horrified by the involvement of one of his sons with marijuana, and real estate developer Joseph Zappala founded Straight Incorporated. (One of Sembler's sons attended The Seed, according to some participants; Sembler says only that he got "counseling."[16]) Shortly thereafter, The Seed stopped "treating" teenagers—though it did continue to "treat" adults for decades.

One early board member of Straight told me that he got involved because he thought Straight would be different. Walter* believed that The Seed had helped his children. At the same time, he says, he was disturbed by some of its methods. He said, "They'd take a little girl in there who led a sheltered life . . . and just rip her to pieces. And if she started crying, they all made fun of her. It was bad." He said that when he joined Straight's board, he'd been assured that such tactics would be stopped. "I had a commitment from them that we would have this wonderful psychiatrist or psychologist [who would] interview the kids and follow along."

But almost immediately, Walter became aware that Straight wouldn't really be different. No leading psychiatrist or psychologist was hired. Just before Straight opened in 1976, its first executive director told the *St. Petersburg Times* in response to criticism of The Seed, "I happen to feel that you can communicate with an individual without degrading him or humiliating him and without depriving him of all his uniqueness." He said that The Seed's attack therapy was done by "untrained, unsupervised and unqualified staff," and vowed that such things were "not going to happen" in Straight. Amazingly, Straight even managed to get federal funding from the same agency that told Congress it would never fund human experiments again after The Seed debacle.[17]

But when the program opened, it didn't abandon a single controversial Seed tactic. No informed consent was given to parents about the experimental nature of the program. The same untrained counselors went on doing what they'd always done. In 1977, after only about a year of involvement, Walter and several other board members resigned. Three quit simultaneously, citing the unqualified staff.

And Straight began to get in trouble with regulators. That same year, for example, several ex-counselors complained to authorities that Straight was maltreating children. They initially felt ambivalent, like Richard had— wanting Straight improved, not shuttered. When the state failed to act, however, they called the press in 1978. One said, "The program was getting . . . so bad that I felt it was hurting more kids than it was helping."[18] Nonetheless, Straight would remain open for more than another decade. In fact, the 1980s were a period of great expansion. Between 1981 and 1989, the program opened sites in Atlanta, Cincinnati, Boston, and Detroit; Orlando, Florida; Springfield, Virginia; and southern California.[19]

Not surprisingly, lawsuits and state investigations immediately fol-

lowed each opening. Straight Atlanta was rapidly sued by the ACLU.
A Cincinnati ACLU official called it "a brutal program," "a concentration
camp for throwaway kids."[20] Mel Sembler told a reporter that the
ACLU's opposition "just shows that we have been doing things right."[21]

AND AS HE continued to protest, Richard Bradbury became increasingly
frustrated. He was working as a maintenance man for six dollars an hour,
spending all his free time and what little money he had on activism.
He'd tried to get media attention, he'd written endless letters, and he'd
even showed up at regulators' offices to try to get them to shut Straight
down. But no one would listen.

Richard's friend John worked as a medical-records clerk at the time.
He thought Richard might be able to gain evidence against Straight by
obtaining its records. He drew up a form to comply with federal laws for
ex-participants to sign to in order to release their files to Richard. Then
Richard could go to Straight and ask for the relevant paperwork. At first,
Straight released some records—and it gave Richard no small satisfaction that they had to obey him for once. But Straight soon stopped complying. Richard went back to the regulators, attempting to have them
force the group to turn over the records and investigate an organization
that wouldn't follow the law. Yet again, no one would help.

AND THAT'S WHY Richard hatched his bizarre burglary plan, which had
him dangling over the blue chairs one cold January night, swimming
across a freezing canal, and then hiding in the palmettos of Pinellas Park.
He did not get caught that evening—although his accomplice did, and
was sentenced to three years' probation.[22] Richard was arrested a year
later—after he disrupted a Straight benefit. On November 12, 1988, he
pled guilty to the burglary. He was sentenced to 1,250 hours of community service and five years of felony probation. He was also barred from
setting foot in Pinellas County, where Straight was located.

Needless to say, the outcome left Richard depressed. He had decided against a jury trial because he couldn't afford a high-powered attorney and felt that the cards were stacked against him in that jurisdiction. He had gotten little publicity. He was now barred from doing the activism that gave meaning to his life. Straight was still open. But Richard had gone back to school and was studying to be a paralegal. A routine business-law assignment soon gave him new hope.

His class had been assigned to draw up articles of incorporation, for either a nonprofit or for-profit business. Richard wrote down the particulars dutifully. And then it hit him: he had to do community service for a nonprofit organization to meet the terms of his probation. What if he created one of his own? "All of a sudden the wheels are turning in my head," he said. Although he only got a C on his paper, the state of Florida accepted his articles of incorporation. Thus was born Community Improvement, Inc. Richard put John Foley, John's father, and a neighbor on his board of directors and named himself executive secretary. The sole mission of the group was to shut down Straight.

Probation may have been the best thing ever to happen to Richard's activism. It forced him to organize. It also gave him time to think, plan, and focus. And in 1990, Straight itself gave him a tremendous opportunity, when it sued seventy families for nonpayment or underpayment of their bills. It sent letters with the brusque salutation "Debtor"—no "Dear," no "sir" or "madam," no pretense of politeness. They read in part, "I still haven't heard from you as to how you plan to payoff your bill owed to my firm for your childs stay and treatment . . . tell me where my money is of yours and when it will be sent to take care of your parental, financial, legal and moral obligation to Straight [sic]."

The court filings gave Richard the names and addresses of these families, the majority of whom, if they hadn't been withholding payment because they'd had a bad experience, had become suspicious of the group when they received these illiterate letters. Richard wrote to all of them. Community Improvement soon had chapters fighting Straight across the country. At that point, Straight had nine centers in seven states and was estimated to be taking in over $10 million annually.[23] Some 50,000 teens had been put through it, according to its own claims.[24]

Richard was finally running a real organization, not just a group of his friends. Other former Straight participants and parents, among them many whose money and education lent the organization credibility and brought much-needed skills, joined in. Soon he had at least a dozen committed volunteers, and many others who would show up for demonstrations or contribute occasionally. His campaign gained momentum.

By July of 1991, he had more than fulfilled his community-service requirement. The judge never cottoned onto Richard's plan: he never recognized that Richard's community service was essentially an extension of his crime. He didn't know that Community Improvement was an anti-Straight group, or that Richard had founded it. All he knew was that Richard had outdone himself in his "rehabilitation." The judge was so impressed, in fact, that he allowed Richard to end his probation early— in two and a half years rather than the full five. At his last court date, the judge commended him for his work and sent him on his way.

Whereupon Richard walked out the door and over to the Community Improvement office. He called the local NBC affiliate, Channel Eight, which spent a whole day taping interviews with Straight victims whom Richard had gathered. Richard said, "That very Friday night, we were out there picketing with not four picketers and not someone I have to pay; I have twenty-five or thirty picketers out there."

RICHARD'S NEXT COUP came later that year. On December 6, 1991, he and about two dozen other protesters were picketing outside Straight St. Petersburg. Suddenly, they noticed a bustle of activity—and four teenagers ran out, followed by a phalanx of angry staffers. The runaways fled past the protesters, not realizing that they were near potential allies. Richard's group prevented the staffers from capturing the kids, and Richard caught up with the runaways at a Burger King. At first, they were too frightened to talk. They couldn't believe that Community Improvement was not in league with Straight. "We didn't know what to think," said Katy*, who was fifteen at the time. "You don't know if they're friend or foe."

This was Katy's second escape from a Straight facility—she'd jumped from a third-floor window at a host home to get out of Straight Dallas, near her home. The police had brought her back after her parents reported her as a runaway. At that time, the Dallas facility was itself being investigated by regulators who found that Straight had used sanitary napkins as gags and tied kids up to restrain them. Katy, who was bruised all over her body from both her jump and injuries sustained at Straight, told police she was being abused. Yet the cops took her back anyway—and her parents had her moved to St. Petersburg when the Texas Commission on Alcohol and Drug Abuse closed the Dallas facility.

At the Burger King, Richard and his fellow activists told Katy and the others that they would not take them back to Straight. All of them had severe bruises, so Richard took photographs and had them audiotape their stories. But then, the protesters knew that they had to have the kids call their parents. Straight had already notified them that Richard had "kidnapped" their children. When Katy's father flew in from Texas, Richard convinced him to take her home. But the other parents were adamant that their kids graduate Straight.

Anticipating this possibility, Richard had the remaining teens memorize the phone number for Community Improvement, promising that if they escaped again, he would prepare a safe hiding place in advance this time. He notified state regulators about the teens' accounts of abuse and their bruises. This was supposed to prompt immediate medical exams. But while the regulators did arrive quickly, they just had the kids brought back to Straight.

Nonetheless, Richard had his photos and tapes—and by the end of the month, the others had escaped again. This time, Richard was ready, maxing out his credit card to feed and lodge them. He'd have them call home every day—but this time, he didn't let the parents know where they were.

A local TV talk show, *Eye on Tampa*, had planned a program on Straight to air live in January 1992. Richard prepared his photos for TV by blanking out the teen's faces. He also brought other documentary evidence and fifty supporters of Community Improvement to sit in the studio audience. And for once, it was the Straight officials who were blindsided. They hadn't packed the audience, as Richard's side had. Their executives had no idea how much devastating information Bradbury had compiled. They couldn't respond to the graphic pictures and the angry onslaught from victim after victim. Richard and all fifty of his teen and adult followers might be lying, of course—but that couldn't explain away the disturbing images of black-and-blue kids.

A second show, demanded by Straight (which had claimed that the first one was biased), only made the program look worse. One Straight official lied on the air about Richard's criminal record. A Straight-supporter father responded to a girl's account of sexual abuse by calling kids in the program "absolute little monsters." But this didn't obliterate the criticism, as Straight had come to expect. This time, there was just too much smoke for there to be no fire.[25]

Shortly thereafter, Richard Bradbury filed suit against Straight for libel, defamation, and slander—and won a settlement because claims that he'd been arrested for contributing to the delinquency of a minor were false. A documentary series made by the same television station put the final nail in Straight's coffin, presenting the charges against the group to then President George H. W. Bush, who, like the Reagans, was a big supporter. Now Bush distanced himself, saying that the program should be investigated.

Florida's inspector general also began to investigate allegations of corruption related to Straight's continued licensing despite documented abuse. By this time, cofounders Sembler and Zappala had become even more powerful in the Republican Party. Each had personally given over $125,000 to Bush's 1988 presidential campaign,[26] and together they headed campaign fundraising for Bush in Florida. They were each rewarded with an ambassadorship. Sembler headed to Australia, while Zappala (who didn't speak Spanish) took Spain. The obviously political nature of these appointments prompted a spoof by Garry Trudeau in his

Doonesbury cartoon, which showed the two bidding for the spots at an auction.

But although the inspector general could not fully substantiate allegations that its political connections had kept Straight open, his report left little doubt that he believed that this was what had happened. To its author's obvious frustration, investigators couldn't definitively prove that it had been political pressure that had allowed Straight to continue its abuses for decades. The report did document phone calls from several state senators to regulators about Straight. It included testimony from employees about receiving calls telling them they had no choice but to keep Straight open—but when they were asked to name who had made the calls, the employees' memories froze up. There was even testimony from one regulator who recalled asking why Straight was still open in Florida, when other states had shut it down. He said he was told he'd be fired "on the spot" if he didn't renew Straight's license—but his boss denied making that threat. The report said, "there were indications that outside influence was involved with this licensing issue. It appears that pressure may have been generated by Ambassador Sembler and other state senators."[27]

But the report concluded that it "cannot be unequivocally corroborated that this outside influence" was what allowed Straight to remain licensed.[28] Sheer ineptitude, or a simple desire by regulators to leave open a program that, no matter how bad it was, was providing a service that was needed, could not be ruled out.

When the report was made public in July 1993, Straight had already closed in Florida. An editorial in the *St. Petersburg Times* on the subject was headlined A PERSISTENT FOUL ODOR. It began conclusively, unlike so much news coverage that had typically presented "both sides" of the Straight debate, "Straight Inc. is dead and buried in Florida, and well that it is." It said that the Inspector General's report "paints an unsettling picture of the possible abuse of political power." It asked sarcastically, "This is regulation?" and called for Florida to do better.[29]

By the end of 1993, all programs with the Straight Inc. name were gone. Straight's executives cited the failing economy as the cause of its collapse. But the group had been run out of Florida, California, Virginia, Texas, Michigan, Massachusetts, Maryland, and Georgia—and in every single state, it had encountered the same allegations of abuse. It had settled dozens of civil claims, paying out millions.

Nonetheless, Miller Newton, Straight's national clinical director, was alive and well and using the blue chairs in New Jersey at a program he founded, called KIDS. It, too, would develop a national network of facilities. On August 14, 1992, the day after Straight closed in Orlando, a new program with the same staff and the same model opened in the same building. It was called SAFE, and unlike Straight, it decided to operate as a for-profit business, not a nonprofit. By October 1993, SAFE had asked the state for permission to use oldcomers to restrain newcomers. Florida denied this "request for deviation" from its standards.[30]

SAFE is still open and still using Straight's methods, according to recent accounts from participants and parents and a shocking local television report in 2000, which showed patients "motivating."[31] And other former Straight staffers still run Straight-like programs across the U.S. in Ohio (Kids Helping Kids), Tennessee (Second Chance, which uses Straight's model but is explicitly Christian), Detroit (Pathways Family Center), Kentucky (Possibilities Unlimited), Georgia (Phoenix Institute for Adolescents), and Florida (Growing Together), and in Canada (AARC). Turnabout/Stillwater Academy in Salt Lake City, Utah, uses a regime nearly identical to Straight's, but it is not known if any former Straight or Straight-descendant program employees are directly involved. Another Utah-based program, the Proctor Advocate, also appears to use the Straight method.[32]

That list doesn't even begin to mention the hundreds of "tough love" programs carried out in the wilderness or in "boot camps," "behavior modification facilities," or "emotional growth boarding schools," which either directly copied or indirectly arrived at many of the same abusive tactics and legal and antiregulatory strategies used by Straight. At least several hundred such programs are currently open in the U.S. (or run by Americans for Americans in foreign countries) today. Unlike the direct descendants of Straight, these programs use different lingo and different "phase" or "level" systems, but the core—attack therapy, rigid rules, and complete isolation from the outside world—remains the same.

So why was Straight allowed to continue its abuses from the '70s until 1993, repeating the same patterns in each state it entered? Why are former Straight staffers still using this dangerous model, under other names, in the twenty-first century, and why are similar programs with different origins still thriving? Why did kids at Straight have fewer rights than even death-row inmates in terms of contact with the outside world and the right to be free of cruel and unusual punishment? If parents treated their own children the way Straight did, they would almost certainly be vulnerable to child-abuse charges, so why were the program and others like it today able to get away with it? And where was the federal government?

Possible explanations include American political phenomena like the ongoing war on drugs, cultural issues like the recovery movement, and the failure by the public and psychologists to demand empirical evidence of effectiveness for talk therapies. Explanations also include the shortage of psychiatric facilities for seriously disturbed children and the historical privileging of parental rights over the rights of children as American citizens. Further, a number of psychological factors make tough love programs inclined to produce enthusiastic converts, even when they don't cure drug and behavior problems. All of these factors persist, enabling continued success for the programs.

Straight was born into a world where there were few options for parents of teens with mental or behavioral problems. The antipsychiatry movement in the '60s and '70s, of which Synanon had been a part, had emptied barbaric state institutions of both children and adults—but the promised community alternatives never really materialized. For-profit psychiatric and drug-treatment facilities thrived during the mid-'80s, but insurers cracked down when providers couldn't prove that their treatments were effective. In fact, one study of some 20,000 admissions in that era estimated that 75 percent of the inpatient psychiatric treatment (including for drug problems) given to teens and children was unnecessary.[33] Length of stay in treatment was determined by how much insurers would cover, not by the severity of the problem. Parents were bombarded with government and media messages suggesting that teens who did drugs needed treatment—but neither those who were simply frightened by exaggerated messages nor those who had kids with genuine problems had affordable, evidence-based options.

By itself, for example, the fact that The Seed was able to simply change its name and dodge regulators for another thirteen years following ten years of scandals is evidence of these themes. Had there been alternatives, regulators may well have been empowered to shut it down. But Straight cleverly capitalized on drug-war panic. Its very name is emblematic of the drug war's goal, whereas The Seed sounded like it could be a hippie commune.

The views of the jurors in Fred Collins's case illustrate just how successfully drug warriors managed to demonize addicts to the general public: they would not have awarded him any substantial amount of money had they believed he'd actually been a "druggie." Addicts deserved whatever could be dished out to them. This was the same era, after all, when Los Angeles chief of police Daryl Gates got nods of approval when he said that even casual drug users "ought to be taken out and shot."

The fact that teenagers were singled out for especially rough treatment in programs like Straight was also not coincidental: adolescence itself is increasingly framed as a pathological state. Studies have found that most media coverage of youth portrays negative and antisocial behavior—and that it doesn't track actual trends. For example, between 1990 and 1998, the national murder rate dropped by one-third—but network news coverage of homicide increased almost 500 percent, according to a study by the Justice Policy Institute. The same report found that while murders committed by youth dropped by more than two-thirds between 1993 and 1999, 62 percent of the public believed that violent crime by young people was rising.[34] And as the drug war intensified, teens came to be seen almost by default as "out of control," "defiant," and difficult; tough measures are far easier to countenance for such folk.

A 1979 Supreme Court decision (*Parham v. J.R.*) affirmed the legality of programs like Straight's to have absolute control over teens with their parents' consent. It upheld the rights of parents to send children to whatever private lockdown residential facilities they believe to be best, just as they are allowed to make schooling and medical decisions. The assumption is that parents won't consent to abusive care. And teens can be committed without a court hearing if a "neutral fact finder" (who can be a facility employee at an unlicensed program!) believes such restrictive care is needed.[35] Teens have no right to appeal their commitment, nor does a teen's institutionalization need to be justified by a diagnosis of potential danger to oneself or others, as is necessary for an adult. This legal setting also permits programs like Straight to thrive with little oversight.

Another key factor that drove Straight's success was the twelve-step recovery movement, which grew as calls for "treatment not punishment" began to be heard in the '80s. While Synanon-style programs were pushed for those who had no choice about treatment—youth, and those forced into it by the criminal justice system—a parallel, more cushy set of rehabilitation centers had sprung up as well. The best known of these are programs like Betty Ford and Hazelden, and they are based on introducing people to the twelve steps of Alcoholics Anonymous.

The twelve steps and the rehabs that promoted them made recovering people and their families, not doctors or psychiatrists, into the "real" experts on addiction. From this point of view, studies were meaningless—only anecdotes of success mattered, and only addicts could understand and help other addicts. The steps are the same no matter whether the addiction is to food or to heroin—and an addict who practices them can help others with compulsive behavior, no matter what their problem. While twelve-step rehabs do promote the idea that addiction is a disease, their treatment of it is meeting, praying, and confession, and this basis in faith allowed many unorthodox practices to enter what was claimed to be "medical" care. Fed by these rehabs and boosted by celebrities, membership in self-help programs skyrocketed to the point that by 1993, more than one in ten Americans had attended at least one twelve-step meeting.[36] Since Straight claimed to be based on the twelve steps (even though many twelve-steppers found it atrocious), it could present itself as mainstream treatment.

In part because of the popularity of the recovery movement, and in part because there are so many competing psychological theories, neither consumers nor the press have demanded real evidence for the safety and efficacy of any talk therapy or behavior treatment until very recently. Freudian analysis, Alcoholics Anonymous and all its brethren, Synanon, recovered-memory therapy, ToughLove—all became mainstream treatments or adjuncts to treatment, even though the only evidence to support them was testimonials. As general medicine found to its dismay, such a standard allows quackery to thrive and does not distinguish between treatments that help and those that harm.

But beyond the lack of alternatives and the lack of a demand for evidence of efficacy—a demand that would have stopped these programs dead in their tracks years ago if it had been required—there are deep psychological reasons why tough love itself continually gains adherents. Tough love programs utilize a number of potent psychological techniques, which reliably produce compelling stories of recovery, if not actual psychological improvement, from participants. Formally, they are known as "thought reform" or "coercive persuasion" strategies; colloquially, some call them "brainwashing." Such tactics are often used by groups like est; religious, political, and therapeutic cults; prisoner-of-war camps; and government interrogators. While Straight's techniques were rarely as heavy as some used by these other groups, the program and others like it utilize every tactic psychologists have identified as important in creating such influence. Understanding these strategies is critical to understanding tough love programs and how they spread, because, unfortunately, with their use of these strategies, these programs produce supporters who are far more deeply committed than are people who have undergone more effective treatments. They yield converts, who will support the programs almost mindlessly, even when their own cases are clearly not successes.

The first critical tough love component is attack therapy. Attack therapies have been promoted as panaceas for everything from dead marriages to failing to meet sales quotas since at least the late 1940s and usually carry euphemistic labels like "T-groups," "encounter groups," or "sensitivity training" when sold to the general public. When pushed for use on addicts or other stigmatized groups like adolescents, however, the euphemisms are often dropped and the toughness becomes a selling point.

As early as the 1950s, however, there were tales from businesspeople of "sensitivity" training or "T-groups" that didn't improve team relationships—but ended them. A 1972 exposé of the Leadership Dynamics Institute, called *The Pit: A Group Encounter Defiled*, told of brutal beatings during its four-day "seminars." It recounted the story of a man who was forced to fellate a dildo in front of a group and others who were made to lie in sealed coffins, hung from crosses by ropes, or locked in cages for hours, even days, without opportunity to eat, sleep, or use a bathroom.[37] The Holiday Magic cosmetics company (later exposed as a pyramid scheme) had required its employees to complete the non-refundable $1,000 course as well as a training seminar called Mind Dynamics. Both Werner Erhard, the founder of est, and John Hanley, who started the similar group LifeSpring, began as instructors in this organization.[38]

It's hard to imagine how people who'd been through experiences like being locked naked in a cage in front of others could turn around and promote them as wonderful and transformative—but some strange quirks of human nature make it not only possible, but quite common. Leadership Dynamics had plenty of self-proclaimed satisfied customers who participated in the same seminars that caused others to file lawsuits. Straight, The Seed, and Synanon similarly polarized proponents and detractors.

A critical part of the explanation for people supporting their own poor treatment is a phenomenon in which people tend to overvalue experiences for which they have paid dearly. This process can be seen clearly in a study where some women were put through a humiliating initiation in order to access a sex discussion group. They found it extremely valuable, even though the researchers had designed it to be dull and useless. Women who hadn't had such an initiation saw it as it was.[39] The same is true for fraternity and secret society initiations: the greater the ordeal, the more valued the group becomes. As a member of Yale's Skull & Bones club (which is rumored to initiate members—one of whom is believed to be George W. Bush—by having them lie in coffins and masturbate) told author Douglas Rushkoff, "Once you do it, you have to believe it was worth it."[40]

Further, psychologists have repeatedly documented how people can come to support their own maltreatment via a process called "cognitive dissonance."[41] What happens is this: human beings have an innate desire to harmonize their beliefs and behavior, but often, it's easier to change a belief than a behavior, especially when that behavior is coerced. When a belief that contrasts with behavior is displayed publicly, people are especially prone to rationalize because they don't want to appear hypocritical or inconsistent.

Studies find that if people are made to take a particular position in front of others, they often come to sympathize with it, even if they strongly disagreed at first. As former Moonie and cult expert Steve Hassan puts it, "Research into social psychology has shown that nothing firms up one's beliefs faster than trying to sell them to others."[42] As a result, while proselytizing rarely attracts new converts, it dramatically increases the commitment and fervor of those who are already in the group.

This phenomenon is visible in Fred Collins's response to Straight. Although at first he knew that he did not have a substance abuse problem, months of being made to stand and identify himself as a "druggie" made him far less sure. In order to get sent home, he had to look and sound as though he genuinely believed he was an addict—he would be attacked or made to stay longer if he came across as "insincere" or "in denial." By the time he left, he had become afraid to drink or smoke pot with his fraternity brothers because of his "problem." The clash between the behavior of publicly calling himself a "druggie" and his internal beliefs subtly shifted his own self-concept, at least for a while.

People also consistently underestimate their susceptibility to simple peer pressure. Yale psychologist Stanley Milgram's studies are famous for giving a dark reply to the question of how many of us would "follow orders" if pressured to harm another person. Subjects were told to administer escalating electric shocks to "learners" (actually, actors who weren't being harmed) for an experiment on learning. They were accompanied by a researcher, who strongly encouraged them to continue increasing the voltage, even when subjects expressed ethical concerns. The device used to "administer" the jolts was labeled starting at 15 volts (MILD SHOCK), 300 volts (INTENSE SHOCK), and 450 volts, which was labeled DANGER: SEVERE SHOCK XXX.

Every one of Milgram's initial forty subjects administered the 300-volt shock, despite increasingly agonized objections and complaints of heart trouble from the "learner." Two-thirds went all the way to 450, even though the learner shrieked, then went ominously silent and fell from view after 330. Variations of the experiment found that people would administer serious shocks when pushed by peers, not just white-coated scientists. This research shows that even moderate pressure from authority figures and groups can rapidly cause adults to question their beliefs and to do as they are told.[43] Teens, of course, are even more malleable.

And with truly hideous experiences, several additional psychological factors come into play. One is the "Stockholm syndrome." This was named for an incident in which hostages held in a Swedish bank robbery came to support their captors. Two female hostages became engaged to two of the robbers. Patricia Hearst's 1974 conversion from kidnapped heiress to terrorist bank robber is probably the best-known example, but the phenomenon is widespread and is seen in cases of domestic abuse and child abuse as well as in kidnappings and terrorist incidents.

Psychologists believe that Stockholm syndrome is caused by being placed in a situation of dependence on others who induce fear.[44] People often adapt to such ordeals by trying to placate their captors—and by becoming grateful for small acts of kindness. By identifying with their captors and trying to manipulate them into providing better conditions, the victims gain a sense of control. Through cognitive dissonance, however, this can cause the victims to support their own oppression by internally adopting the stance of their oppressors. It is less psychologically stressful for the victims to adopt the captors' perspective than to dwell on their own helplessness. Consequently, victims come to believe that they deserve harsh treatment.

This belief also plays into what psychologists call the "just world" hypothesis.[45] The idea is that people want, above all else, for the world to be fair. When that doesn't hold true, it is easier to reframe the situation in a way that makes things seem fair than it is to question this basic and reassuring worldview.

So, researchers find that when people are punished without good reason, there is a tendency to see the victim as "asking for" maltreatment. Milgrim's subjects became extremely harsh in their judgment of their "victims" once they had "shocked" them, just as Straight parents readily came to accept practices for use on their children that they would have previously found abhorrent because the organization constantly reinforced how badly their children had behaved.

The natural human need to create meaning can also cause victims themselves to embrace cruel treatment. Most people want their suffering to have served some purpose, rather than to see it as useless and unnecessary. As a result, we tell ourselves that pain leads to growth and that even the most awful agony teaches a useful lesson. People often do learn and grow from painful experiences, of course. But while few would argue that Elie Wiesel or Primo Levi didn't learn a great deal in the concentration camps, even fewer would claim that this means that setting up similar camps would similarly produce wisdom in their inmates and be beneficial to society.

When you combine all of these sophisticated psychological factors with the simple joy of pain ending when an ordeal is over, you have a powerful recipe for something that can appear in the end to be transformative and helpful but in fact is simply abusive. Graduates of Straight—because they'd gotten the reward of release—were often truly grateful, and they expressed this gratitude in a way that would ensure that they would not be returned to the program. In other words, they said it had saved them—and kept insisting this was so, even if they relapsed into worsened addictions or developed genuine drug problems for the first time after attending the program.

What this all adds up to is that when people choose attack therapy for themselves or their children, powerful psychological forces incline them to find great good in it. These forces are so intense that people will continue to insist on the value of such therapy even in the face of demonstrable negative results or the absence of any noticeable benefit.

And Straight and its descendants don't just rely on the effects of peer pressure and attack therapy alone. They also use a set of interrelated tactics that makes change nearly impossible to resist by maximizing the effects of the psychological forces noted above.

The earliest classification scheme to describe these methods is probably still the best. It was devised by Robert Jay Lifton, a former Air Force psychiatrist and current Harvard professor, who interviewed some forty Chinese intellectuals and Westerners subjected to Chinese thought-reform regimes in prison in the 1940s and 1950s. From their experiences, he drew out a number of "themes," or techniques, which have since proven to be common to mind-control systems.[46] Obviously, Straight and other tough love programs don't use torture as extreme as the Chinese communists used—but the same tactics can be identified in their regimens.

Lifton's first "theme" is called "milieu control." By this, he meant that an organization uses total control over the subject's social and physical environment—particularly absolute regulation of communication—to change behavior. At Straight, there wasn't anything—from food to sleep to contact with the outside world to scheduling—that it didn't attempt to control. And almost every strategy for controlling the environment, by itself, has profound psychological effects.

Take diet. Many Straight participants reported that from the very start, they were underfed. Richard Bradbury described spending the end of his morning stint in the blue chairs carefully plotting how to get the peanut-butter-and-honey sandwich with the most filling. He said that most teens would deliberately eat the crust from their sandwiches first, to prolong the meal. Because of the diet's poor quality and monotony, they dreamed and fantasized about food and thus were much more responsive to promises of food rewards.

Hunger, by itself, even when not extreme, can destroy concentration and affect mood, making those subjected to it more malleable. A study of thirty-six young, healthy men who agreed to a semi-starvation diet (half their normal caloric intake) reported exactly what Richard did: they developed extreme preoccupations with food, dreamed about it, and began to lengthen and ritualize meals.[47] Sleep deprivation has a similarly insidious impact. It adversely affects concentration, reaction time, memory, and mood. As a CIA interrogation manual explains, little force is actually needed to derange higher thinking and decision-making: "Relatively small degrees of . . . fatigue, pain, sleep loss or anxiety may impair these functions."[48]

Straight didn't stop at just controlling its participants' environment, however. In order to advance past first phase, participants had to engage another of Lifton's themes, what the psychologist labeled "the cult of confession." Confession served multiple purposes. For one, it was taken directly from one of AA's twelve steps, making it seem legitimate. But in thought reform, confession also has a more sinister aspect.

In Richard Bradbury's case, it gave the group a very personal way to control him. Once he'd revealed that he'd been sexually abused by men, Straight could constantly intimidate him by implying that this meant he was a homosexual. It could offer him hope—by claiming that its program would cure him of what they said was a deviant sexual orientation. Sexual humiliation, it turns out, is one of the best-known ways to induce false confessions of other behavior, according to experts on interrogation.[49] And not only did confessions give the organization information it could use to batter its participants directly, it also provided ways to discredit them if they tried to go public with complaints.

Another of Lifton's themes, what he called "loading the language," was also evident in Straight. For instance, the group called verbally and physically attacking someone "helping" him. One of Lifton's subjects of Chinese "reeducation" could just as easily have been describing Straight when he said that in his captors' language, "to help means to maltreat people."[50] The concept of truth itself becomes distorted this way. At Straight, what had really happened to Richard didn't matter. His truth—that he had dropped out of school because he'd been sexually abused—wasn't acceptable. Straight's "real" version of the story was that he'd dropped out because he'd been getting high—and so this was all he was allowed to say about it. "Getting honest" at Straight didn't mean telling the truth; it meant telling only stories in which you behaved poorly, in ways about which you now felt guilty and from which the program had saved you. Anything else was "lies" or "denial."

Another Lifton tactic that Straight utilized was "mystical manipulation." This technique uses the absolute control the group has over its participants to make them feel as though God himself is aligned with its goals. At Straight, this involved being told repeatedly "everything happens for a reason." Any positive coincidence was a sign that God was working through Straight to further his goals; any negative event was a test. In other words, if a parent brought someone to the program late and he was punished for it, he needed a lesson in humility; if the traffic allowed a to-the-minute arrival, God had guided them on their anointed mission. In this way, even the most trivial event becomes imbued with meaning and the program can be made to seem to have control beyond its worldly powers.

Mystical manipulation also involves promoting dedication to the cause of the organization as the ultimate good. To Straight, teen drug use was not just dangerous or unhealthy, it was evil. Consequently, it needed to be fought by any means necessary, and if that meant breaking the law, beating a child, kidnapping someone, then that's what Straight would do. By framing each person's story as part of a great struggle between good and evil, mystical manipulation ups the stakes involved in both compliance and rebellion.

When this technique is successful, it produces in its victims what

Lifton called "the psychology of the pawn." Once someone comes to accept that Straight's goal is of cosmic significance, his compliance becomes ever more complete. Not "motivating" enthusiastically enough, not "turning yourself in" for sexual or drug-related thoughts, not immediately restraining a "misbehaver" becomes not just a deviation from one's own goals, but from God's plan. This ideology leads many people to abandon their previous value systems, to do things that they would otherwise find wrong in service of what they now see as the greater good. The noose of thought reform is tightened by making its victims into perpetrators.

The climate of guilt and shame that insistently pervaded Straight Incorporated also vividly demonstrated Lifton's notion of a "demand for purity." This means that no shameful confession is ever enough. In the world of the program, there's always more to the story, some damning detail you neglected to reveal. Participants are always generating new secrets—for example, thoughts about wanting to leave (even counselors were considered "selfish" for thinking this way) or doubts. Even normal sexual desires must be confessed, because Straight's policy was that teenagers should not have sexual feelings. If these treacherous thoughts weren't revealed, such "druggie" thoughts could doom Straight itself and therefore those who so needed its help. The group demands absolute purity because its goals are said to be threatened if everyone does not "open up" entirely.

Those involved become so focused on perfecting their own thoughts and behavior that they have no time to consider whether the group's demands are appropriate. Once inside, the program's structuring of their lives and its mental control over their fears and obsessions leaves little room for critical thinking. As Richard Bradbury put it, "They could have put a gun in my hand and said, 'Kill somebody for us,' and nope, I wouldn't even have questioned."

The fact that the group itself is the only place to go for absolution from the shame it induces creates a cycle of increasing dependency. As Lifton noted about Chinese thought-reform victims, the more an individual experiences guilt and shame—and people vary greatly in this propensity—the more vulnerable that person is to this process. Because Richard Bradbury had had such a shameful experience as a child, he was almost a perfect target for Straight. Less sensitive teenagers and those who had not had significantly shaming experiences in their pasts might have been able to shrug off Straight's attacks, but they went right to the core of Richard's fears.

Ironically, of course, this means that programs like Straight are most likely to harm the kind of people who do not need "rehabilitation"—i.e., people with a strong conscience, people who are highly empathetic, who are eager to please others, and who feel shame at not measuring up to their own standards of goodness. A genuine sociopath, who is willing to do anything for his own selfish ends, won't agonize about applying himself to the group's great mission. If he can't escape, he'll tell the lies necessary for advancement, and then enjoy the power and control he gets to wield over others.

Conversely, then, the type of person that society would most like to "brainwash" is probably the least susceptible to the attempt. In fact, exposure to thought-reform tactics can make antisocial behavior worse, by giving sociopaths new tools for controlling others. Research on sociopaths in a "therapeutic community" that apparently used Synanon-like tactics, in fact, found that it made them worse than if they'd had no treatment at all.[51]

Every single one of Lifton's themes played itself out at Straight and would appear in its many descendants. Especially prominent was what he called "sacred science," which means elevating the group's own doctrines and practices to the status of gospel truth, impervious to empirical evidence. Straight supporters ignored "research" and "cold statistics." To counteract hard evidence, they'd use phrases like "If it helps just one person . . ." and dismiss their critics.

Lifton's final theme, "the dispensing of existence" shows the most serious repercussions of mind-control techniques. What this chilling phrase means is that when all these forces combine, the group will believe that outsiders are literally not as worthy of life as are insiders. If one rebellious teenager or angry parent or stubborn bureaucrat gets in the way of the great goal of saving thousands of innocents, it no longer seems wrong to lie to him or to threaten or rough up or detain someone who might block such an important and worthy project.

While Lifton's themes have been criticized when applied to religious organizations that members join by choice, because voluntary belief in the group's ideas can occur without and even in spite of coercion, their applicability to groups into which people are placed involuntarily and treated violently is much less controversial. Whether or not such "brain-washing" can force the unwilling to permanently change their opinions and behavior, it can certainly produce compliant teenagers in the short run—especially when many of those sent to such programs (like Richard Bradbury and Fred Collins) are not severely troubled in the first place.

And as a result of all of these complicated influences, an increasingly bewildering variety of tough love programs have been introduced over the last three decades. When one form falls from favor, another gains momentum to rehabilitate the tough love concept. And as Straight Incorporated's network began to wither, the wilderness boot camp took center stage.[52]

THREE

Into the Wilderness

S ALLY AND BOB BACON'S Phoenix home looks like something out of *Architectural Digest.* It is airily spacious, with two large living rooms filled with colorful, original objets d'art and spotless sectional couches. Sally is a jewelry designer and Bob is an architect. The beauty is almost intimidating, but Sally herself is warm and welcoming. And she doesn't blink when her large, exuberantly shaggy Bouvier des Flandres jumps up on the white couch. Rather than shoo the dog off, she curls up and strokes him.

In the outer living room, right near the studio where Sally creates her elegant jewelry, there's a basket containing some photos and mementos of her son, Aaron. Many show a skinny, smiling, compellingly attractive young man with long honey-blond hair and brilliant blue eyes.

But among them is one photo that no parent should ever have to see. It's the last picture ever taken of Aaron. He looks drawn and skeletal. His eyes are piercingly haunted, looking at the camera as though he knows he's going to die but wants desperately to live. It feels like he knows the picture is evidence, his only way to tell of what has happened to him. People often almost blithely compare images to those from the Holocaust, but the Aaron Bacon in this picture truly would not have looked out of place at Auschwitz. It seems impossible to look at the photo and not make the comparison. The just-under-six-foot sixteen-year-old weighed 108 pounds. His arms and chest are achingly thin, with his ribs painfully protruding as he holds his shirt up to display them to the camera.

The people who ran the tough love wilderness program he attended, however, who could have saved him from dying of an easily treatable ulcer, were convinced, some even to this day, that he faked and/or deliberately caused his own illness. The photo was taken, in fact, while Aaron was being taunted by a staff member about intentionally starving himself; the man who took it said he was going to send it to his parents and girlfriend "so they'll know what you're up to," according to an account of Aaron's death by journalist Jon Krakauer.[1]

AARON BACON WAS, by every account but those of the people who killed him, an extraordinary person. Even as a small child he was unusually empathetic. When he was little, the Bacons lived in a Phoenix neighborhood called Encanto, a picturesque historic district that had a high concentration of homeless people. Because Bob was working in Japan at the time, Sally was especially frightened that some of the vagrants might mug her or break in. She couldn't understand why they seemed to gravitate toward her home. Their sleeping bags and other limited possessions were always in the Bacons' yard. Eventually, she discovered that young Aaron had been leaving peanut-butter sandwiches for them in the slot outside formerly used for milk delivery. He was unlocking the guesthouse to allow them to take showers.

"I sat him down and said, 'Look, you can't do that,'" Sally says. "We don't know if these people will harm you. And he looked at me and said, 'Mom, we have a house. We have love. We have each other. They don't have anything, and I won't stop.' And I'm like, What do you say to a child that says that?"

Aaron wasn't being kind just for show. Sally didn't learn until his funeral, for example, about a small act of kindness that had moved the mother of one of his friends. In third grade, Aaron was in a tight-knit group with three other boys—his best buddies. One day, two of the others decided that the third kid was "a geek," and told Aaron that they weren't going to speak to him any more. Aaron went to the school office, asked to use the phone, and called the child's mom, describing what had happened and saying that the boy would "need a little extra love today." He didn't drop his friend.

Aaron was not only mature for his age; he was also highly intelligent and had great powers of persuasion. When he was older and attending a private school, the headmaster called his mother in for a conference. She believed he was listening to "negative music," and didn't like his long hair. She told Sally that Aaron liked Ozzy Osbourne, then known for once biting the head off of a bat. Sally insisted that Aaron be allowed to defend himself, so he quietly asked the assembled adults if they'd ever actually listened to Osbourne's lyrics, which tend to oppose war and violence. He told them that the rocker had long repudiated the bat-biting incident. He impressed the school officials so much with his reasoned arguments that they backed off completely, even about the hair.

But Aaron's high intelligence, his self-determination, and his own strong moral compass were all part of what set him up for trouble as he approached adolescence. The black-and-white certitudes of prepubescent life, where drugs are bad, cops are good, and girls are boring were starting to be replaced by a world where the truth isn't so clear.

Aaron became upset when he learned that his older brother James* was smoking pot and taking acid. Aaron was now in eighth grade; his brother was in high school. As kids, they'd had posters on their walls that read DO DRUGS. DO TIME. Their father, Bob, was an alcoholic in long-term recovery. He had long warned the boys about the dangers of addiction. Bob had been very open about the effects of alcohol on his extended family and had steeped his boys in the culture of recovery. Sally, too, came from a family with a history of substance-abuse problems and had had her own youthful drug experiences, though she had stopped without treatment. The possibility that genes might put their kids at great risk of addiction made the entire family especially sensitive to drug issues.

So when James began regularly smoking pot, and no one confronted him about it, Aaron worried. He told his mom that he thought the family was "dysfunctional" because they hadn't stopped his brother's drug use. Shortly thereafter, James told Sally that he needed help and was sent to the highly respected Minnesota rehabilitation center Hazelden.

Six months later, however, Aaron began to smoke pot and take psychedelics himself. James, too, had continued his drug involvement after Hazelden, straightening himself out only several years later as he matured. James's rehab stay hadn't made any noticeable difference, and Sally now believes that Hazelden should never have accepted him because he was not a drug addict.

But while James had kept up his honor-student grades while he was taking drugs, Aaron's grades started to plunge when he hit his sophomore year of high school. He also began taking the car out at night, driving it, dinging it, and then denying what he'd done. This made Sally crazy: she'd worked really hard to teach her children honesty, to have open communication with them—things she'd felt she'd been denied during her own childhood. She couldn't take being lied to; she felt particularly betrayed by a son she'd felt especially close to since his birth. Aaron, who'd always been so bright and open, now seemed sullen, depressed, and irritable.

Sally became ever more concerned, especially after an incident in February 1994 in which Aaron was attacked in the Central High parking lot by members of the Crips gang, which had recently expanded from L.A. into Arizona. A witness reported that it was more than a random mugging; that Aaron seemed to know the gang members well, and that they'd called him by what seemed to be a gang nickname, "Rabbit."

Aaron had recently transferred to Central from an exclusive private

school. He was sixteen. He and his parents both knew that the real reason he wanted to change schools was to spend more time with his girlfriend, who attended Central. But he'd nailed his case for the switch by
arguing that he wanted more "socioeconomic diversity" and saying he
felt stifled by the privileged atmosphere at Pacific Country Day. Hanging out with gang members wasn't exactly what they thought he'd had
in mind. Though Aaron denied involvement with the Crips, his simulta-
neous abrupt change in demeanor made Sally unsure about what to
think.

The Bacons were already in family therapy, having started after the incidents with the car. Sally didn't think Hazelden—whatever its effect on
their older son—would be right for Aaron. However, she'd heard from a
close friend about a rigorous wilderness program for troubled teens
called North Star Expeditions. The friend said it had had remarkable results on the son of one of her friends. It sounded perfect for Aaron: "Oh!
Just to be out there with God and nature and himself writing," Sally says,
calling up her original image of the program. "Aaron loved solitude, the
kid liked to be alone, loved to write. Aaron's lifeline was his pen and paper." She adds, now startled by her own naiveté, "When he left, I was
afraid he would think he did all this stuff and now I'm sending him on
this great vacation." She told one journalist, "I pictured Aaron sitting
around campfires, being nurtured by nature. I thought I was sending him
to a little slice of heaven."[2]

She imagined Outward Bound or a Boy Scout camp, with the addition
of trained therapists. She knew the conditions would be spartan, but she
pictured well-provisioned campers, navigating the unpredictable but
character-building challenges of the wild. She looked at North Star's
slick brochure, which pictured a boy with a backpack on top of a mountain, pointing eagerly at a twinkling star. She thought that yes, this might
be just what Aaron needed.

But Sally Bacon wasn't impulsive in her decisions about care for her
kids. She checked everything out by the book, whether she was looking
for a private school or a physician, even when she was worried and
frightened. Like many of the Straight parents, she'd checked out the

treatment program she was considering for her child in the ways most experts recommend: by asking her family therapist's opinion, talking to parents of kids who'd been through it, and having long discussions about critical issues with the people who ran the program.

On February 28, 1994, Sally and Bob met with two of the owners of North Star, Lance Jaggar and his wife Barbara, for several hours. When Bob said that Aaron wouldn't react well to threats or scare tactics, they heard in soothing tones about Lance Jaggar's "special gift for working with kids." Sally said that she told the Jaggars that her biggest concern was that Aaron would lose weight in the program, because at five-eleven and 134 pounds, he was already far too thin. "They grabbed my hand and held [it]," Sally told me, "and said, 'We would never let your son lose weight.'"

Sally asked about whether there was a complaint process, about what would happen if, for example, a kid said he was being sexually abused. The Jaggars responded that someone from the office would be immediately sent into the field to interview the child and investigate. Over and over, the Bacons were told almost exactly what the experts had said they should look for in a program: that it was not a harsh boot camp, that Aaron would be well cared for, that he'd be hiking in beautiful desert areas by day, discussing his issues with a therapist around the campfire at night. When they left the meeting, Sally told Bob she was concerned that Jaggar was "not exactly a rocket scientist" and that he might respond poorly to Aaron's intellect. But Bob said that maybe what Aaron needed was to be less caught up in his thoughts for a while.

And so they signed him up—going so far as to take a second mortgage on their house in order to pay the $13,900 fee. They assumed that the high cost must cover trained staff and top-of-the-line equipment, which they'd been told would be provided. And because the Jaggars recommended it, rather than bringing Aaron to the camp themselves, they agreed to have Jaggar and his brother-in-law "escort" Aaron to the program, for an extra $775. Says Bob, "When parents are in that state of distress, they can easily imagine that a several-hour trip in the car with their child on the way to such a program would be an extremely tense and dif-

ficult ride. You fear that now that you've struggled over making this decision that you're going to be talked out of it. And when they suggest
that the way that's overcome is by [picking the teen up], you're like,
'Oh, all right.' And it kind of is an indication that these people do have
experience with these things. They understand the kind of situation that
you're in, so, you know, of course you buy into it."

AT SIX A.M., on March 1, 1994, Aaron Bacon was woken up by Mae,
one of the Bacons' three Shar-peis, who was whinnying outside his bedroom door. Soon, Bob Bacon and two large strangers poured into his
room. Bob told Aaron that the men were from North Star. He assured
his son that he loved him, but that Aaron needed to shape up and go
with them to the program that his parents had mentioned they were
considering for him.

Aaron started to get out of bed, but Jaggar, 280 pounds to Aaron's
134, roughly grabbed his arm. When Aaron attempted to pull back, Jaggar said, according to one magazine account, "You're coming with me. If
I detect any resistance, I'll assume you are trying to get away and I'll take
the appropriate action. Do I make myself clear?"[3] Minutes later, an obviously terrified Aaron was led from his bedroom. Sally tried to hug him,
but Jaggar didn't let Aaron hug back. She gave him a kiss, said, "I love
you," and told him not to be frightened. Aaron, probably angry and certainly disoriented, didn't reply. He was driven to the airport and then
flown in a single-engine Cessna to an isolated airstrip in Escalante, Utah.

Escalante is a tiny Mormon town, with a population of about 800, located in the red rock country of southern Utah. The Escalante Chamber
of Commerce describes the region as one marked by "great distances,
enormously difficult terrain, and a remoteness rarely equaled in the
lower forty-eight states."[4] The red rock canyons, plateaus, scrub pines,
and large stretches of desert give the area an alien feel; in many spots, the
landscape looks almost Martian. March is definitely a winter month
there: at night, the temperatures are often well below freezing.

Upon his arrival at North Star's base, Aaron was strip-searched. He was given a pair of cheap boots that were too small, a sleeping bag rated to twenty degrees below zero, and a backpack. Then he was driven farther into the desert. His first few days were supposed to be for "acclimatization" to 5,600-foot elevation and cold temperatures, but Aaron was never given warm enough clothing. His first journal entry reads,

> I've been shaking from the cold since I got here, my body being used to the weather in Phoenix . . . I feel like I'm going to die. My whole body is goose flesh and I feel like it's being stretched over my body like the skin of an animal over a drum.[5]

Aaron was made to write an essay upon arrival that explained why he believed he'd been sent to North Star. He wrote,

> As of yet, I'm not sure why I'm here. My parents, as far as they're concerned, have no other options. My parents aren't ready to handle the universal problems that come with parenting a child today. In my opinion, marijuana use, and my drug involvement, is no reason to be here. I think my parents are making a mistake. I wouldn't think so if something could be changed in me. I have no willingness to change because as I see it, I have no need to. But if I am forced to change, this program seems to be ready to FORCE me. This is not their last resort. Child abuse, which I think this program is, is never a resort, it only results in the opposite.[6]

That essay, and this passage from his journal written later that day were clearly not intended to endear him to program staff, who read everything the teens wrote. Aaron wrote of Jaggar, "He proceeded to tell me that I would be escorted by whatever means necessary . . . He quoted Malcolm X and seemed to live by Machiavelli, but I'll bet my own dime that his redneck hillbilly ears have never heard of either."[7]

Several days later, in an entry which joked about the unpleasantness of the topic he was discussing, he first noted serious gastrointestinal distress:

"I drop some serious logs at home and here I just did this little bitty super concentrated turd. Yucky. My stomach really hurts."[8] This was probably the first sign of the intestinal ulcer that would ultimately kill him. At this point, a simple over-the-counter medication like Tagamet could probably have saved his life. Nonetheless, when he was taken back to town for a preprogram physical, he was cleared by a physician's assistant. His blood and urine tests revealed nothing but marijuana. His long hair was shorn.

He noted, "When I was at the clinic getting my physical, there was a box of extra chewy Chips Ahoy! and a bunch of assorted chips. I asked but [the staff] wouldn't give me any. When we were in the office, [staff] were eating huge sandwiches, lots of meat and lots of soda . . . of course we can't have anything." Trying to make the best of the situation, he conceived a rationale for the cruel treatment.

When we were hiking, I got to realize why or at least one advantage to it. While we are here, we aren't around drugs so it's pretty easy not to use. But when we get home, we'll be around them again. We "jones" for [a drug-culture term for "crave"] good food now because we don't have it and it's around. If we become immune to the jones or able to overcome it, it is more likely we'll be able to overcome the weed jones. Well, at least it makes some sense.[9]

What didn't make sense to him were the lectures he received while they trekked farther into the canyons. In a letter he wrote home on March 8, but was not allowed to send at that time, he said,

I love you both very much but I still don't think this was the right decision nor do I think this was your last choice. I'm trying to work this program as well as I can but their philosophy about everything seems so different from anything that I've been taught. I can't believe you want me believing this stuff . . . I've been told that "all therapists, counselors, psychologists and psychiatrists are quacks." I've been lectured on the stupidity of believing in them.[10]

His journal entry from later that day reveals a continued obsession with food. "I'm pretty excited that I'm gonna eat soon because I got to taste some of the leftover pan scrapings from the staff's dinner." The kids were given lentils, rice, oatmeal, trail mix, and cornmeal, with smaller quantities of fresh vegetables about once a week. But they were not well instructed on how to prepare it, nor were they told how to ration it. If the campers couldn't learn to make a fire with a Native American bow drill technique, much of the food was inedible. After initial instruction, no one was allowed to "use" the fire if he couldn't make one himself. Aaron would never master fire-making with a bow drill.

Three days later, already hungry, he was moved to the second phase of the program, "Primitive," which began with a two-day fast called "Impact." His "counselors" were Craig Fisher, Sonny Duncan, and Jeff Hohenstein—who didn't have a year's experience in leading wilderness expeditions or counseling troubled teens between the three of them. Fisher was nineteen, Duncan twenty. Hohenstein, the oldest and most experienced, had worked at North Star for three months and was just twenty-one.[11]

Attempting to put a good face on it (or possibly, just trying to please the staff), Aaron wrote,

> I can tell already that it is going to test my physical limitations and broaden them. I am pretty scared of the next couple of weeks. I've been sick all day with a horrible stomachache. It's been heck hiking as much as we do. We are on "impact" getting rid of all the toxins in our bodies by not eating. I suppose it won't be bad because I don't know how to cook well enough yet. I feel really bad after eating.[12]

He also wrote about his parents, who had been told, unbeknownst to Aaron, not to write to him.

> I wonder if they miss me? They haven't written. I should have told them that I love them, and I'm sorry I didn't. I didn't even hug them

and that was terrible. I sure wish I could hug them and tell them I
love them now.[13]

By now, Aaron's group, which consisted of six students and two
staffers (Duncan, Fisher, and Hohenstein rotated shifts) was deep into
the wilderness, in a region of burnt-orange sandstone made even more
otherworldly by narrow slot canyons. The terrain features jagged rocks
and steep cliffs. Ancient petroglyphs of animals left by the Anasazi
people line some of the rock faces. The hiking had left Aaron's feet severely blistered by the tight boots and he could barely stagger along under the weight of his forty-five-pound backpack.

Soon, he began to slip and fall repeatedly. On March 12, he wrote, "I
fell twice on the trail today. The first time I could not get up because the
pack was too heavy . . . I fell again because my legs were so weak. My
whole body became numb that time, and I was so weak I couldn't lift my
arms."[14]

Because of North Star's philosophy that any problem was a matter of
mind, not body, Aaron was constantly urged to try harder, to keep going,
and worst of all, to stop being so lazy. The staff assumed that his complaints and repeated falls were all part of a ruse, an attempt to get released early from the program. Without any effort to check whether or
not he was actually ill, they began calling him a "whiner" and a "faker."
Each time he reported or showed symptoms, he was punished and lectured more. He wrote that he felt bad for being the "wimp" of the group.
Soon, other campers and staffers began calling him "gay," implying that
his increasing weakness meant he was effeminate, not a real man.

On March 13, having gone without food for two days, Aaron continued to repeatedly stagger and fall. While attempting to climb through a
slot canyon area called Little Death Hollow, he gashed open his chin on
the slickrock (which takes its name from the coarse, uneven, windswept
surfaces that didn't provide good traction for settlers' metal-shod
horses). As he landed, he broke a gallon container of water meant to be
used by the group. He wrote,

I'm just so enveloped in pain . . . I felt so stupid but I hit my face on
the rock and that hurt more than I felt stupid . . . I'm glad I can't
see it because I bet it looks horrible. The staff didn't seem to care
one bit . . . We get absolutely zero positive reinforcement and that
really bothers me.[15]

Two days later, he abandoned his pack, having become too weak to
carry it. That meant having to go another two days without food until
the group returned to the point where he'd left the pack on their way
back. As of March 17, the only sustenance Bacon had had in five days
was a can of peaches, a six-inch-long raw lizard, and a cooked scorpion.
When he retrieved his pack, he was able to eat some cooked food that
helped restore his strength. He did well on the trails, for once not trip-
ping and falling. That day, he wrote, "was my first good day here at North
Star."[16] It would be his last.

The following day, the group crossed a deep stream. Aaron was too
weak to lift his pack over his head like the rest of the group did. Everything, including his food and his sleeping bag, got soaked through.
Worse, because he still hadn't been able to make a fire, that evening he
wasn't allowed close to the group's fire and wasn't allowed to eat what
was cooked there. Still wet and shivering, he wrote, "I am so scared of
everything, staff, slickrock, the cold, my pack, everything."[17] The low
temperature that evening was 36 degrees. His remaining diary entries
are spotted with blood from recurrent nosebleeds. His spelling and
handwriting would deteriorate progressively as his illness became worse.

On March 19, Aaron's group was visited by another North Star staffer,
Brent Brewer, who once again encouraged him to work harder. Clearly
continuing to attempt to please his keepers, Aaron wrote,

I know he's right and I should. I will. But I think I have been. He told
me I was definitely going to lose something when I next saw him.
Something that I really like. I'm freaking out about that. I don't want
to lose my pack for a blanket pack [a wool blanket, sewn together, instead of the weather-rated sleeping bag]. That would be horrible.[18]

The next day, Brewer took Aaron's sleeping bag. The evening temperatures dropped below freezing, but he was made to sleep away from the fire, outside the group's tent of tarpaulins, with just a wool blanket. The blanket was so cold to the touch that when he actually did lie down to sleep, he didn't even wrap it around himself. He wrote,

> I don't really get what I'm doing wrong or why my parents want me here. I know they want me to change, get off drugs, quit lying and be trustworthy, but I don't see how any of this stuff is going to help with that. This seems more like hiking and camping school.[19]

That same day, he received a tough letter from his mother, who'd been told by program staff that Aaron didn't need to be pampered or told he was loved. She told me, "They said Aaron does not need to hear how much you love him right now. Right now he needs for you to be tough. Well, I bought into that. I bought into that because our whole life was upside down, we weren't communicating, I didn't know how to reach him." She figured since she'd always been a soft touch and that didn't seem to be working, it was time to try something different.

Aaron wrote in his journal,

> She didn't tell me that she loves me or that she misses me. It was mostly a letter that she hates who I have become and loved me when I was little. I've been wanting to hear "I love you" or "I miss you" for so long now that I'm not sure that she does.[20]

By this time, Aaron hadn't eaten in twenty-four hours and had had few meals in days. At some point, intestinal fluids had begun leaking into his abdominal cavity through the ulcer, causing exquisite pain and gradually poisoning his blood and organs with intestinal bacteria. Hunger would have exacerbated the condition and sped the progression of the infection. He wrote,

> I feel like I am losing control of my body. I've peed in my pants every night for the last three nights and today when we started our

little hike, I took a dump in my pants. I didn't even feel it coming, it just happened. I told Jeff, because I thought he might be more sympathetic and easy on me, but he yelled to Craig, "Hey, he took a dump in his pants." All the other students started to laugh . . . I've been telling [the staff] that I'm sick for a while and they say I'm faking it.[21]

Instead of receiving medical attention, Aaron was told that his incontinence meant that he had no "self-respect." And so even when he wasn't explicitly being punished, other campers refused to sleep next to him in the "burrito" formation they usually adopted to conserve body heat under the tarps.[22]

The next day, his last entry, streaked in blood and nearly impossible to make out, read in part, "All I can think about is cold and pain . . . I miss my family so much. My hands, my lips and my face are dead."[23] That same day, one of the North Star staffers wrote about Aaron in his own journal, "I have finally wiped the smile off the Bacon boy's face. I have finally broken his spirit."

It is not known if other journal entries for the last ten days of Aaron's life were destroyed, or if he was too weak to write by that point. The conditions, incredibly, became even worse. The group climbed to the summit of the Kaiparowits Plateau, one of the most remote regions of the American Southwest. The Southern Utah Wilderness Alliance calls the mesa a challenge for even the most experienced hikers, and the ascent to 7,000 feet must have been excruciating for Aaron. He abandoned his pack again. Nighttime temperatures for March 22 to 25 were often well below freezing, but Aaron was still denied food and access to the fire. He was given neither a sleeping bag nor a blanket to keep warm at night.

On March 25 alone, his group hiked eight miles. One boy, risking punishment, did sneak him powdered milk and brown sugar on the 23rd, but that was all he would eat until the 26th. The group met up with Lance Jaggar, who once again called Aaron "a whiner and a faker"[24] and told him to stop pretending to be ill. On the 26th, the boys were made to do 100 jumping jacks, 100 leg-raises, 100 sit-ups, and 50 push-ups, as they had hiked only two miles that day because of Aaron's difficulties. Aaron was "helped" to complete the exercises since he could not do them on his own. He was given rice and lentils, but vomited and said he had stomach pain.

For the descent from the plateau, because of his lack of bowel and bladder control, Aaron was now made to go without pants. This meant not only public humiliation, but more physical discomfort in the cold. The group returned to where he'd left his pack, but Aaron was still too weak to retrieve it. And the others were prohibited from helping him. Seeing what Aaron was being put through for breaking the rules, none dared try. The next day, his only meal was prickly pear cactus and pine needle tea. The day after that, although he was given rice and lentils, he was not permitted to drink because his "Gookinade," an energy drink similar to Gatorade, had been lost or stolen.

By March 29, Aaron was so sickly that he could walk no farther. The other campers carried him back to base camp. He vomited all over them, babbling incoherently about seeing purple stars in a purple sky. Again, he asked for medical attention and again, despite obvious evidence to the contrary, he was called a faker by program staff. The other campers—who'd seen Aaron naked when they'd done "full body hygiene" and stripped to wash both their bodies and their laundry—were already describing Aaron as "weak and brittle" and like "a skeleton" or an "old man" or someone "from Ethiopia."[25]

MIKE HILL, a nineteen-year-old Apache from Arizona's San Carlos Indian Reservation, had been recruited literally on the street and offered a job at North Star without a résumé or qualifications. So had his best friend, Sonny Duncan, one of the "counselors" assigned to Aaron's group. Both had been trained on the job by simply being left to supervise students in the desert.

Hill had met Aaron Bacon when the teen had first entered North Star, and while he'd had little contact with him because he'd been given a different group, he had instantly liked the boy. When he met up with Aaron's group on March 30, he was horrified by the changes he saw in him. He described Aaron then as "anorexic-like, with bones showing everywhere."[26]

Even those in charge of Aaron's group became concerned now. They called in Georgette Costigan, a certified EMT, to give Aaron a checkup. But shockingly, for reasons that may forever remain obscure, she didn't physically examine him. She didn't take his pulse, didn't examine his abdomen, didn't take his temperature, didn't listen to his complaints of stomach pain or gather reports about his incontinence and vomiting from the staff. She simply handed him a piece of cheese and made him promise to keep hiking. When staffer Craig Fisher asked her to take Aaron back to town with her, she demurred, saying there was nothing wrong with him.

By the next day, when Aaron couldn't walk for more than a few minutes without collapsing, the staff had had enough. They decided they would start "the faker" over—take him back to Escalante to redo the entire program, starting with acclimatization. Duncan radioed Hill and asked him to bring his group over to where Aaron's group was and watch the boy until a truck could drive out from town to pick him up.

Hill found Aaron sitting on a pit latrine. Whenever he tried to stand, he collapsed into the filthy ditch, staggering and disoriented. He had no control over his bowels, and had lost consciousness repeatedly while attempting to crawl to the latrine earlier that day. Staff had finally carried him there, and left him. As Hill approached, Duncan was standing nearby, mocking Aaron, and laughing while imitating his pitiful attempts to right himself. He told Hill that Aaron was starving himself, trying to commit suicide. Hill couldn't believe what he was hearing, and he asked some of his campers to carry Aaron away from the latrine. They laid him down in a shady spot beneath a juniper tree, and there Hill took the haunting photo of Aaron that I later saw in Sally's basket.

Hill seemed at first to buy the idea that Aaron was suicidal, and joined his friend Duncan in taunting him. He said he was taking the picture to show Aaron's parents and his girlfriend how he was harming himself. But Hill wasn't completely convinced that Aaron was deliberately hurting himself. He asked the teenager whether he really wanted to die. Aaron, already losing his hearing to his illness, asked Hill to repeat the question. Nearly shouting because he couldn't even pick up his own voice, Aaron said, "Please speak louder, sir, I can't hear you," still using the respectful form of address the program required.

"Are you doing this because you want to die?" Hill shouted.

"No, sir, I don't want to die, sir," Aaron pleaded.[27] But Hill suddenly realized that there was a real possibility that Aaron was, in fact, in such bad shape that he might not make it. The realization stunned him: What if this boy was not defiant, not faking, but deathly ill, possibly starving? He prepared some oatmeal for Aaron, and a fellow camper tried desperately to feed him. After eleven spoonfuls, the boy couldn't eat. As the horror of what was happening, of what it might mean if Aaron really did die, began to dawn on him, Hill panicked. He tried to take Aaron's temperature, but the thermometer he'd been given by North Star was broken. Aaron said hoarsely that he was losing his eyesight, that all he could see was a "white glare."[28]

Hill had no idea what to do. He took a yellow Apache "healing" powder from his pocket, sprinkled it around Aaron's body and asked the other campers to gather around to pray. Aaron couldn't keep from urinating on himself as Hill lay down next to him, and another camper began to cry.

And still, the ordeal wasn't over, and still no one with the power to make a difference sought real help. Emergency medical care, certainly the day before he died, possibly even hours before he last collapsed, could have made a real difference. While the death rate for severe peritonitis can be up to 50 percent,[29] the disease usually strikes the old and infirm. Intravenous antibiotics and supportive measures could potentially have given a young man like Aaron a good chance of recovery, even after the disease had progressed this far.

As the truck approached the campsite from Hole in the Rock Road, Eric Henry, son of North Star's co-owner Bill Henry, radioed Hill, telling him to get the "faker" ready. Because Aaron couldn't walk, Henry dumped him into the cab of the truck, and unforgivably, spent fifteen minutes or more talking and joking about Aaron's feigned illness while he literally lay dying. Why Hill didn't push Henry to get Aaron to the hospital immediately, when he was clearly at least somewhat aware of the gravity of the situation, is another of many unanswered and probably unanswerable questions surrounding Aaron Bacon's death.

When Henry and Hill looked inside the truck, after hearing the boy bang his head repeatedly against its back window, they found Aaron unconscious. His heart had stopped; he had no pulse. They put him on the ground and radioed for help while Hill attempted CPR, but he didn't really know what he was doing. He had no training. The physician's assistant who had OK'd Aaron for the program arrived, and didn't recognize the teen he'd examined three weeks earlier. Georgette Costigan, the EMT, was called, too, but her skills weren't of any use. She kept yelling "Oh, shit," as the group realized that the boy was dead and, possibly, that they bore no small responsibility for what had happened.[30]

It had been glaringly obvious for at least two weeks that Aaron Bacon was severely ill. All the kids in his group were devastatingly aware of it; none of them had wasted away as much as he did. They had watched him try and fail daily to control his bodily functions. It seemed clear to them that no one could—or would ever want to—fake the disgusting symptoms and the progressive deterioration he had undergone. Many had mentioned his health complaints and weak, sickly demeanor repeatedly in their journals, and they had no medical training at all. None was needed to see that this boy was direly ill. Costigan would later be charged with witness tampering, for allegedly trying to force the teens to alter journal entries she deemed too incriminating, but there was not enough evidence to make the charges stick. And that would not be the only disappointment for the prosecutors who would seek to bring Aaron's killers to justice.

When Sally Bacon got the call from North Star, saying, "Aaron is down. We can't get a pulse," her mind simply refused to make the logi-

cal jump that the caller, Barbara Jaggar, expected. Sally thought her son
was sick or injured, maybe severely. "Aaron's been airlifted to the hospital in Page, Arizona," Jaggar said.[31] Sally couldn't imagine that it was
even possible that he was dead. How could it be? She was told to call her
husband, who'd been given the hospital phone number. Bob repeated
what he'd been told more straightforwardly. Some sort of awful accident
had occurred; maybe Aaron had eaten something poisonous. According
to North Star, he had collapsed and died suddenly. From what the Bacons were told, the program had tried everything possible to revive him;
nothing more could have been done.

Sally thought back over the phone calls she'd made to North Star.
She'd only been allowed to check in once a week, and even then, she'd
talk only to the base camp, to Barbara or another staffer, Daryl Bartholomew, never to Aaron or his group leaders. After being told that Aaron
had arrived safely, she was notified about a conversation he'd had with
Barbara. He'd tried to apologize for having been rude to her during the
trip to the program. He'd told Barbara that he didn't usually act that
way, but that he'd been angry. In response, she had said, "You're so full of
shit, Aaron—you're trying to manipulate me." When Barbara related this
incident to Sally, expecting agreement about the boy's devious tactics,
Sally protested, saying that Aaron always took responsibility for his actions and was not insincere. Sally thought Barbara's treatment of Aaron
was despicable, but she rationalized it, figuring that the program was
used to dealing with kids who really were underhanded. Now she said,
"I should have been clued off right there."

In their next conversation, Sally was told that Aaron was uncooperative and malingering. Bartholomew called him "belligerent and a whiner."
He was refusing to carry his pack; he was always complaining. The other
kids hated him. Sally replied that this didn't sound like Aaron; that while
he'd sometimes been difficult with his parents, he was always a good, respectful kid in school and to other authorities. And with other kids?
Aaron had always, even at his most troubled, been popular and even a
leader among his peers.

"They said everything was fine," Sally said, emphasizing over and over that they kept telling her Aaron was OK and that the unusual behavior was to be expected, that she shouldn't worry. But looking back now, she sees red flags everywhere that she will forever regret missing. She said that once they'd called her and asked if she actually had a rare form of epilepsy, which could sometimes cause loss of bowel control. "And I said, 'Yes, that's true. Why?'" They'd told her that Aaron had soiled himself; that he'd told them she had the condition and he was afraid he might have inherited it. She'd responded that he'd never showed signs of it before; he'd never soiled himself past infancy at home. She recalls,

> [They said,] "You know what? Kids do this here all the time to get out of the program. A lot of times if they're hiking, they have to go to the bathroom, they don't get to stop, [so] sometimes they go to the bathroom on themselves." And I said, "Well, why wouldn't they get to stop?" "Well, if they were hiking up a hill, blah blah blah." But they didn't lead me to believe he was losing control of his bodily functions.

On March 30, when unbeknownst to her Aaron was already close to death, Sally had had lunch with James. They'd discussed why she'd sent Aaron to North Star, and James said he didn't think it had been necessary. He mentioned his own rebellious period, saying that even though she'd sent him to Hazelden, even though she'd thrown him out of the house when he continued to smoke pot afterward, he didn't stop until he was ready. And that Aaron would do the same. He didn't need help, James said, he just needed time. This conversation would later haunt her.

> The night before he died, I called them and they said, "Aaron is belligerent, he is not cooperating, he's bargaining for food, and he's going to have to repeat the program." And I said, "Why would he be bargaining for food?"
>   "Well, he's not cooperating, and he's trying to get the other kids to give him some of their food." Not that he's not getting any food, but that he's trying to get the kids to give him their food. And I said,

"You know what? Something's not right. You're describing a child I don't even know," and they said, "We're going to make him repeat the first leg of the program." I went to bed that night and I was sobbing, and I said "God, something's wrong with Aaron. I want you to put your arms around him and hold him and protect him." He was dead the next day.

All Sally wanted now was to reclaim Aaron's body, to hug him and tell him she loved him and say all the things she wished she'd said, all the things she wished she'd done, before he'd left. But three days later, when she first saw his body in a Phoenix morgue, it was unrecognizable. This violently battered corpse couldn't possibly be Aaron's remains, she thought. It was only when Sally noticed a childhood scar over his right eye that she could begin to tell that it was he.

He had lost twenty-three pounds. He was bruised black and blue "from the tip of his toes to the top of his head,"[32] not only from falls, but from the clumsy attempts at resuscitation. His arms and legs looked like toothpicks, his face like a hollowed-out skull; other parts, like his knees, were grotesquely swollen. And she says with incalculable pain, "If you would have seen my son's feet . . . my husband held and kissed his feet. The sores on Aaron's feet, he was wearing shoes at least two sizes too small for him. That they made him hike in. When I ripped the sheet off of Aaron's body, there were sores from his groin down, open sores." She shrieked a mother's unearthly cry of pure rage and hurt as it began to dawn on her that what had happened had not been an accident or an unavoidable tragedy at all.

The Bacons called the sheriff investigating the case, to ask about the sores and about the shocking condition of the body. They were told that the sores were from urine; that Aaron had had both urinary and fecal incontinence for the last two weeks of his life. The police were already treating the death as suspicious. One of the many things for which Sally cannot forgive North Star was their not giving her any warning at all about the horrifying condition of Aaron's body.

SEVERAL DAYS LATER, the Bacons got a call from a local television reporter, asking for their reaction to the fact that there had been two previous deaths in Utah wilderness programs. Both deaths had been linked directly to employees of a now defunct program called the Challenger Foundation. North Star, they now learned, was run by two former top Challenger staffers. The reporter's question was the first time they'd ever heard about any of this. Ironically, before he'd been sent to North Star, Aaron Bacon had seen a TV exposé on Challenger, which had looked at these deaths and exposed additional abuses. And they all seemed to start with Challenger's founder, a man named Steve Cartisano.

UNTIL STEPHEN ANTHONY CARTISANO entered the picture, wilderness programs and boot camps had largely been separate and not particularly profit-focused enterprises. Boot camps had been devised as an alternative to prison in which offenders would be rehabilitated by military drills. They tended to be run—or at least paid for—by states. Teens who participated were usually sent by judges, not parents. The camps were located in fixed sites, the way prisons are.

Wilderness programs, on the other hand, used the unrelenting power of nature to show teens that their actions—for example, not preparing to deal with cold weather—had consequences. They tended to be privately operated, and parents paid a few hundred dollars to teach their kids some lessons about survival. They involved nature treks and camping at various locations. Cartisano would be the first to explicitly put the two ideas together with the glue of "tough love."

Both wilderness programs and offender boot camps had become popular as fears about teens and drugs escalated through the '80s and into the '90s—and as the scandal over Straight caused it to wither and ultimately die. The first youth boot camp was started in Orleans Parish, Louisiana, in 1985, and soon close to 100 such programs, designed as alternatives to incarceration, opened across the country. Many remain open today. Not only were these programs seen as "treatment, not punishment," they were also cheaper than prison. The combination proved irresistible to policymakers, faced as they were by ever-mounting criminal-justice costs.

As soon as rigorous evaluations were conducted for the U.S. Department of Justice, however, just as with previous tough love miracle claims, the "results" vaporized. The four best major studies on youth boot camps were reviewed for a 1998 report to Congress, "Preventing Crime, What Works, What Doesn't, What's Promising." Three showed no significant differences in recidivism between boot camp participants and those sent to juvenile prison. One found that 72 percent of boot camp participants re-offended—but that only 50 percent of juvenile detention inmates did. The Justice Department lists boot camps for youth as an intervention that doesn't work.[33]

The problem appears to be that while boot camp can work miracles for the military, basic training is not what makes so many aimless youth who join the armed services into responsible adults. Those who conceived boot camps as a form of rehabilitation forgot several critical factors. For one, once someone completes military boot camp, he isn't returned to the street, he's given a job and an identity to be proud of: a defender of his country. Secondly, boot camp developed over centuries as a way to train people to kill—the toughness is not arbitrary, but instead an essential part of training people to survive and win wars. And finally, the military is full of checks and balances, as rusty as they may sometimes be. Soldiers with medical complaints are seen by doctors even if their commanders believe they are faking, those who feel they've been abused have an appeals process, and they are not entirely cut off from contact with the outside world. In today's volunteer army, in fact, they are free to drop out.

Says Assistant Utah State Attorney Craig Barlow, who would help prosecute Aaron Bacon's killers, "I've been through army boot camp. The purpose of army boot camp is to prepare you to be a soldier after significant additional training, and you're also nineteen, twenty, twenty-one. Not thirteen, fourteen, fifteen. The army has been doing that kind of stuff for years, and as harsh as army boot camp is, I was never tortured. The berating was more in the nature of high school athletic coaching than the kind of sadism that you see in some of these programs. And most of my drill sergeants were in their late twenties and early thirties, not nineteen [as Aaron's counselors were]."

The first wilderness program used for rehabilitation also had military origins. Outward Bound was designed in Wales during World War II. Its original goal was to toughen up British forces, to improve survival skills. In 1946, the Dallas Salesmanship Club, a group of Texas business leaders, founded the first yearlong therapeutic camp for troubled children, which is generally acknowledged to be the first wilderness program specifically for youth in crisis. But it was not until 1968, when Larry Dean Olsen of Brigham Young University took his first group of failing college kids on a tough wilderness course and found that their grades improved afterward, that the idea really began to get traction.

Olsen left BYU in the 1970s, in the wake of allegations of sexual misconduct.[34] In 1988, he founded what has become probably the most respected wilderness program in the U.S., the Anasazi Foundation. Anasazi, in fact, was founded as an explicit alternative to the "tough love" practiced by military-style programs. "A boot-camp philosophy was in vogue and that was offensive to me," Olsen told the *Salt Lake Tribune*, "There were companies springing up with the idea that 'all you had to do was herd kids around the desert and they were going to be fixed.'"[35]

Anasazi holds its founder's philosophy that nature can nurture and bring people closer to God through its beauty. Such ideas, of course, have deep resonance: from the earliest sparks of human spirituality in wood spirits and sea gods to the wandering of the Jews in the desert and Christ's wilderness awakening, every religion has a vital role for the power of Nature. And of course, these notions dovetail with the great American traditions of Emerson and Thoreau, with their reverence for the insights revealed outside civilization. They can be seen as returning a bit of the pioneer spirit—the Wild West of both the cowboys and the Indians—to anyone who seeks it.

Wilderness programs sold themselves to parents with the full force of these ideas. They sold themselves as alternatives to soulless, sterile psychiatry and its potentially dangerous medications. For liberal types, they had the appeal of "back to nature" and environmentalism; for conservatives, they had the boy scouts' emphasis on self-sufficiency, self-discipline, and preparedness.

The Anasazi program, and others like it that developed either from the Dallas Salesmanship Club or the BYU group, don't just use the rough conditions and harsh challenges of surviving with little in the wilderness to force teens to surrender. They try to inspire joy and wonder as well. Anasazi uses trained counselors, as do some other wilderness programs based on its model. But even in the gentlest programs, the idea that nature's unforgiving consequences can promote spiritual awakening poses problems beyond the ordinary risks of wilderness survival. When you add the element of pushing people who don't want to be there to do things they aren't necessarily physically able to do, the difference between "natural" consequences of lack of preparation like being soaked because you forgot your rain gear and arbitrary rules like "If you can't make a fire, you can't sit near the group's fire" gets elided. If "natural consequences" are to be used to change the behavior of those who can't or won't comply, you can easily create a situation in which small cruelties can be countenanced as necessary. Soon, even if you believe in kindness as the primary way to help people, if your campers seem resistant and you aren't extremely well trained, you have no way to tell when "I can't" means "I won't." And worse: if you've been told that troubled teens are by nature manipulative and lazy, you will see all complaints as rebellion.

Even the most respected programs like Anasazi use food and sleep deprivation that few people would voluntarily choose to undergo. They often include a two-day fast like North Star did. Participants can be made to live for weeks on inadequate diets that they are forced to supplement with foraged food like lizards and prickly pear cactus. Grueling, meaningless tasks like dragging heavy, wooden handcarts back and forth across tough desert terrain are common.

And Steve Cartisano would give tough love an even more savage twist. He would bring the in-your-face boot camp into the unforgiving wilderness—and "consequences" would now unquestionably come from both Man and Nature. When you add this militaristic, "make a man out of you" machismo to the notion of the goodness of "natural conse-quences," the small risks that are inevitable in the wilderness multiply into life-threatening hazards. And, in fact, the wilderness boot camp was where tough love began to move beyond hurting kids—and into killing them.

Cartisano would make wilderness programs both more dangerous and more profitable. He recognized that high cost can be a selling point, as-suaging parental guilt about sending kids away by making them pay for what they assumed must be the best treatment, since it was so expen-sive. As Jon Krakauer wrote in an article about Aaron Bacon's death, Steve Cartisano "single-handedly made tough love wilderness therapy a high-revenue proposition." Before Cartisano started his operations in 1987, even for-profit wilderness groups charged just $500 for a month-long expedition. Cartisano started by charging $12,500.[36]

Cartisano seemed to have the perfect background to bring him to the controversial role he would play in the industry: he had been a troubled teen himself. His mother was a Cherokee Indian, who died in a car acci-dent when he was seventeen; his father was of Italian-American origin.[37] While in the Air Force, he was exposed to the Mormon religion and soon converted. He enrolled at Brigham Young University. Although he didn't graduate, he did work for the school as an instructor in a wilderness course as part of his coursework. He soon decided to found his own, for-profit wilderness program in Hawaii.

With some help from a friend, the Iran-contra figure Oliver North, Cartisano began generating big-time publicity. He soon appeared on ma-jor talk shows, including *Donahue* and *Geraldo*. By the end of 1988, he'd moved from Hawaii to Utah, grossed more than $3 million, and was employing fifty people. And if merging boot camp with wilderness courses had been a marketing stroke of genius, the marriage of such pro-grams with talk shows was even more perfect. Since the shows were studio-based, they were especially starved for photographic variety to break up the monotony of the talking heads. The highest-rated shows featured titillating glimpses into the sex lives and drug use of teenagers. What could possibly be better suited to their needs than a show full of stories of degenerate teens, followed by footage of their humiliation by drill sergeants and messy outdoor ordeals—which ended with them happily returning to their parents, reformed? "They loved me," Cartisano told Krakauer, adding that he'd bring the talk shows "beautiful fourteen- to fifteen-year-old girls who'd talk about how they'd been out on the street stealing and doing drugs and turning tricks until Challenger changed their ways."[38]

While there was no scientific evidence that wilderness programs and boot camps had any positive long-term effect on teens, they did prove a major ratings boost for talk shows, becoming a staple. And this gave them even more legitimacy, because parents didn't think they'd be featured on TV if they hadn't been proven to work.

A 1989 video of Challenger shows stunned teens arriving in the desert in a van in the middle of the night. Pounding on the windows and demanding ever-louder "Yes sir's" from the group is a large, grizzled man, who calls himself "Horsehair." He faces the camera and says to his charges dispassionately, "I'm going to love you till it hurts." Lance Jaggar, who would soon go out on his own and open North Star, was Cartisano's field director. North Star's Bill Henry also helped in supervising the operation.

By mid-1990, Challenger employees had seen how easy it was to sell the program and how cheap it was to operate. There were no limits, no regulations. It was like growing money on trees. While The Seed and Straight had had the clever notion to use parents' own homes as a way of providing low-cost inpatient "care," Cartisano made teen programs even cheaper to run. A boot camp wilderness program required no physical facility at all. Denying even minimal food to the kids could be rationalized as part of "treatment," as could lousy equipment. There was virtually no overhead. "Counseling" staff were paid just $800 a month.

Cartisano's admissions director, Gayle Palmer, was the first to jump ship, opening her own program in May 1990. She had no outdoor experience or training in psychology. She simply copied Challenger. And soon there was a new gold rush in the West, mining the deep vein of difficult adolescents, as dozens of similar programs followed suit, charging exorbitant fees for what were essentially undersupplied, undersupervised remote wilderness expeditions.

Michelle Sutton, a blond-haired, blue-eyed fifteen-year-old girl, was one of the first five students in Palmer's program, called Summit Quest. Palmer charged $13,900 for each teen. She'd hired two minimum-wage "counselors" for her inaugural sixty-three-day outing. Unlike most teens sent to wilderness programs, Sutton had enrolled voluntarily. She'd been date-raped, and she felt low. The mother of her sister's fiancé, a friend of Palmer's who'd sent her two daughters to Challenger, recommended Summit Quest. Michelle had wanted to live in nature and lose weight in time for the following school year. She'd been crushed when a boy she idolized had called her "a fat hippo."

On Palmer's course, just like Cartisano's, weight loss would have been one goal she'd have been assured of meeting: it's hard not to slim down on a diet of lentils and lizards. But Sutton never completed the program: just seven days in, on May 9, 1990, she died of dehydration. Of course, the real cause of death was the same as it would be in Aaron Bacon's case: refusal by adults in charge to believe that medical complaints and pleas for basics like water weren't teenage "faking."

Responding to media reports, Cartisano was almost gleeful about the mishap that would tar the name of the ex-employee who'd dared to compete with him. He boasted, "At Challenger, a tragedy like the one that killed Michelle Sutton could never happen."[39] But he was wrong. Less than two months later, Kristen Chase, a sixteen-year-old girl from Florida, died suddenly after only four days in his program, her complaints of nausea and pleas for water and relief from the heat having also been ignored.[40]

FOUR

"They Used Tough, Not Love"

AFTER THEY'D HEARD from the reporter about the prior wilderness deaths, the Bacons received a call from Michelle's mother, Cathy Sutton, who has become one of the fiercest advocates for reform of the tough love industry. She'd set up the Michelle Sutton Memorial Fund with the $350,000 settlement (the max of Summit Quest's insurance) of a federal civil suit she'd filed against the program after her daughter's death. She'd been devastated that Michelle's killers hadn't been criminally prosecuted. And like Sally Bacon, she hadn't sought tough love because she didn't believe it helped. She says now,

It makes them worse. That's why I say, pain upon pain is never gain. That's why I used to walk around babbling in my house. All I could say, continually, I'd be folding clothes, doing my housework and I'd just start crying and saying, "How could they treat my child this way? She was already hurting. How dare they? All in the name of what? Power? Control? Money?"

Michelle's death was the first to hit the booming for-profit wilderness industry. Rather than trying to make a case, law enforcement and child welfare officials saw it as a tragic but probably unforeseeable accident. Despite evidence that Michelle's complaints had been ignored, state officials reckoned that her counselors had simply made a terrible misjudgment. They didn't see evidence of malice or depraved indifference. They didn't know that the "counselors" had had no real psychological or wilderness training. They didn't know that Cartisano had explicitly taught his staff that there would inevitably be a "window of loss," that, as one former staffer later put it on CNN, he'd told them, "We're going to help so many kids that it's worth the loss [of a few]."[1]

But when Kristen Chase died in such similar circumstances so shortly after Michelle Sutton had, Utah officials became much queasier. One death from dehydration and hyperthermia in a troubled teen program might be an accident; another, little more than a month later when anyone caring for youth outdoors should have been hyper-aware of those dangers and erring on the side of caution, was quite possibly criminal.

Both Cartisano and Lance Jaggar were charged with negligent homicide and nine counts of child abuse in Chase's death and in the treatment of her and three others on the expedition beforehand. Seeing which way the wind was blowing, both Jaggar and Bill Henry agreed to testify against their boss. Though the prosecutors had much more direct evidence against Jaggar because he'd been in the field, they wanted to get Cartisano, who really ran the show. Unfortunately, Cartisano's first trial ended in a mistrial due to a judge's error. In the second one, Cartisano's high-paid New York defense attorney managed to tar the teenage witnesses as liars and fakers and raise medical doubt about the cause of Chase's death.

It also didn't help that there was no support from Kristen's parents, neither of whom attended the trial. Kristen's mother, Sharon Fuqua, initially refused to blame Cartisano or Challenger for her daughter's death, telling the press, "I have never met any more dedicated, loving people striving to help children."[2] However, when Kristen's father, Ronald Chase, later filed a civil suit against the program, Fuqua demanded and won 70 percent of the settlement in a nasty court battle.[3]

After six hours of deliberation in Cartisano's criminal trial, he was acquitted. One juror told the press, "We weren't saying Cartisano was innocent, we were saying the prosecution didn't prove he was guilty. . . . We all felt like the program had some real problems."[4]

But now Cartisano felt bulletproof. He charged the prosecutors with misconduct. He swore he would open a new program, saying, "No one's seen me run from a fight yet. Why run now that I've won?"[5] Utah regulators, however, were not convinced that teens would be safe in his care. They barred him from ever working again with children in Utah. Challenger itself was bankrupt; Cartisano would be charged with writing bad checks. He even refused to pay his defense attorney. The lawyer, who'd once called Cartisano a savior for troubled teens, now used very different language to describe him.[6]

Through the '90s and into the twenty-first century, Cartisano has since operated "programs" in Puerto Rico, Costa Rica, and Samoa—all producing reports of hideous abuses. In Puerto Rico, for example, teens were found bound and gagged with nooses around their necks.[7] The FBI has investigated him and he is still at large, possibly even "treating" American kids under an alias abroad.[8]

LANCE JAGGAR AND BILL HENRY, meanwhile, opened North Star Expeditions in October 1990 without difficulty, despite the fact that both had been seriously implicated in Chase's death. Denouncing the practices of their former employer, Jaggar and Henry supported the Utah Department of Human Services' efforts to develop the first set of detailed regulations for teen wilderness programs in the country. They would ensure, through tough regulation and oversight, they claimed, that what had happened to Chase and Sutton could never recur.[9]

One of the key requirements for licensing, regulators decided, would be that programs must provide a minimum of 1,800 calories' worth of food daily. While this was better than allowing program staff to deny food entirely, the World Health Organization sets the minimum for boys fourteen to sixteen years old at 2,650, even if they aren't going to be especially active, and for girls that age at 2,150.[10] The new regulations also barred deprivation of other essentials, like appropriate sleeping bags and clothing. They mandated that backpacks not exceed 30 percent of a teen's body weight. They required that physical tasks and weather endurance not exceed the limits of the group's weakest member. Any single violation of these rules could prompt a suspension of the program's operating license.

But it was made clear to staffers from the start that these rules had been made to be broken, that they'd been designed just to please the suits in the state offices. As before, Cartisano's attitudes set a tone that was not easily altered. He'd told the media in 1989, "There's no way on earth I'll ever allow any petty bureaucrat to . . . turn [this program] from a survival camp into a summer camp."[11] Jaggar and Henry didn't seem to feel differently. Cathy Sutton had seen their defiance and arrogance on display at Cartisano's trial in Kristen Chase's death. She'd begged Utah regulator Ken Stettler not to license them. But Stettler told the media that Jaggar was "cleared on the system" and that North Star was "squeaky clean."[12] In Aaron Bacon's case, North Star repeatedly broke every single regulation its owners had claimed to support.

WHEN AARON BACON'S DEATH was reported, Garfield County Sheriff Than Cooper, Deputy Sheriff Celeste Bernards, and County Attorney Wallace Lee were called to the scene. Though they had been told that he had died without warning, they were acutely aware of the previous deaths in similar programs. Wilderness therapy was big business in Utah—and they knew that their investigation would have to withstand close scrutiny. At first, everyone's stories matched up. The staff and kids seemed cooperative. The day after Aaron died, Bernards took written statements and collected the journals of both campers and staff. These would ultimately provide crucial—and damning—evidence against North Star.

In contrast to what Bernards was first told, the autopsy results were not consistent with sudden death. Aaron had died from complications of a perforated ulcer, and the resultant peritonitis was not confined to a small region; one medical examiner described his abdominal cavity as containing "festoons" of pus.[13] Such a widespread infection could not develop instantly.

After burying their son the day after Easter, the Bacons drove to Escalante to see where he had died. They did not confront North Star's owners, but met with the three law enforcement officials, who did their best to support them. Bob asked about the investigation, and was told that it was continuing. The sheriff's department had serious concerns about what had happened to Aaron. Wallace Lee handed them Aaron's journal.

The Bacons had both thought that viewing Aaron's body had been the most painful experience of their lives—but it was nothing compared to sitting in a strange motel room in Utah and reading that journal. The steno notebook was spotted with blood from his nosebleeds, but the content was even more upsetting. Reading about Aaron's physical decline, his mental anguish, and his brave attempts to make the best of his situation was devastating. When they learned how they'd inadvertently added to his pain—for example, when Aaron had received Sally's tough letter after saying he needed to hear he was loved, they could hardly force themselves to read further. The idea that their child had died alone, frightened, helpless while his killers mocked him—in a program they'd chosen—was just too much to take. Their grief alternated with lacerating anger at North Star.

The only consolation they could take from the diary was that Aaron had recognized that his parents hadn't intended to send him to such a program, that he'd known they were unaware of the abuse. He'd written that he understood why his parents had been angry with him, and that, at least, offered some solace.

Meanwhile, Bernards was cross-referencing all of the journals into a calendar, along with the weather conditions reported in the region on each day. She worked out, confirming Aaron's account, that he had been made to go entirely without food for eleven days, had eaten a lizard and a scorpion as his only meal on one day, and had endured four additional days with only one meal. He'd been deprived of his sleeping bag for fourteen of the twenty days he'd spent hiking and had been left without even a blanket on four days, three of which had temperatures lower than freezing.

Soon, Sergeant Diana Hollis of the Children's Justice Division of the State Attorney General's Office was brought into the investigation. Lee had called in the big guns, knowing that the case would require all the manpower it could get.

Six months after Aaron's death, North Star was still open. It held about twenty kids. Most had not been there when Aaron died, but by now, the attorney general's office had grave concerns for their safety. Ken Stettler had again immediately cleared Jaggar and Henry, days after Aaron's death. Even though the regulator's own site visit had revealed obvious violations at that time, Stettler still believed that North Star's owners were fundamentally good people. Before he found out about what the journals contained, he believed they would be fully exonerated and even said in a letter to the program that he wanted to "commend the staff for their cooperation" in dealing with this "difficult thing."[14]

In a telling interview with CNN after Bacon's death, Stettler was asked why he hadn't shut North Star immediately. "Because that's in the—in our laws, we can't do that," he stuttered. "Basically, there has to be a right for a fair hearing." Unable to believe this, the reporter asked whether the state of Utah was more concerned about the program's rights than the safety of the children. Stettler replied, "Well, it would appear that way, although our—you know, our department is dedicated to protecting children in every instance."[15] He didn't mention that he'd been involved in writing the rules[16] or that those charged with killing Bacon had been major proponents of those laws.[17]

Pressure to keep North Star open had also come from parents who hadn't removed their kids. They believed, just as fervently as the Straight parents had, that North Star was the only thing that could keep their kids alive. In fact, Hollis was told so many times by parents that their teens would die if they didn't complete the program that she began reading obituaries to get a rough sense of how common teen death was in general. "I read obituaries for probably two years after that case," she said. "I was kind of obsessed with it then. I'd go, 'Look, not one today! Not one!'" In fact, the death rate for youth aged fifteen to nineteen from all causes, not just risky behavior, in the United States is minuscule: fewer than seventy teens per 100,000 for 2001, according to the CDC.[18]

HOLLIS INTERVIEWED the kids remaining in the program whose parents were still gung-ho, despite Bacon's death. Many of the youth were genuinely profoundly troubled, and they responded rudely and angrily to the questioning. After all, not only had they had to deal with their own ordeal in North Star and whatever problems had pushed their parents to send them, but they also knew that at least one child had already died there. They clearly felt a need to distance themselves from what had happened to Aaron. They seemed to fear saying anything negative.

When those who had been in North Star while Aaron died were questioned, however, it became apparent that they had known pretty much from the start that Aaron wasn't faking. These interviews also showed that while some of the campers had tried to help—by doing things like giving him food and allowing him to sneak his feet under their blankets at night—they were usually too frightened to do so because of the fear of consequences.

Hollis questioned the emergency-room doctor who had been on call when Aaron's body had arrived. "He became emotional and just teared up," she said, describing him as a new, young doctor. "He said this didn't have to happen. Even if we'd had him twenty-four hours before, he would have lived."

She also dug deeply into the program's finances, doing a complete "source and use" analysis. She found that North Star grossed about $1.68 million a year, charging between $13,900 and $14,600 per person. On each two-month expedition, there were usually between twenty and twenty-five kids. But North Star had only thirty staffers—and most of them were paid no more than $800 per month. Since those meager salaries were the company's largest expenditure, the program could easily clear $1 million to $1.5 million per year in profit. By comparison, at the time, the Aspen Academy wilderness program, which was not considered a fly-by-night operation, charged $15,900 to $17,000 for an expedition of similar length. It had nearly three times as many staff, and all counselors were required to have at least a master's degree, which required greater compensation.

Of course, North Star didn't tell parents that the staff who worked directly with the kids were themselves barely educated teenagers who hadn't had criminal background checks and were sometimes literally hired off the street. In fact, investigators discovered that North Star had out-and-out lied about staff qualifications, claiming that they were trained in both therapy and survival skills, and that a psychologist called "Doc Dave" worked with the kids. But "Doc Dave" Jensen didn't have a doctorate. He was a certified social worker. And he only saw each teen once, at the beginning of the program.[19]

The investigators had clearly developed an extremely strong case against North Star. But they also ran into several serious problems, all of which would affect the case. For one, only one staffer initially agreed to testify against his bosses. On paper, Mike Hill, the Native American staffer who'd been the first to recognize that Aaron was in serious trouble, seemed like the perfect witness. He hadn't been involved directly in Aaron's care, so there was no need to immunize him in exchange for his testimony. Also, he was wracked with guilt about the way he'd seen Aaron treated: unlike Jaggar and Henry, he didn't feel the need to badmouth the victim and didn't have any particular investment in "tough love." He'd basically been a kid himself who took a job offer and found himself in way over his head.

Hill soon took to calling Sally and Bob, seeking forgiveness. But it turned out that he had another reason to feel guilty: he'd sexually abused a boy in a previous group. Worse, he'd had him perform sexual favors for extra food.[20] When he confessed this to Sally and told the investigators, they had a major problem on their hands.

When prosecutors had first heard rumors about Hill's problems, they didn't know whether they were more smear tactics by the defense, like the claims that Aaron was a violent hard-drug user whose parents were addicts, that North Star and its supporters made to the media. But now that Hill had confessed, they'd have to give evidence of the crime to other prosecutors. It was an unrelated crime that they wouldn't prosecute themselves, given their need for him as a witness. Hill's history didn't really have any bearing on whether he had seen Aaron harmed or not, but if allowed into evidence, it might not look that way to a jury. A jury might think there'd been some kind of bargain for his testimony that hadn't been disclosed, or might automatically reject any kind of testimony from an admitted child molester.

Still, the prosecutors didn't have any other line staff who were not defendants who would talk. They figured they could get the judge to exclude at least the details of the charges against Hill. They also had precious few teens who agreed to testify. Diana Hollis had been shocked by the uncaring attitudes of the parents of the boys who'd been in the program when Aaron died. They were all from out of state, so they couldn't be forced to testify without an involved bureaucratic hassle.

Hollis says that even when she showed the autopsy photos to the parents, they would say things like, "Well, that's not my kid and I don't care." They seemed furious that anyone would dare interfere with the program. It didn't matter that it had killed another boy, so long as it would stay open to treat their own precious children. They didn't seem able to empathize, to think that if it happened to Aaron, it could happen to their kids, too. Hollis eventually came to believe that some of these parents were abusive themselves, and had deliberately paid for abuse.

Incredibly, these parents also expressed their anger directly to the Bacons. Sally said, "I suffered the wrath of these people—my son is dead, and these people were angry with me because I was having North Star closed?" she asked, still unable to believe it. One woman, whose son had actually held a gun to her head before being taken to North Star, told

Sally that she'd "ruined everything," because without North Star, she'd have nowhere to send the boy. Sally said that this woman had asked her caustically,

> "Where did you think you were sending him, a daycare?" They knew their son was going to a boot camp. Why didn't I know that Aaron was going to a boot camp? Because they wanted a boot camp and that's what they were sold. I didn't want a boot camp so that's what I was sold [a gentler program]. And see, that's what they didn't understand. These people sell you whatever you're looking for.

Adds Cathy Sutton, "I think in five minutes these people can figure out what you want to hear and that's what they're going to feed you and sell you to get what they want, which is your money."

AFTER MUCH DEBATE, prosecutors decided to charge the North Star employees with "abuse and neglect of a disabled child," a felony count introduced by a 1988 law, which had never been tested in court. It carries a five-year maximum sentence. Curiously, under Utah law, negligent homicide is a lesser offense, a misdemeanor. The maximum sentence is one year. It is generally used in situations in which someone is killed by thoughtless, but not intentionally homicidal behavior, like speeding and killing a pedestrian.

The prosecution felt that the perpetrators in Bacon's case were more culpable than that. They thought North Star's operators deserved much longer prison sentences. Aaron had been killed by repeated negligent behavior by all of them, not by a one-time, isolated, careless bad act. Any reasonable person certainly should have known that what North Star was doing was not only cruel and abusive, but potentially deadly. The problem was, so many people had "cared" for Aaron that the diffusion of responsibility made it difficult to prove "depraved indifference" on the part of any particular person, especially among the higher-ups who weren't in the field. Consequently, they couldn't file a more serious homicide charge.

The team reasoned that Bacon became a "disabled child" the moment he came under North Star's control. His disability was caused by the conditions in the program, which made him unable to provide his own food, clothing, and shelter and prevented him from seeking medical attention. And, they argued, even if he hadn't been disabled upon admission, he was certainly disabled when he became ill.

The defendants included Lance Jaggar and Bill Henry; Henry's son Eric, who'd driven the truck to pick up Aaron; Aaron's "counselors" Craig Fisher, Sonny Duncan, Jeffrey Hohenstein and Brent Brewer; and Georgette Costigan, the emergency medical technician who had failed to examine the teen the day before he died. Costigan was also charged with felony witness tampering for allegedly telling teens to alter their journals to make them "less incriminating."[21]

Jaggar and Henry hired a private attorney, Sheldon Wellins, who had recommended the program to a client for his son and believed strongly in it. Wellins had told the *Salt Lake Tribune* that he thought about "all the lives that have been saved by North Star" and intended "to fight this forever. I don't feel I am representing Bill and Lance alone. I have the burden on my shoulders of all those kids who have gone through and had their lives turned around, and all that won't."[22] The rest of the defendants were left to rely on public defenders.

The prosecution passed its first big test, which was a five-day preliminary hearing to determine whether there was enough evidence for trial. Two of Aaron's fellow campers, whose names were not released because of their ages, testified the first day. Ironically, one was the son of the client whom Wellins had referred. The boy, whom Wellins saw as a North Star "success," had witnessed Aaron's death. Both campers said that Aaron had been mocked and dismissed. One admitted, upon being shown Aaron's last photo by the prosecution, that he'd done his best to block the experience from his memory. When the defense pressed the boys to admit that everyone in the program suffered hunger pangs and indigestion, the witnesses remained steadfast that Aaron seemed far sicker and weaker than anyone else.[23]

Sally Bacon testified the next day, describing the horror of seeing her son's body. "His face was unrecognizable. He had these sunken cheeks and his eyes, he looked like a skeleton, his hands were all bone. I ripped the sheet off and the autopsy [incision] was the best looking part of him."[24]

Defense attorneys questioned her about Aaron's behavior, having her describe his pot smoking and depression. They said that simply sending Aaron to a program showed that she, too, believed in tough love. "Well, it's hard to use tough love when you don't love the person, and they obviously didn't love my son," she shot back. "They used tough, not love."[25]

The final witness in the hearing was Mike Hill, who was grilled repeatedly about his own failure to act, if, as he claimed, he knew that Aaron was seriously ill. The sex abuse charges against him were not revealed, just that he was under investigation for an unrelated crime. All he could say was, "I should have done it [sought immediate help], that's why I'm really upset at myself." He described Aaron's final hours, saying that he had bouts of severe pain interspersed with "bursts of energy." "This is the thing—he wanted to walk," Hill testified. "He kept saying, 'Let me do it.' Then he'd stagger and fall down." This was the child the staff had labeled uncooperative and belligerent, that they said had given up. Hill tried to explain that his bosses had told him not to intervene with kids who were not in his hiking group. "They always told us these kids were manipulators. That word was constantly used."

In closing arguments, the prosecution said, "Once it was decided that Aaron was a faker, a manipulator, that was the party line at North Star. They said, 'We ignore Aaron because he's faking.' I don't know how you fake a twenty-three-pound weight loss in twenty-four days."

Judge K. L. McIff was skeptical of the defense's theory that Bacon didn't appear sick enough to need help. "Isn't Aaron Bacon in an impossible situation?" he asked sharply at one point. "He's accused of being a complainer and uncooperative so he starts responding with terms like 'yes sir.' Now we're down on him because he doesn't complain loud enough." When a defense attorney noted that Aaron just didn't seem "deadly sick," McIff interrupted pointedly, "Do you have to think he's deadly sick [to seek medical attention]? What if he's [just] real sick?"

The defense argued that the consequences of Aaron's actions had to be reenforced and that Aaron knew that he'd have to go without food, for example, when he abandoned his pack. The judge shot back, "Isn't there a point where you must step in and say we just can't let that person starve himself to death?"

Defense attorney Floyd Holm replied that that would defeat the whole purpose of North Star. "If you can never use negative consequences, it completely guts the program."[26]

ENDING THE HEARING, McIff ruled that the North Star program was "fraught with a desensitizing mentality which a reasonable jury would conclude contributed to the offenses in this case." He bound the defendants over for trial, dropping only the witness-tampering charge against Costigan for insufficient evidence. Sally Bacon says that one defendant, Craig Fisher, unseen by the judge, sneered at her and gave her the finger.

The defendants were immediately arraigned and pled not guilty, with Wellins declaring defiantly "I don't believe for a moment that we'll ever be convicted."[27] And he had good reason to feel confident—despite the strong case against his clients. The tiny local jury pool was filled with North Star supporters. When Jon Krakauer asked a waitress at the nearby Circle D restaurant about Bacon's death, she told him, "That's a real touchy subject around here. He was a drug addict, his parents was drug addicts and now that he's dead they want to blame somebody so they're trying to wreck the lives of the folks who was trying to help him."[28]

The local paper, the *Garfield County News,* took the same line. It repeatedly ran stories of parents who felt wronged by the closure of North Star, who believed the program had saved their children's lives. Its publisher told Diana Hollis that the paper felt obligated to "compensate for the anti-defendant publicity" in the national press. *Outside* magazine, CNN, the talk show *Leeza,* and the *Los Angeles Times* had all run stories that did not make North Star look good.

Garfield County Attorney Wallace Lee also reported signs of community bias. He said he'd been threatened by a local resident who said he'd "better think twice" about filing charges against North Star because its staff were "just good people trying to help kids."[29] The local Mormon church took up a collection to support the defendants.[30] And whenever the Bacons attended legal proceedings, they were treated with contempt. The prosecution team was appalled by the attacks on a couple that, no matter what one thought about wilderness programs, had suffered the greatest loss a person can experience. Defense attorney Sheldon Wellins's lighthearted courtroom demeanor—he wore a tie with a different cartoon character on it on each day of the preliminary hearing—was also far from respectful.[31]

As a result, as trial approached, the prosecutors tried to get the defendants to take a plea. They wanted to spare the Bacons a long trial, which would inevitably reexpose them to repeated attacks on Aaron's character and their own and to horrifying details about his death. While it is usually the defense that demands a change of venue because the jury pool may be tainted, in this case, the prosecution successfully argued that given the massive community support for North Star, its case could not get a fair hearing. The trial was moved. And the plea deals suddenly looked a lot more appealing to the defendants.

ULTIMATELY, six of the seven North Star staffers pled guilty to the reduced charge of negligent homicide. Henry and Jaggar also pled guilty to operating a program that violated licensing requirements. But one staff member, Craig Fisher, who'd been one of Aaron's rotating group leaders, refused to take the deal. So the Bacons ended up with the worst of both worlds: having to attend a trial and knowing that the defendants who pled out (who included Jaggar and Henry) would get only a year in prison at most.

Pretrial maneuvering in Fisher's case was fierce. By this time, the Bacons had won a large civil settlement, and the defense wanted to introduce evidence about that case to suggest that they had ulterior motives. The prosecution argued that this was harassment of the family, but said, to shouts of protest from the defense team, "If you really want, we can talk about why two insurance companies paid the Bacons a lot of money after they independently concluded that Jaggar and Henry caused the death of Aaron Bacon."[32] The civil case was excluded.

And at the trial, much of the testimony from the preliminary hearing was recapped. The boys testified, Hill testified, some of the defendants who'd pleaded guilty testified for the prosecution. Sally told of seeing her son's body. Fisher's attorney tried to use the Nuremberg defense: "Who was really making decisions how this kid was to be treated out there in the wilderness?" he asked rhetorically. "It was not Craig Fisher's decision and it was beyond his control." He said that Fisher was "trying to help" when he yelled at Aaron.[33]

Sally Bacon observed the defendant's family, who'd come to support him. She said, "I remember watching Craig talk and I was looking at his mother and I started to cry. I thought, 'You know something, I would rather Aaron be the dead one than be sitting where she is. I don't know what the heck I'd do if my kid treated another human being like that.'"

The jury concurred: Fisher was rapidly convicted. After the verdict was read, Fisher tried to hug Sally, saying that she had to believe that he honestly didn't know Aaron was dying. Sally said that everything he'd done had been to harm her son, not help him even if he wasn't aware of how ill he'd been. She told him she only hoped that he would never treat another human being that way again—and hugged him back. Her next thought was that Aaron's brother would be furious at her for doing so.

It turned out he was right to be. Sally felt bitterly used when Fisher's attorney used the hug as evidence of remorse in his presentencing statement. In her own victim impact statement, Sally mentioned that Fisher had given her the finger in court. But it didn't matter: none of the North Star defendants would serve real prison time. Jaggar, Henry, Costigan, Duncan, and Hohenstein, who'd pled guilty, served no jail time at all.[34] They were given one-year suspended prison sentences, fined $2,500 each, and given three years' probation. Their sentences also included community service ranging from 720 to 1,440 hours and restitution for legal costs, which ranged from $1,200 to $3,600.[35] Fisher was sentenced to one year, but served only a few months.[36]

Incredibly, Bill Henry violated his probation by completing only 86 of the 1,440 hours.[37] He violated it again by moving out of state, to be with his wife, who had been hired by another wilderness program, the Sage Walk School in Bend, Oregon. Bill Henry was prohibited from owning, operating, working for, or even volunteering for any youth program during his probation. But Patti Henry, who had also been a top North Star executive, had not been charged in Aaron's death. She was under no such restrictions.[38]

Within six months, their son Eric Henry had violated his probation and was hired as a counselor himself at Sage Walk. He was never incarcerated for these violations. In 1998, he began working for the Obsidian Trails wilderness program, also in Oregon, but he left in 1999 for undisclosed reasons.[39] The owner of Obsidian, Gregory Bodenhamer, the author of a 1995 book called *Parent in Control* that recommends that parents restrain their own children and called today's teens "the worst-behaved generation of children in American history," had written a blurb for the brochure that convinced the Bacons to send Aaron to North Star. It said: "The best way to gain control of incorrigible, out-of-control teenagers, who are running away, using drugs, committing crimes and making life miserable for everyone else in the family, is with a well-run wilderness program like North Star Expeditions Inc."[40] Bodenhamer, who is still in the business, conducted two-day "seminars" for parents of North Star students. In 2000, a fifteen-year-old boy named William "Eddie" Lee, died in a facedown restraint at Obsidian Trails.[41] The program settled a suit with his parents for an undisclosed sum.[42]

AFTER THE VERDICT, the Bacons appeared with Leeza Gibbons on her talk show, where they were once again attacked by North Star supporters. Sally said that several of the women asked to meet with her afterward. She reluctantly agreed. One young woman, who'd gone through North

Star herself, tried to convince Sally of its value. Sally responded: "I said to her, 'If North Star is responsible for the beautiful young woman you are today, that's wonderful. But it doesn't relieve them for what they did to my son. It's like a priest who has helped a dozen people but he molested a few boys, it doesn't make him not responsible for what he did to them.'"

The girl backed off, crying, but others then berated Sally, saying she'd feel different if she'd been there when the kids "ran in" from the camp to their parents' arms. Sally asked sadly, "Don't you think I wanted to be there?" To de-escalate the conflict, she asked how the women's children were doing now. To her shock, one mother said that her son was living on the street; the other said her son had killed himself and his girlfriend in a car accident during the previous month.

WHEN BOTH *Outside* and the *Los Angeles Times Magazine* featured the dramatic story of Aaron Bacon's death, the writers and the Bacons were besieged by requests for film and television rights. Sally says she even received a call from Barbra Streisand. Eventually, the rights were sold. But no movie has ever been made. The ending—what happened in court after those stories were written initially—is just too depressing. Justice was not served.

And since Aaron's death, at least nine other teens have died in wilderness programs. The vast majority of these deaths occurred when the victims' requests for food, water, or medical attention were denied. At least five teens have also died in fixed-site boot camp programs—for virtually identical reasons. In a death that sadly echoed Aaron's in its prolonged, gruesome, and utterly senseless nature, sixteen-year-old Nicholas Contrarez of Sacramento, California, died of a massive infection at the Arizona Boys Ranch in 1998. As in Aaron's case, his illness had made him incontinent before he died, and he'd been made to do push-ups with his face over a basket that contained his soiled and vomit-covered clothes. He'd been ill for about two weeks prior to his death, and at autopsy, his chest contained two and a half quarts of pus.[43]

Heat-related deaths like those of Michelle Sutton, in which teens' calls for water and rest were ignored, have also continued to plague these programs. At least four have occurred since 2000.

Complaints ignored also play a critical role in the eight known restraint deaths that took place in teen boot camp and wilderness programs. In one shocking case, twelve-year-old Mikey Wiltsie was killed in a camp run by Eckerd Youth Alternatives, because his 320-pound counselor sat on him to restrain him and thought he was "playing possum" when the 65-pound boy went still after saying he couldn't breathe.[44]

As I write, there is still no federal regulation to protect children in privately run wilderness programs and boot camps. A 2000 survey identified 116 "outdoor behavior health" programs aimed at treating troubled teens—and estimated that these programs alone generated $200 million in annual income.[45] Another survey that year identified more than forty correctional boot camps for youth, mainly state-funded programs.[46] While Aaron's death resulted in yet another tightening of Utah's regulations, this did not prevent two additional deaths in the state in 2002. There is also still no peer-reviewed controlled research showing wilderness programs to be superior to other treatments or to no treatment at all. Reviews of the studies that do exist find most of them to be poorly designed[47]—and the better designed the study, the less likely it was to show positive results from the programs.[48]

While some programs have begun to conduct new research, the organizations involved are those that claim most strenuously that they do not use deprivation or harsh tactics—so these evaluations, while possibly useful in showing whether the gentler programs work, would not offer evidence that the tougher ones do. So far, they have yet to produce controlled studies or to publish in peer-reviewed psychology or addiction journals.

One recent study of outcomes at seven wilderness programs (Ascent, Anasazi Foundation, Aspen Achievement Academy, Catherine Freer, Redcliff Ascent, Sunhawk Academy, SUWS, Three Springs, and Trailhead Wilderness School) did find a significant reduction in psychological

symptoms and problematic behavior among teens a year after participation in a wilderness program. But the study was plagued by poor response to follow-up: though 858 parents (one participating parent per
child) agreed to take part, the researchers obtained complete outcomes
data for just 271 parents and only 139 kids.[49] A common problem with
outcomes studies is that the people who respond to them tend to be
those who are doing the best; this may make the programs appear to
help when, in fact, it only looks this way because people who didn't have
such good outcomes are not heard from. Although the researchers tried
to control for this, with such a large loss of data, it's hard to know what
to make of the outcomes. More important, without a control group, it's
impossible to know whether the kids simply got better as they got older.
The study was self-published by researchers at the University of Idaho.
While it lists a group of "peer reviewers," all of its members are strong
supporters of wilderness programs. The study was funded by the Outdoor Behavioral Health Industry Council—in other words, by the programs themselves.

Without better regulation and oversight, of course, it is impossible for
consumers to know whether they will get treatment advertised as nurturing and evidence-based rather than tough anyway. Kinder, gentler
wilderness experiences might prove to be helpful—but if there are no
regulations to drive out those who just pretend to offer such treatments, and no ways to ensure that individual counselors in kind programs don't decide to get tough, parents still risk being victimized. The
rhetoric of the "gentler" programs still regards teens as "manipulative"—
and on a *Primetime Live* broadcast that favorably profiled the Catherine
Freer program, kids were shown being denied water when one member
of the group refused to keep going.[50] Just as that show was being produced, fifteen-year-old Erica Harvey died at Catherine Freer. A lawsuit
her parents have filed claims that her complaints of feeling unwell were
ignored and she was left alone for forty-five minutes before she died of
heatstroke and dehydration on her first day in the high desert.

As the wilderness deaths accumulated and tough love in the woods moved from its "miracle" period to its "controversial" one, tough love for teens once again took on a new form. This was the "specialty school," sometimes called a "behavior modification" or "emotional growth" boarding school. Such organizations had existed since the late '60s and took their cues directly from Synanon. The CEDU chain (which includes Boulder Creek Academy, Rocky Mountain Academy, and the ASCENT Therapeutic Adventure program), for example, was founded by Mel Wasserman, who'd been involved with Synanon himself, and some former Synanon members in 1967. Their programs include lengthy, confrontational large-group sessions called "Propheets" similar to Synanon's "game." They also involved exercises like those in est and similar encounter seminars. The Academy at Swift River is similar, run by former employees of CEDU.[†][51]

Another program, the Elan School, was founded in 1970 by a dropout from a direct Synanon-descendant program. He'd been sent to that program for robbery, not just heroin addiction, and most of his staff were former addicts and ex-cons with no training. Until late 2000, Elan used a disciplinary procedure called "the ring" in which a student being confronted would be made to wear boxing gear and fight fresh opponents until he verbally agreed with whatever the group had said about him.[52] The opponents were fellow program participants, made to fight on the "side of good." This school and practice became famous because a cousin of the Kennedys, Michael Skakel, had been sent there.

After one "ring" session, Skakel admitted to murdering fifteen-year-old Martha Moxley, who'd been bludgeoned to death in 1975. He says he made the confession to end the beating. For six weeks afterward, Skakel was made to wear a sign saying I AM AN ARROGANT RICH BRAT, CONFRONT

---

†In 2005, just as I was completing this book, CEDU, which had been facing abuse lawsuis, suddenly shut down. However, there are currently offers to reopen it and the academy at Swift River is still open.

ME ON WHY I KILLED MY FRIEND MARTHA[53] and to repeat his admission in greater and greater detail. Though his statements were obviously tainted by the use of force, he was later convicted of the murder based largely on what he'd admitted at Elan. Despite current complaints and reports of serious physical abuse going back to the early '70s (including beatings that resulted in hospitalizations), Elan is still open.

Maine officials did not find abuse at the school in a 2002 investigation. They did require the school to refrain from using "the ring" and from employing "excessive use of mechanical restraints," although they said they could not substantiate "individual" accounts of such practices.[54]

Former staff and participants have detailed to the media how they fooled prior investigators,[55] so it's hard to know whether to accept the new investigation as the final word. This is especially true since online accounts of recent abuse are still appearing.[56] And there are dozens of similar programs, some running several sites, some with just one facility.

Like Synanon itself, programs like Elan and CEDU capitalized on the antipsychiatry movement, eschewing diagnoses, individualized treatment, and especially the use of psychiatric medication in favor of a group regime designed simply to improve behavior. Opposition to medication was often one of their biggest selling points, in fact. For parents who feared that rising use of drugs to treat conditions like attention-deficit disorder was simply drugging kids into submission, or who thought that medications allowed kids to avoid responsibility and continue bad behavior due to their "diseases," the programs became particularly attractive. Some of these programs also pitched themselves as wilderness treatment or boot camps when those became fashionable, because of their secluded and often rural locales.

But it wasn't until the mid-'90s—just after Aaron Bacon's death, in fact—that the group that is now the largest player in the industry, WWASP/Teen Help, began to take off.[57]

FIVE

The Sting
of the WWASP

I N JUNE 1997, Laurie and Michael Berg and their two young sons were living in Snohomish, an upscale suburb of Seattle. Michael was a mortgage broker; Laurie was a stay-at-home mom who volunteered as a children's pastor for the Foursquare Church. One weekend just after school let out, Laurie tried to phone fifteen-year-old Paul Richards, intending to ask him to do yard work. Paul had been a regular babysitter for the Bergs. He'd mentioned that he wanted to earn extra money. But Paul's older sister told Laurie that her brother wasn't home. She said he'd been sent several nights earlier to some kind of behavior-modification program. She didn't offer more details.

Concerned, Laurie asked the girl to have her mom or dad call her back. The Bergs knew that Paul often clashed with his parents, and had even offered to take him in if they needed a respite from each other. Privately, they thought the Richards were too strict. Paul was an honor student, one of the top in his class, as well as a star basketball player. He had never experimented with cigarettes, let alone alcohol or other drugs. Paul was a popular teenager, and the only people the Bergs say they saw him unable to get along with were his parents. He says he rarely even fought with his siblings, a sister three years older and a brother five years younger.

His parents, Bruce, an engineer, and Karen, an occupational therapist, see things very differently. They say the Bergs and Paul's basketball coach and teachers didn't know the real Paul, who was troubled and angry from early on and often physically attacked them. They say that as a toddler, Paul "bashed the head of a preschool classmate into a brick wall" because the other child wouldn't let him ride a Big Wheel. At six, he "brandished a butcher knife against a babysitter." At nine, according to his parents, Paul wrote a Mother's Day card which read, "Happy Mother's Day to the Bitch." In ninth grade, they say he assaulted a teenage girl at a bus stop, and her parents told them "her ribs were bruised black-and-blue." Paul, they wrote in a letter to a newspaper, "makes it appear as if [he] is the innocent victim of his parents' overzealous discipline and unrealistic expectations."

Bruce and Karen say that Paul frequently broke school rules and received numerous detentions and a daily "behavior contract" with all his teachers in eighth grade because of his argumentativeness and inattention.[1] They say they ran a tight ship, but because Paul's two siblings didn't have any problems following their rules, they did not expect Paul to have problems, either. They came down harder and harder when he resisted.

One counselor described Paul at age ten in his medical records:

[He is a] 10 YO boy with above average intelligence who seems to be in a somewhat dysfunctional setting, where there is the vicious cycle of conflict, creating antagonism with each side digging in, waging war, trying to control with an escalation of limits and the potential to degenerate into a 'win the battle and lose the war' situation. . . . My perceptions are that that family discipline style needs to loosen up, become more creative, less involved in who wins and more involved in the process of negotiating limits with well-defined consequences which are appropriate . . . and do not come across as angry and punitive.[2]

Eventually, the Richardses had a typewritten list of twenty-two "behavioral expectations" for Paul. It included ordinary things like cleaning up after himself and taking proper phone messages but also required that Paul ask permission before using the phone or turning on the TV, stereo, or computer, and that nothing ever be left out of its "assigned storage closet."[3] At least in part as a result of the sheer number and specificity of these strictures, Paul was frequently grounded and kept from watching television for months at a time.

Paul met the Bergs because of his devotion to basketball. Michael Berg is a passionate player: Laurie says he's out the door as "soon as he hears a ball bouncing." He frequently played with the neighborhood kids in pickup games at a nearby house that had hoops. The Bergs themselves also had an "open yard" policy for sports, and Paul often came by. They saw no evidence of the violence and refusal to follow rules that the Richardses reported.

Paul's problems with his parents only worsened as he moved further into adolescence. One time, his mom ran onto the basketball court in the middle of one of Paul's games, interrupting play and causing confusion in the bleachers. She demanded that the umpire stop the action because Paul wasn't supposed to be there. In another cringe-inducing incident for an adolescent, his mother once called him at a friend's house when he was in seventh grade and demanded that he come home immediately to wash some dirty dishes he'd left in the sink. He refused, and his mother threatened to have his friend's mother call the police and report him for trespassing if he didn't leave at once. Embarrassed, he left, but stayed out until eleven P.M. Upon arriving home, he found his parents had locked him out. He broke into the room where the family's hot tub was located and went upstairs to bed. The next morning, his parents grabbed him on his way to school, he says, and confiscated his house keys. Frustrated and furious, he took a baseball bat and smashed the windshield of his father's BMW.[4]

For their part, the Richardses didn't understand why their second son couldn't behave as well as their other children. They had been frightened when Paul had threatened to take an overdose of an over-the-counter painkiller after a particularly ferocious argument. They felt he was often genuinely suicidal and say he made at least one attempt. The violence of Paul's attack on the BMW and the intensity of his anger about their disciplinary practices terrified them. At six-four and 170 pounds, he was physically intimidating. Karen later told *48 Hours,* "I can tell you he was capable of inflicting physical harm as well as property damage."[5] When describing the concerns they'd had about their son to the Denver *Rocky Mountain News,* Bruce said later:

> Would you rather be the parents of the [Columbine] kids who were killed or the parents of the kids who did the killing? If you were the parent of one of the kids who did the shooting, and you had any inkling that your son or daughter needed some kind of help and you didn't take action as a parent, then you have to live with that for the rest of your life. And Karen and I were not willing to do that.[6]

At first, the Richardses responded to Paul's increasing disregard for their rules by making his punishments stricter and the rules ever more precise. Yellow Post-it notes soon protruded from many household items, laying down the law for Paul in relation to them. By his freshman year of high school, Laurie says, even Paul's bedroom and most of his possessions had been taken away. He now slept in the basement on a mattress, in a bare room containing nothing else but piles of his clothing.

The more his parents sought to impose their will, the more Paul resisted, and neither parents nor child seemed able to find a way out of the vicious cycle. As advancing adolescence led Paul to demand more freedom, his parents were afraid to provide it to a young man they saw as unstable and impulsive. And Paul's behavior toward them certainly didn't discourage this perception. The Richardses' increasingly stringent attempts at discipline seemed only to reinforce his immaturity. The struggle made both sides increasingly stubborn and uncompromising.

By the early summer of 1997, when the NBA playoffs were on TV, Paul and his parents were thoroughly fed up with each other. They'd repeatedly tried counseling—but Paul says his parents would always quit whenever a counselor suggested that Paul might not be the only one who was being unreasonable. His parents, of course, have another perspective. They say, "In our personal opinion, Paul was not a willing participant (in some cases, he physically refused to accompany us, in other cases, he was present physically but checked out mentally) since he took and still maintains the position that there is nothing wrong with him that needs changing and the family problems are his parents' fault."[7]

Paul had been on television "restriction" for months—he couldn't see the end of his penalties. And he really wanted to watch the games. Violating the terms of his punishment, he turned on the set. His mother turned it off. He put it back on. Karen says he shoved her, and she called the police, demanding that he be arrested for assault. But when the cops arrived, Paul's brother corroborated his account that he had not hit or pushed his mother. They took a report and left.

As Laurie Berg describes it, "I had always known Paul to be a kid that would honor his restrictions, but there came a point, probably a few months before he was shipped away, where he kind of threw his hands in the air and said, 'What does it matter? I'm going to be on restriction until I'm eighteen anyway.'"

Deciding that Paul had "oppositional defiant disorder," a behavior disorder marked by rebellious and antisocial behavior toward all authority figures, the Richardses came to believe that he needed residential treatment. As Bruce Richards described the situation to *48 Hours*, "We felt as though if we didn't take some kind of intervention, that the next one might be an irrevocable event."[8] Paul's parents took him for an evaluation, which, according to Paul, quickly found that he did not meet the criteria for oppositional-defiant disorder, since he behaved well at school and didn't persistently break the law. His parents disagree, saying that his behavior met more than enough criteria to qualify him for the diagnosis.

The "oppositional defiant" diagnosis is controversial, even within psychiatry, because many believe it is overused to classify teens who behave badly but do not meet the criteria for other psychiatric disorders, teens who would formerly simply have been described as obnoxious brats.

But many forms of residential care don't require a diagnosis, anyway. Even in 2004, many seemingly-mainstream teen "treatment" programs say they don't believe in counseling, psychology, or psychiatry, and see these disciplines as worse than useless. To avoid the regulation that comes with running a "residential treatment program," these groups often call themselves "specialty schools," "therapeutic boarding schools," and "emotional growth" or "behavior modification programs." What they really are is tough love, with new labels.

In the 1990s, a chain of these programs based in southern Utah came to prominence. Now the biggest association of tough love programs in the U.S., its main arm was known primarily as Teen Help when Paul's parents became involved. The Richardses discovered that Paradise Cove, a Teen Help affiliate located in Samoa, would take Paul based on their account of his problems. As had been the case with Straight and with North Star, nothing was required for admission other than the parents' belief that their child was trouble and, of course, their ability to pay the fees. For Paradise Cove, these were roughly $2,000 a month. The program was expected to last at least a year.[9]

On June 19, 1997, at 3:16 A.M., as Paul tells it, "I was rudely awakened only to be kidnapped against my will . . . by three fully grown men and my parents. . . . I was told to get up and get dressed. I replied, 'Leave me alone, I'm trying to sleep. . . .' They then proceeded to tear the sheets off the bed, exposing me lying in my underwear. . . . This is where the humiliation and emotional abuse first started for me in the program."[10] When Paul said he had to use the bathroom, the men refused to let him go unobserved, even though the bathroom had only one possible exit.

Paul's parents had hired an "escort service" recommended by and affiliated with Teen Help, which would take him, in handcuffs if necessary, to Teen Help's "evaluation" facility, Brightway Adolescent Hospital, in southern Utah. The Richardses believe the treatment they sought for Paul was worth every penny and say that he was not abused in any way in the process.

Paul and his three keepers made the eighteen-hour drive from Washington with only two stops for food, at a McDonald's and a Burger King. At Brightway, Paul was made to strip and shower while observed. He had to wash his hair with delousing shampoo, and show the staff that it fully covered his head. He was given a hospital gown, which he found embarrassingly short. Although he stayed for ten days, he was never allowed outside, never allowed phone calls, and wasn't evaluated for any psychological or psychiatric conditions, he says. He also says he saw other children forcibly medicated for refusing to follow the rules—and other teens confirm his account. Brightway would later close after regulators found that it had failed to report accusations of child abuse and had rubber-stamped admissions—referring almost every patient, no matter what the diagnosis, to long-term treatment at Teen Help facilities.[11] Paul Richards would be sent to Samoa.

WHEN LAURIE BERG spoke with Karen Richards after Paul's disappearance, Laurie reiterated her offer to take him in rather than have him stay so far away. She also noted that one of his basketball coaches had made a similar offer, and that Paul could stay there instead if Karen was uncomfortable with the Bergs. Says Laurie, "[Karen] said, 'No, Paul is going to do this thing, he's going to do it.' She told me at that time that [the program she'd sent him to] had told her to expect letters that said things like, 'Mice are crawling on me, I call for help and no one comes,' and that she was told all the children write things home like this and that's only manipulation. I caught my breath and said, 'You're telling me that you can't have contact with your child?'"

Berg had intuitively grasped that without direct contact with the teen and in an atmosphere in which all complaints are put down to "manipulation," true reports of abuse cannot be heard. She was further horrified when Karen Richards left a newsletter called "WHUTZ UP in Paradise Cove" in her mailbox. "She'd put a little note in there that said she thought I would enjoy reading this," Laurie says, "and it made me sick to my stomach."

Full of spelling and grammatical errors, the newsletter wasn't exactly an advertisement for the program's educational values. And worse, Karen had highlighted what the program presumably thought was a model exchange of letters between two parents and their child, showing how adults can resist teen "manipulation." It is headlined, seemingly without intended irony, LOVE LETTERS IN THE SAND. The teen writes,

> It is not the camp you promised . . . It smells here and I am forced to sleep on the floor . . . The Samoan fathers [program staff] are mean and beat me when I do something they don't like. They even threw a sea urchin at my head. I have learned my lesson. I love you guys and my sister and will do good in school. I am ready to come home.

The parents reply,

> Sorry about the sea urchin. You should work hard on your program. You will be home when you are recommended [by the program to be ready to graduate].

In another exchange, the child writes, "The flies are eating my cuts. . . . [A staffer] screamed so loud and hurt my ear so now I can't hear out of my left ear. Now I can't hear them call me stupid." The parents reply, ". . . Things are the same. Work your program." When the teen writes that he is almost eighteen and can't wait to return home, addressing them as "Dear, most revered Mom and Dad," the parents reply as if by rote, "Don't worry about eighteen. Finish the program."[12]

Some of the complaints in the newsletter were clearly designed to be obvious lies or perhaps humorous exaggerations—for example, at one point, the child writes about cannibals on the beach. But the beatings, the bloodsucking flies and the sewage smells would prove to be all too real. And even without knowing whether the child's account was true, Laurie found the "model" parents' compassionless responses chilling.

The Richardses, however, say that they found that the program offered exactly what they had been promised. They visited and said that the staff were "competent, committed and caring individuals" and that while the facilities were "primitive," they were "safe and sufficient," as was the food.[13] They note that during his stay Paul wrote a positive article about the program for its newsletter.[14]

Berg, however, began to investigate what she could do to free Paul. She feared for his safety, both emotional and physical. She would soon be involved with local child protective agencies, state courts, the U.S. State Department, members of Congress, national media—and anyone else she could find who would listen and potentially offer assistance. She would find herself up against a network of behavior-modification programs that grosses over $80 million annually. It is run by a group of Mormon men, linked primarily by blood ties and marriage in Southern Utah, which has changed names over time as regulatory and legal actions have led to the closure of several of its facilities.

In 2004, some 2,500 students were in programs affiliated with what is currently known as the World Wide Association of Specialty Programs (WWASP).[15] They are linked with at least six programs in four states and two countries: Cross Creek Manor and Majestic Ranch Academy in Utah; Spring Creek Lodge in Montana; Carolina Springs Academy in South Carolina; Academy at Ivy Ridge in New York; and Tranquility Bay in Jamaica.[16] The key players in the group have been affiliated with at least nine others which are now closed: Brightway Adolescent Hospital[17] and Red Rock Springs Academy in Utah;[18] Bell Academy in California;[19] Sunrise Beach, Casa by the Sea, and High Impact in Mexico;[20] Dundee Ranch Academy in Costa Rica;[21] Morava Academy in the Czech Republic, and Paradise Cove in Samoa.[22]

WWASP is linked with a series of interconnected limited liability corporations—over which true ownership is unclear but which include the same cast of leading characters. In 1997, its central referral group was called Teen Help. Like Straight and The Seed, WWASP/Teen Help has roots in the behavior modification programs of the 1970s, which all trace their roots back, directly or indirectly, to Synanon. WWASP's most immediate predecessor is Provo Canyon School, a Utah behavior modification facility that opened in 1971. At the time, there was widespread public interest in "behavioral technology" and whether people's beliefs, behavior, and even their personalities could be changed by controlling their environment and the rewards and punishments it delivered. There was also a great deal of concern, as we saw earlier, leading up to the 1974 Ervin Report on Behavior Modification, about possible abuses of such techniques.

In 1982, the U.S. Court of Appeals in the 10th Circuit upheld a decision against Provo Canyon (*Milonas v. Williams*). The program had been accused of torturing children. A class action suit had been brought against it by an advocacy group, the Youth Law Center, and a consent order had been imposed to stop a practice of dragging kids around by their hair (called the "hair dance"), mail censorship, and the punitive use of isolation and restraint. But it wasn't a clear-cut victory for a teen's right to be free of such punishments: the Court had decided that because many residents had been court-mandated into the program or sent by school districts, the facility was acting "under the color of state law"—essentially, as an agent of the government. The American government is not allowed to violate its citizens' constitutional rights, so the school's actions were deemed illegal, despite parental consent. The decision was ultimately appealed to the Supreme Court, which rejected the school's arguments and upheld the 10th Circuit's decision.[23]

But the actions of private companies are not so closely confined by the Constitution. If they do not operate "under the color of state law," they have much more leeway. As mentioned earlier, in *Parham v. J.R.* in 1979, the Supreme Court ruled that parents can involuntarily and indefinitely commit children to any programs they believe appropriate so long as the facility will accept them.[24] There have been no more recent federal cases that have addressed youths' rights in these programs—and Provo

Canyon is still open (though under different management) and still generating complaints from teens about maltreatment.[25]

By the mid-'80s, several of Provo Canyon's employees seem to have realized the potential for profit in such an unregulated—and apparently limitless—market. It was clear that programs could get away with doing almost anything in the name of "treatment" for teenagers—and that even if serious abuses and human rights violations were found, the punishment wouldn't be more than an order not to do it again and, perhaps, a fine. Both Robert Lichfield and Karr Farnsworth, who would go on to be major players in WWASP, worked for Provo Canyon when the abuses at the school documented in *Milonas v. Williams* were occurring. According to his own court testimony, Farnsworth worked at Provo Canyon for seventeen years before leaving in 1988, which puts him right in the frame of *Milonas v. Williams*.[26] Lichfield worked as "Director of Residential Living" at around the same time but, as the *Salt Lake Tribune* put it, "eluded the school's legal troubles."[27] Neither of the men has a college degree, nor is either qualified to work as a therapist.

In the mid-1980s, Lichfield attended an encounter-group seminar held by David Gilcrease, who would soon also play a major role in WWASP. Gilcrease had been a trainer for LifeSpring, a Large Group Awareness Training organization similar to est, from 1974 to 1981.[28] The founders of both est and LifeSpring had been trained by the Mind/Leadership Dynamics groups, and both organizations' seminars, like their predecessor's, involved brutal psychological attacks on participants.

Bob Lichfield was so impressed by the Gilcrease seminar (apparently, Gilcrease was taken with Lichfield as well) that they decided to work together on a new project: opening a network of schools for troubled kids that would center their "emotional growth" programming on such seminars. In 1987, Lichfield founded Teen Help, which would soon encompass a collection of behavior-modification schools and related services, such as marketing, referral services, and "escorts" to bring unwilling teens to the facilities. It would link up with Gilcrease's Resource Realizations, which would provide seminar leaders as needed. As Jay Kay, the director of Tranquility Bay, told *48 Hours*, "The cornerstone of the program is the seminar. That is really the driving force and motivating factor behind kids making changes."[29]

WWASP has made varying claims about graduation rates and success rates, with Bob Lichfield saying that 60 percent of teens drop out without completing the program,[30] while Jay Kay's father, Ken Kay, has claimed that only 40 percent fail to graduate. Lichfield told *Dateline NBC*, "Having worked with five thousand or so children in my career, I don't think there's any child that I've met that hasn't been positively influenced."[31] Predictably, there is no research to support these claims.

Costs to parents for WWASP programs range from roughly $2,000 a month for the foreign programs to $4,000 a month for Cross Creek Manor in Utah. (Cross Creek, unlike the others, does have full-time credentialed therapists and is regulated as a residential treatment facility by Utah). Since the recommended stay is typically a minimum of eighteen months, and since many teens actually spend two to three years away, this means parents are looking at a minimum of $36,000. And that's before costs for things like "escorts" (which can run up to several thousand dollars), incidentals like shampoo, which generate extra monthly charges, and travel to visit the student and participate in parent seminars is taken into account. Except for Cross Creek, health insurance almost never covers the programs because they present themselves—at least to regulators—as comparable to boarding schools and military schools, not as residential treatment.

In 1990, Lichfield incorporated his first treatment center, Cross Creek Manor, in La Verkin, Utah.[32] In 1993, he signed a contract with the Utah Alcoholism Foundation, which owns Brightway Adolescent Hospital, to run and manage that facility.[33] Over time, Teen Help and its various services became part of a group of limited liability corporations, including WWASP. The same people—J. Ralph Atkin, the founder of SkyWest Airlines, Robert Lichfield, Karr Farnsworth, Brent Facer, Ken Kay, Jay Kay (Ken's son) and Narvin Lichfield (Bob's brother)—appear repeatedly as officers of the various companies (which number at least in the dozens), though the names and titles often change.[34]

As a result, it is very difficult to trace the finances and the actual ownership of the facilities, especially the foreign sites. Utah state prosecutor Craig Barlow, who prosecuted North Star employees in Aaron Bacon's death, and has investigated WWASP's Majestic Ranch, described the group's structure to the *New York Times* as "a lateral arabesque with no hub except for these connections in Utah."[35]

The owner of a website aimed at parents looking for help for troubled teens wrote, "It has been stated to me over and over again by Narvin Lichfield and others associated with the group that the reason for the convoluted ownership situation is to shield Bob Lichfield from liability . . . I know of no other treatment organization which has gone to the great lengths this group has to obfuscate the question of who is legally and morally responsible for the welfare of the children."[36]

Teen Help's first foreign facility, which opened in 1994, was Paradise Cove in Samoa. The tiny South Pacific country is slightly smaller than Rhode Island and was known as Western Samoa until 1997. Because of its tropical climate, temperatures there are typically in the eighties, with extremely high humidity. While the palm trees and beaches provide tourists an idyllic Eden, many teens say Paradise Cove was closer to an earthly hell.

PAUL RICHARDS SAYS that when he arrived in Samoa, he was at first too stunned to take anything in. "I was homesick, I was confused. I thought it was all a dream and I would wake up," he said. He found himself spending his days in a ten-by-ten-foot straw-roofed hut called a *fale*, along with eight to fifteen other boys. There were numerous similar huts in the compound, which encompassed three separate stretches of beach. Each group of huts was surrounded by barbed-wire fencing on all sides but that facing the ocean. Between 300 and 350 boys were in the program.

On arrival, Paul was strip-searched and given a Samoan skirt to wear, known as a *lava-lava*. He was made to sleep on a straw mat on the floor, in a large room in a concrete-floored building. He shared sleeping quarters with between fifty and seventy other boys. Even at night, fluorescent lights burned steadily, in order to help the staff maintain control and prevent escapes, but this also attracted mosquitoes. And the room they slept in had only one door, which was often locked from the outside, presenting a Straight-like fire hazard.

WWASP programs use a level system, similar to that utilized by Straight. However, since there are no host homes, the kids don't get to return to their own beds until they graduate the program. On level one, as in Straight's phase one, communication with the outside world and speaking without permission is banned. Although there is no belt-looping, a higher level "buddy" (comparable to the Straight "oldcomer") is always in close proximity to new participants. The "buddy" can impose punishments for rule violations.

"It was a very difficult time for me," Paul told Lou Kilzer of the Denver *Rocky Mountain News*, who wrote a series of revealing exposés on WWASP. "I cried myself to sleep just about every single night. I cried many times during the day. I didn't have anybody I could talk to . . . I was depressed for a good while from having the brunt force of it."[37] He told me, "It was incredibly frustrating because I just have an outgoing personality and I like to talk and it was really hard to not be able to say anything. . . . I was always getting in trouble for it."

In a letter written in response to Kilzer's story on Paul's plight, the Richardses wrote,

> Regarding . . . the comments that Paul "cried himself to sleep" for eight months, does [Kilzer] care how many YEARS of tears have been shed by us, his parents, because of his oppositional defiant actions? Does [Kilzer] care that we have lost countless hours of sleep because of heartache and anguish over our son's spiteful behaviors and verbal tirades?[38]

A graduated series of "consequences" are imposed by WWASP programs to punish transgressions like Paul's talking out of turn, depending on how serious they are seen to be and how often they are repeated. The consequences vary slightly from program to program, but they have the same general structure. For talking without permission at Paradise Cove, kids would get a "warning," and if they got three warnings, they would be given a "category one" consequence. This meant they would have to sit Indian-style on the floor of a small room and listen to ten thirty-minute self-help or motivational tapes, typically Tony Robbins or Stephen Covey. Each tape was followed by a quiz on its contents, and all of these had to be passed in order to complete the punishment. Another common consequence for misbehavior entailed having to handwrite a several-thousand-word essay.

If they didn't sit in the right position, didn't do the writing or pass the tests, or continued to break rules, students would initially be given additional periods of "cat one" punishment or made to do many repetitions of strenuous exercises. If participants continued to refuse to comply with lower-level punishments or if they couldn't complete required exercise, they were sent to some form of solitary confinement. More serious transgressions, such as fighting or planning to run away, resulted in higher-category punishment. This meant immediate solitary confinement without intermediate consequences. The conditions of this confinement vary from program to program, but it is usually called "observation placement," or OP.

In Samoa, the isolation room was known as "the box." It quite literally was a box, three feet by three, of plywood, windowless, with a concrete floor, in a small building. Students would sit or stand in their underwear until they'd finished their assigned time. The heat and humidity made the close conditions especially difficult. The only food teens were given while in isolation was a small quantity of rice and water. And some boys spent weeks in the box, freed only for one daily shower break and for trips to the bathroom at the staff's discretion. Masturbation, which was considered to be a particularly heinous sin in WWASP programs as it had been in Straight, resulted in an automatic three days in the box.

Days were rigidly structured. The youth would wake at sunrise, stand for a morning roll call, and eat breakfast, usually buttered saltine crackers or boiled milk with rice. They'd attend "school" for an hour and a half: this involved reading textbooks and taking the same quizzes on each chapter repeatedly until achieving at least a B grade. There were no U.S. qualified teachers. Cleverly, WWASP's promotional material calls its educational program "self-directed schooling"[39] and uses this as a selling point. It boasts that teens can progress at their own pace.

After the morning "school" session, the kids were made to exercise for an hour and a half, running and doing sit-ups and push-ups. "We didn't have shoes," Paul explains. "We had optional sandals, but those would wear out and so, walking on coral and dirt and rocks, our feet would just get cut." And this would attract more of the island's numerous, large insects. "They'd just swarm on you," Paul says.

A lunch of butter sandwiches—or, if they were lucky, Spam, mackerel, tuna, or peanut butter and jelly—would follow. Some days, the midday meal consisted of Top Ramen noodles. Like the Straight and North Star kids, Paul and the others at Paradise Cove were constantly hungry. "I was starving," Paul says. "Right now I'm six-six, two hundred and thirty pounds, and I'm skinny. Over there I was six-five and one-fifty." He adds, "You could see my collarbone through my shirt when I wore a shirt, you could see all my rib bones. It was just sickening." His parents dispute this account, saying that he gained weight in the program.

The rest of the day was devoted to more "school" time and group "therapy." This was composed primarily of attacks by the kids on one another. "They'd try to pick on you for fun, or theoretically to try to make you 'see the light,'" Paul says. "They just circle you up and they all start yelling at you at the same time and say how shitty a person you were." He'd continually be told things like, "You're worthless, you're pathetic, you're a piece of shit, you're a compulsive liar and nobody likes you," until, he says, "they broke down [my] self-esteem."

As had happened to Fred Collins, Richard Bradbury, and so many others, Paul was told over and over that he was a drug addict, that he'd gotten bad grades, that he was a criminal—because his parents couldn't possibly have sent him to Paradise Cove otherwise. His peers and the staff wouldn't believe his repeated claims that he was an honor student who hadn't even tried cigarettes.

Dinner was one piece of boiled chicken and a handful of rice. The "kitchen" area was unclean, refrigeration was nonexistent, and the drinking water wasn't sanitary. Part of the reason for Paul's claims of weight loss while in Samoa was diarrhea, which continued persistently for the first two months of his stay. He blames it on the dirty water. Paul says he was not given medical attention for his bowel problems, nor for tonsilitis, until the throat condition caused swelling so severe that it interfered with breathing. In addition, Paul had recurrent scabies. Scabies is a parasitic illness, caused by a mite similar to the one that causes mange in dogs, and it produces severe itching. It is easily treatable, but since the facility lacked hot water for washing, the parasite lingered in clothes and bedding, causing reinfection. In Paul's case and that of many other boys at Paradise Cove, numerous boils developed on their skin as well—either due to irritation and scratching from the scabies or because of other cuts that became infected.

BEFORE ATTEMPTING to have Paul brought back, Laurie Berg wanted to be sure that she was right, to be sure that he wasn't psychologically troubled in ways she had overlooked. "I felt I knew this kid's heart," she told the Denver *Rocky Mountain News*. "I started asking around the neighborhood. Had I misread him . . . ? Were there problems at other places? And I found out that there really weren't."[40]

Laurie began to gather information. She discovered that in Washington, a parent cannot have a child committed unless it is "medically necessary," and that state child-welfare officials may check "periodically" to determine whether ongoing confinement is still indicated. Just after she'd become aware that Paul had been taken from his home, Laurie had called the county sheriff's office, asking them to check on his safety under this provision. They contacted Utah authorities, who interviewed Paul. He says he requested to go home. But by the time the police followed up, Paul had been sent to Samoa, where they had no jurisdiction.

Now Laurie began corresponding with the U.S. State Department, attempting to make them aware of the problems with Paradise Cove. She was told that there was a procedure the department had developed to do "welfare checks" on minor citizens who lived in foreign countries. But

getting the State Department to act was a slow, grinding process. To bolster her case for quicker action, Laurie began to contact other people
who had had run-ins with Teen Help. Her brother sent her a newspaper
article that detailed a case in which a teen and his grandparents had unsuccessfully sued his parents, attempting to win the boy's release from
Teen Help's Jamaica program, Tranquility Bay. She contacted the California district attorney in that case and was given the name of a lawyer
who had represented another man who was fighting the organization in
a California custody battle. Stanley Goold III, then sixteen, had been
sent—against his father's wishes—by his mother to Paradise Cove in November of 1996. Goold Senior eventually won his case to bring his son
home—but not until Stanley III had spent eleven months in Samoa.

Stanley III told Laurie what he'd later tell *Forbes* magazine. "It was
worse than being in prison, because we didn't know when we were going to leave. . . . I saw a few kids punched, kicked, and thrown," he said.
In the worst cases, "they'd put duct tape over the kid's mouth, hog-tie
him or put on handcuffs." He described the "box" and said that the food
was meager, the conditions filthy.[41]

Laurie says, "He told me pretty much that it seemed that some of the
things in the newsletter could be true," adding that she found him very
credible. Horrified, she tried to get the Washington courts to act, filing a
"third-party dependency petition," which essentially claimed that Paul's
parents were not acting in his best interests by keeping him in Samoa.
She constantly searched online, ultimately connecting with Maine social
worker Donna Headrick, who soon became one of the most dogged investigators of Teen Help.

Through these and other connections, Laurie found out that
WWASP/Teen Help had briefly been affiliated with a facility in Mexico,
called Sunrise Beach. Opened in 1995, it was a girls' program near Can-
cún run by Glenda and Steve Roach. In the spring of 1996, a Mexican
newspaper published an exposé, alleging child abuse. Police conducted a
surprise raid on May 10 of that year. They found that girls had been held
in isolation rooms in stressful physical positions for days. The Roaches
were arrested, but they were later freed.

One WWASP official told a journalist that he blamed the problems in Mexico on disgruntled former employees who had convinced Mexican authorities that Sunrise Beach was "a house of ill repute."[42] Another said that the group chose to shut the facility after the raid, rather than fight to keep it open, because "the local legal system may not have been above-board."[43]

But that would not be the last time Glenda and Steve Roach tangled with foreign police due to abuse allegations at a WWASP-linked facility that they ran. In January 1998, the Roaches opened Morava Academy in Brno in the Czech Republic. By October, they had problems with "disgruntled employees" again. A woman they'd hired as a teacher, Hana Simonova, reported repeated physical and psychological abuse to Czech authorities.

In early November, police raided the site. They interviewed twenty-five students—eight of whom said they'd been mistreated.[44] For punishment, they said they had been confined in a room with covered windows and a bare mattress. Often, they were made to lie on the floor on their stomachs for days. One girl was denied bathroom access until she defecated on herself.[45] Simonova described Glenda Roach to the Czech papers as a real-life Cruella DeVil. Simonova said, "I think she hates people," adding that she never saw Roach laugh or smile, except while punishing kids.[46]

The Roaches were arrested again on November 9. They were charged with human-rights violations.[47] As before, program officials placed the blame elsewhere. WWASP's Karr Farnsworth compared Czech officials to the KGB, saying that they'd only acted because they "don't like Americans."[48] He said that the kids were lying, calling them "master manipulators." He also claimed that Czech authorities had simply misunderstood the program's perfectly reasonable use of "time-outs."

"We overlooked the possibility that the Czech authorities might not consider time-out to be an appropriate way of dealing with kids," Farnsworth said. "They just don't understand that time-out is exactly what parents all over the world use to discipline their children."[49] Or perhaps they didn't understand how keeping a teenager locked in a

windowless room for days could possibly be seen as analogous to sending a four-year-old to a corner for ten minutes.

AS THE MONTHS passed by and 1997 turned into 1998, the state department began to respond to the activists' prodding. Documents received by Berg and Paul Richards under the Freedom of Information Act
reveal the following chronology: In late 1997, the chargé d'affaires of the
American Embassy in Samoa, Bill Warren, expressed concern that the
welfare checks Laurie sought for Paul might leave the embassy open to
legal action by Paradise Cove. Officials in Washington refuted this. A
November 1997 communiqué from Washington to Samoa notes:

> The department is far more vulnerable to legal repercussions for
> failing to perform appropriate welfare checks when a concern exists
> than for performing checks that do not uncover negative informa-
> tion. . . . Congress, in reviewing disasters like the Jonestown
> tragedy, reinforced the US government's mandate to provide pro-
> tection for Americans—especially in communities aboard with
> large numbers of Americans and especially towards minors.[50]

The communiqué went on to say that the State Department had responsibility to protect American children, even if their parents tried to
deny access to them, as had happened at Jonestown. In 1978, a total of
276 American babies, children, and teens had been killed, poisoned,
stabbed, or shot there, many of them by their own parents. Six hundred
thirty-six adults had died by their own hands or at the hands of other
cult members. The State Department had had numerous reports of
abuse from ex–cult members and their families prior to the massacre,
but had failed to investigate them thoroughly.[51]

Despite this awful precedent, however, the right of American children
held in foreign behavior-modification facilities to contact the State
Department—and to be given private hearings—has nonetheless only
rarely and slowly been enforced since. The chronology of the State De-

partment's failed dealings with Jonestown, in fact, echoes many of its interactions with WWASP.

After receiving the November 12, 1997, communiqué, Warren insisted that Paradise Cove allow him to inspect its facility. A report from a visit he conducted on February 25, 1998, stated that many of the boys had serious skin problems, including scabies and boils—and Warren told director Brian Viafanua that these problems could not be cleared up unless hot water was provided. Warren spoke with Paul Richards, but did not inform him that the police back home had requested a welfare check, because he apparently believed that the request had been withdrawn. He said that Paul "appeared in good health," but noted that, after a year in Samoa, he was still on the program's lowest level.[52] Paul claims he was never permitted to speak with Warren alone, and that Viafanua "was standing right over my shoulder the entire time I was talking to him." A review of the State Department's actions before the Jonestown massacre found that there as well, State Department employees announced their visits in advance and had allowed them to be supervised by the very people they were supposed to be investigating.[53]

The other boys Warren interviewed spoke glowingly of the program, so much so that he wrote that he "wondered aloud to [an employee] whether some of them might not be perhaps too enthusiastic about the program, like religious converts." He was told that it was part of the boys' "rehabilitation" that they were "expected not to be negative." He noted that the boys "might be somewhat less enthusiastic" if interviewed privately. Nonetheless, when he coincidentally ran into several parents at a local pizza restaurant, who also passionately supported the program, he wrote that this confirmed his impression that there were not "any areas for major concern."[54]

PAUL, MEANWHILE, had come to believe he'd been abandoned to his fate—and was trying to decide whether to just accept it and tough it out until he turned eighteen or continue to resist. A letter he sent via his parents to a friend back home reflects his ambivalence. The first page is an account of recent failed attempts by other kids to run and have the program sued and shut down after they'd left. It includes a passage on something Paul would have in ordinary circumstances found abhorrent. The program's censors had tried to black it out, but the impression he made with his pen was so deep that it was legible.

He wrote that the boys of Paradise Cove believed that "if one dies here, the program shuts down for a minimum of six months."[55] Consequently, he'd heard about a plot by some of the teens to kill a fellow inmate to spur such a shutdown. Accounts by other teens who had simultaneously attended the program confirm his story and show that the boys had actually chosen a victim, S., the youngest boy there. He was twelve or thirteen and, according to Paul, "weighed about eighty pounds, wet." The youths had sharpened a broken toothbrush into a shank, planning to stab S. in the throat with it. They figured they could escape a murder charge by pleading insanity brought on by conditions at Paradise Cove. Paul's letter gives no details of the plot, simply mentioning it as one thing that might bring him home quickly. Disturbingly, it contains no sense of moral outrage or discomfort about possibly benefiting from murder—or indeed, any kind of emotion at all about being in a place that made people so desperate.

Several paragraphs later, he writes, seemingly without awareness of how strange the contrast might be, "I'm glad I came here 'cause I have learned a lot."[56] The letter was received in November of 1997. By December, Paul says, he'd come to a decision to simply do his time until his eighteenth birthday. The murder plan had been discovered before anyone was harmed; the conspirators had been punished. Paul continued to make the odd effort to be freed, but no matter whom he asked about contacting anyone outside the program, the answer was always no. He wouldn't get the "privilege" of even speaking on the phone with his parents until he "earned" it. And he refused to adopt the attitude of happy submission that the staff saw as evidence of "progress."

ON SEPTEMBER 11, 1998, just when Hana Simonova was preparing to blow the whistle on WWASP's Czech facility, the State Department in

Washington sent a communiqué to its Samoa office, saying that it had received "credible allegations of physical abuse" at Paradise Cove. These included allegations of "beatings, isolation, food and water deprivation, choke-holds, kicking, punching, bondage, spraying with chemical agents, forced medication, verbal abuse and threats of further physical abuse." Washington told Warren and his staff to formally request the Samoan government to investigate, again mentioning the Jonestown tragedy as a cautionary tale.

The communiqué stated that there were multiple allegations from independent sources that corroborated one another.[57] The State Department had probably also been contacted by CBS's *48 Hours*, which was producing an exposé on Paradise Cove. When it aired on October 15, 1998, the broadcast included footage of "the box" as well as stories from several boys about having been left hog-tied in it. PC's director and owner admitted on camera that boys had been bound with duct tape, although he claimed that this had only been done when the program had first opened. The show also told the Bergs' story of fighting for Paul's freedom.[58]

While *48 Hours* was filming other areas of the facility, Paul was kept in "the box." He was not permitted to be seen or interviewed. S., the kid who had been targeted for death by the other boys, was also hidden away. He would ultimately spend five years, from age twelve to age seventeen, in at least three different WWASP facilities, and he currently suffers from profound post-traumatic stress disorder.

48 HOURS did bring Paul some good news indirectly, however. The day after it aired, he was handed a fax from his parents. It disparaged the Bergs, saying they were hurting the family. Upon reading the note, Paul burst into tears. He says, "The director gave it to me . . . and I started crying. He was like, 'Yeah, I know, it's a bad thing,' and I was like, 'No, this is the greatest day of my life, I can't believe how happy this makes me.'" Apparently, Viafanua had believed that Paul would be just as distressed as his parents were that his neighbors were trying to interfere with "his program." Paul was just delighted to know that he hadn't been forgotten.

The news made his last four months in Samoa more bearable. And, perhaps wary about the public concern for him, staff began giving him special privileges. Deciding that dealing with other kids' rebellion might make Paul more compliant, they put him in command of the most difficult teens. Paul told his charges that as long as they didn't make obvious trouble, he wouldn't report petty offenses. The kids had to help build stone walls—sometimes, they simply had to move heavy rocks back and forth. But when one kid's refusal to work threatened to get the whole group punished, Paul felt he had no choice but to turn him in.

Shortly thereafter, he says, the boy stabbed him four times—in the hand, forearm, and lower back—with a plastic pen that he'd sharpened into a shank. At this point, the staff finally stepped in to restrain the boy. The director refused to remove him from Paul's living compound. "I lived in fear for the remainder of my stay at Paradise Cove," Paul says.

WHILE THE SAMOAN GOVERNMENT started investigating Paradise Cove, it also began looking into two other American-run teen behavior-modification programs that had set up shop there. One, the New Hope Academy, was operated, at least in part, by Steve Cartisano—who'd been barred from working with kids in Utah after the death of Kristen Chase in 1990. In February 1999, during the Samoan government's investigation, Cartisano fled, leaving five emaciated teens on the beach.[59] He later returned, under an assumed name, and became involved with another program, Pacific Coast Academy, from which the U.S. embassy pulled twenty-two maltreated students in 2001.[60]

Laurie Berg, meanwhile, was still fighting for Paul. Her petition to have Washington State intervene had been denied. While she was pleased that the State Department had forced Samoa to investigate, the fact was that Paradise Cove was still open for business and Paul Richards was still there after twenty months.

Good news came in the form of a letter from Paul himself, mailed surreptitiously as he was moved from Samoa to a WWASP facility in Utah. On February 22, 1999, he wrote, "First off, thank you very much for all that you have done for me since I have been here. . . . It meant the world to me, knowing that there was someone still there who cared."[61] Since he was now back under American jurisdiction, Laurie reactivated the Washington sheriff's investigation, aimed at determining whether Paul's treatment was "medically necessary."

Paul was put on "level zero" for his continuing resistance. He was made to sit in a chair and stare at the wall for twelve hours a day. He later told the *Rocky Mountain News* that staffers kept asking if he was bored.

And I would give them some spiel about how it was so tantalizing to be able to analyze a pattern . . . that it amazed me that cumulus clouds form so rapidly. I was bored out of my mind and they knew it. But I wouldn't give them the satisfaction. . . .[62]

I had been planning to leave all along when I turned eighteen, and then as eighteen rolled around, I talked to my parents. [They said,] "Everybody at home has given up on you, your grandparents don't care anymore, they're not going to pay for your college, the Bergs lost all interest, they lost in court, nobody cares back at home, but if you decide to stay and graduate then we'll pay for your entire education."

Paul was advised that if he chose not to stay after age eighteen, his parents' "exit plan" gave him $100, money for six meals, and a bus ticket from Utah to Washington. No college money, no further support, period. The "exit plan" was a new strategy, devised by David Gilcrease for WWASP in late 1998. Gilcrease had noticed that some of the older kids, like Paul, were not fully submitting, preferring instead to wait the program out. To deter such resistance, Gilcrease suggested that parents announce an "exit plan," which would expel the child from the family unless he agreed to stay, even after his eighteenth birthday, until the program deemed him ready to graduate. Further, if they did not comply exactly with their parents' rules after graduation, the kids would either have to leave home and be denied all parental support for at least six months or agree to return to WWASP. Straight had arrived at virtually the same policy more than two decades earlier.

Not seeing a choice and desperate to go to college, Paul agreed to stay. Staff had made a deal with him: Behave for four months and we'll graduate you. But on June 21, days after his eighteenth birthday, Laurie and Michael Berg arrived with Paul's uncle and several friends. They asked for Paul, but WWASP's Karr Farnsworth threatened to call the sheriff to arrest them for trespassing.

Instead, Laurie called the sheriff herself and the group was allowed in. Laurie wept when she saw Paul. In a four-hour discussion, the Bergs told him that he would not be homeless if he left and could live either with them or his former basketball coach. He'd dreamed of attending his final year of high school with his class: though he was eighteen, the date of his birthday put him in line to graduate the following year. The adults agreed with his high school plans. They also told him that his grandparents had promised to fund his college education, no matter what. Paul left with the Bergs, furious with his parents.

The Richardses immediately instituted the exit plan, refusing even to talk with him on the phone. When he ran into them at a basketball game several months later, he tried to hug them. They walked away. He received a two-page letter, which read in part:

> We want you to know that we thought it was extremely inappropriate for you to feign friendship in public by hugging and shaking hands with us. We were extremely uncomfortable with this situation because we are no longer willing to participate in a dishonest relationship. . . . We have chosen to be honest in our lives, and this does not include the kind of deceitfulness you exhibited by acting as if nothing was wrong.[63]

Though Paul says he continued to try to reach out to his parents, his attempts were rebuffed. A psychiatrist diagnosed him with post-traumatic stress disorder, and he required talk therapy for it for a few months. He says, "I was having flashbacks, like if I saw a scene [in a movie or on TV], or something made me think of [Paradise Cove], I'd have a flashback and my stomach would go queasy and I'd get sweaty palms and go white." He also had frequent nightmares about being returned to the program. He says, "I'll wake up and it'll be freezing cold in a full sweat and I'll be gasping for breath. They're a lot less frequent now, but they're still there, unfortunately."

When he tried to return to high school, he found that WWASP had one more nasty surprise in store: his school had been sent a diploma which claimed that he'd already graduated. Paul insisted that the diploma was bogus. His high school principal couldn't believe his ears: for the first time in twenty-five years on the job, here was a kid who wanted to finish school, when he could avoid it. Paul was allowed to enjoy his senior year. At eighteen, he had his first kiss.

And in December 1999, Laurie and Michael formally adopted him. He says, "At that point, there was kind of closure. I was just really happy and thankful. I had this new family and somebody could love me and I could love them." He adds that he's still not perfect and still sometimes argues with his adoptive parents: "We're like normal people, we disagree on some things, but we're civilized and they respect me and we talk about our differences and you know, life goes on."

The Richardses, meanwhile, defend their actions, saying that Paul needed help and that he would have been dangerous to others without the program. They write, "Since placing [our] son in this program in June, 1997, we have had to endure cruel and endless accusations against us of kidnapping, child abuse, child neglect, child abandonment, lack of love for our child and personal dysfunction. . . . *Time, People, Diablo, Spin, Fortune*, and *Seventeen* as well as the *48 Hours, Dateline*, and *Primetime* television programs . . . all reported how terrible it is to send children to programs like this without their consent . . . [but] when tragedies such as the Littleton massacre occur, the first question in anyone's mind is always, 'Why didn't the parents do something to help their child prevent this tragedy.'"[64] "These programs WORK," they add, maintaining that if the Columbine high school shooters had been sent to a WWASP program, the shootings would never have happened . . . We have personally met many upper level students and graduates of the program and it is hard to argue with the successful, demonstrable results. Although they were suicidal, depressed, angry, spiteful, addicted to drugs or alcohol, hated their parents and themselves, [and were] school truants/dropouts and/or juvenile delinquents . . . most of these teenagers returned to their families as successful, confident, motivated, loving, honest, respectful, mature individuals.[65]

Paul earned a 4.0 average for his senior year. He won a place at West Point, but he decided to stick closer to home and has just completed a degree in engineering at the University of Washington. He is allowed to call and see his younger brother, but his older sister avoids all contact. He is still estranged from his parents.

OTHER RESPONSES to WWASP's "exit plan" have split families in even more heartbreaking ways. There have been at least two suicides. One seventeen-year-old boy, Corey Murphy, shot himself in the head with a .38-caliber handgun after his mother, Laura Murphy, told him she would institute the plan. She told reporter Lou Kilzer that she believed her son had put the gun to his head, not to kill himself but "to manipulate me into sending him back into the program."[66] He'd already spent thirty-two months in WWASP facilities, twenty-two of them at Paradise Cove.

Laura Murphy told Kilzer that she fervently believes that without the program, Corey would have killed himself even earlier. She says it was the only thing that ever helped in his lifelong struggle with depression. She cited his upbeat letters home from Samoa as proof. She had a Teen Help staffer officiate at his funeral and has supported a scholarship in his name, which funds treatment in WWASP programs for kids whose parents could otherwise not afford it.

But Paul Richards and Laurie Berg see it differently: Paul attended Paradise Cove with Corey. He says Corey put on a happy face in his letters for the same reason all the other boys did—in order to get out. The last thing he would have wanted, they believe, was to return to Teen Help or to have other children sent to its programs in his name. Another boy, who committed suicide after being pulled from a WWASP program when his parents could no longer afford it, has his name attached to such a scholarship. There have also been at least two known suicides that occurred while teens were inside WWASP programs.[67]

In June 1999, the State Department's Bill Warren sent a communiqué to all the countries in which WWASP was known to be operating or to have operated, warning them about what had happened in Samoa and saying that the WWASP-affiliated programs in "Samoa, Mexico and Jamaica (and the former program in the Czech Republic) are interrelated and appear to be under the same ownership and control." It went on: "There have been credible allegations of abuse. Instances of poor sanitation and food have been raised by the embassy with the camp staffs and with Samoan health authorities. There are valid concerns that isolation as a punishment for nonparticipation is a human rights abuse." Warren's communiqué also noted that while many participants said they felt the program was "life-changing," there was no research on long-term effectiveness, and that "at least on the part of the owners and directors . . . profit [seemed] to be their most important product." The message went on to reassure the other outposts that their worst fears—that these programs might produce another Jonestown—would not be realized. "There are no signs . . . that the kids themselves are involved in any apocalyptic or mass-suicide religious indoctrination. Post suspects that the kids at the camps, most of them very street-savvy, would react to a call for mass suicide with a hearty 'Up yours!'"[68] The upshot of all this is that the State Department has yet to push for investigation into WWASP's Jamaican program, Tranquility Bay, nor did it push investigation of the Mexican facility Casa by the Sea, which remained open until late 2004, when Mexican authorities raided and shut it following abuse reports.[69] In Jamaica, activists say that the State Department won't even enforce the rules that require teens at Tranquility Bay to be allowed to contact the embassy.[70]

SIX

"Based on the Results, You Have Exactly What You Intended"

Because WWASP and similar programs are still thriving, Laurie Berg continues her activism, even after Paul has graduated from college. While fighting for his release, she contacted a California woman named Karen Lile. She and her husband, Kendall Bean, had posted a lengthy account of their disturbing experience with WWASP and its seminars on the Web. The couple had sent their daughter, Kyrsten Bean, to Tranquility Bay. Their story illustrates further how WWASP manages to get under so many people's skins.[1]

Unlike Paul, Kyrsten had indisputably been in serious trouble. At fifteen, she was drinking a twelve-pack of beer daily and living on the streets of San Francisco. Kyrsten would use almost any drug, once even injecting heroin. In the spring of 1997, she was picked up as a runaway and taken to the psychiatric ward of Walnut Creek Hospital. A psychiatrist there told her parents that Kyrsten "would probably be dead within a year" if she did not get long-term residential treatment. The doctor then gave them the phone number for Teen Help. Tired of the streets, Kyrsten agreed to go to Jamaica—expecting a cushy rehab.

"[I was] dreaming of eating healthy food, exercising in a big gym," she wrote in an account written upon arriving at Tranquility Bay. And her dreams weren't out of line with the program's promotional material, which features kids on Jet Skis and tropical beaches. But after being driven hours into rural Jamaica to a dilapidated-looking facility, she says, "my first remark after being asked how I liked it was, 'I'm in hell.'"[2]

Kyrsten was rapidly introduced to WWASP's strict rules. She was told that she couldn't speak without raising her hand for permission, and that looking out windows or at boys would result in "consequences." Teens had to move from place to place in straight lines, saying "Excuse me" to any adult they passed and keeping their eyes down like penitents. At first, she says, she thought the program was "insane." The rules seemed to change constantly, and she initially learned them by breaking them. She soon discovered that one punishment, called "observation placement," was a bare, tiled isolation room in which kids were made to lie still and silently on their stomachs with their arms at their sides or behind their backs. Tranquility Bay's director, Jay Kay, told one journalist that the "record" for consecutive time spent in OP was eighteen months.[3]

But after her initial shock and confusion, Kyrsten threw herself into the program completely. She decided that the rigid structure was exactly what she needed to overcome the lackadaisical, free-form life of the streets. And the tough therapy allowed her to express emotions that she had previously felt obligated to suppress. As a result, she grew to like and approve of the program's philosophy.

WHEN KAREN AND KENDALL placed Kyrsten at Tranquility Bay, they had no reason to suspect that it was unlicensed. After all, they'd been referred by a doctor at a hospital covered by their insurance (the hospital would later be cited by the state for making the referral without knowledge of what really went on at the program).[4] The couple also says they were led to believe that the line staff of Tranquility Bay were licensed therapists.

Karen and Kendall did think, even at the time, that the contract they signed for treatment was rather strange. In one clause it said:

> When it becomes necessary, in the sole discretion of the Program, to restrain a Student, the Sponsors authorize the Program to use pepper spray (or electrical disabler, mace, mechanical restraints, handcuffs) as means to or alternative to avoid, whenever possible, the potential for injuries, complications, and/or altercations that can arise from the Program staff having to physically restrain or wrestle with the student in order to subdue the student."[5]

Concerned, Karen asked what this meant, but was told, "Well, they never do that stuff, it's just in the contract." She adds that they had less than a week to decide on further treatment for Kyrsten and trusted that the doctor covered by their insurance had made a good recommendation. When asked about this clause on a show aired in January 1998, Jay Kay would tell *Primetime Live,* "Do I have handcuffs here? No, I don't. Do I have electrical disablers here? No, I don't. Do I have pepper spray? You bet I do. And I haven't used it in five and a half or six months."[6]

In the "Parent Manual," which they saw only after Kyrsten had been in the program for several months, Karen and Kendall also found what they would later realize were red flags. The section on medical care, for example, reads, "We try to make our decisions taking into consideration a balance between added costs to the parent for medical care, and true medical need of the Student. The staff, like any parent, can miscalculate the timing or need of medical intervention. Such miscalculations can result in the student not getting medical care as soon as would be recommended or to avoid complications." It goes on to say that as a result of such "judgment calls" by nonmedical staff, if the child is harmed, the program should be held free from liability. Ordinary school or treatment contracts, while often containing legal waivers, rarely even imply that cost will be considered before a child can get medical attention.

The Parent Manual also contains a grotesque parody of Elisabeth Kübler-Ross's stages of grief, applied to how teens react to being sent to the program. Rather than offering ways for parents to empathetically address the natural grief a child might feel at being exiled from home, it instead aims to inoculate them against believing any complaint whatsoever of abuse, neglect or shoddy treatment, telling them to expect "denial," "bargaining," and false accounts of abuse.[7]

But worried as they were about Kyrsten, and knowing that at least she wasn't on the street, Karen and Kendall accepted the document. "We read through it and were surprised by many things," Karen says, "but we really felt that we were not expert enough to judge what was best for our daughter and were relying upon people we thought were experts."

The couple felt especially grateful to WWASP/Teen Help, because it had arranged a barter deal with them to pay for Kyrsten's treatment—a transaction they didn't know was forbidden by most mental-health ethics codes.[8] But, of course, WWASP wasn't actually providing mental-health treatment: when pressed by journalists about the lack of trained mental-health professionals working with the kids in its programs, WWASP officials call the programs "non-therapeutic."[9] Explaining the rationale for their system, WWASP associate Brent Facer told a journalist,

> Automakers learned a long time ago that if the right system is engineered, everyone who works on the assembly line is not required to be an engineer themselves. These programs have been carefully engineered by many professionals in the field, who not only have extensive educational backgrounds, but also have scores of years of experience.[10]

However, none of the key players in the WWASP programs appears to have even an undergraduate psychology degree, and many lack any college degrees.[11] Only David Gilcrease, who designed the program's intensive seminars, has a graduate degree: in engineering.[12]

The group's spokesperson, Ken Kay, during a brief split with the organization, told the *Rocky Mountain News*:

These people are basically a bunch of untrained people who work for this organization. So they don't have credentials of any kind. . . . We could be leading these kids to long-term problems that we don't have a clue about because we're not going about it in the proper way. . . . How in the hell can you call yourself a behavior-modification program—and that's one of the ways it's marketed—when nobody has the expertise to determine: Is this good, is this bad?[13]

Karen and Kendall didn't know any of this as the months went by and their daughter stayed at Tranquility Bay. They were disturbed that their contact with Kyrsten was limited to letters and very brief, obviously supervised phone calls, but at the time, they still believed that the program and its "experts" knew what was best. That all changed in January 1998, when they checked into the Livermore, California, Holiday Inn to attend their first "parent seminar."

Participants in WWASP's seminars—including both parents and children—are made to take a vow of secrecy about what actually takes place. They are told this is necessary to protect the confidentiality of others, to avoid "spoiling" it for future participants, and to avoid revealing trade secrets. They make this agreement within the first hour of the seminar.

Nonetheless, dozens of parents and teens have described their experience publicly, believing that they made their promises of silence under duress, without being fully informed about what they were about to undergo. Their stories reveal that many of the exercises and the seminar philosophy have been taken almost directly from the LifeSpring seminars.

LifeSpring, a Large-Group Awareness Training (LGAT) similar to est, was founded by John Hanley in 1973.[14] David Gilcrease, who orchestrates WWASP's seminars, worked for seven years as a LifeSpring trainer.[15] LGATs are designed to produce profoundly emotional experiences. Like similarly confrontational encounter groups, they have long been linked with psychological casualties, including psychotic breaks in previously normal adults. LifeSpring alone has been sued more than thirty times for psychologically damaging participants, with most cases settled out of court in favor of the plaintiffs. It has even been charged with causing suicides: the family of a man who died after jumping from a fourth-floor window following a LifeSpring training session won an undisclosed settlement from the organization in 1982. A 1993 case resulted in a $750,000 judgment for a participant who was institutionalized for two years following a LifeSpring training.[16]

Consequently, many remaining organizations selling such seminars (LifeSpring itself seems to have split into several competing groups) now require participants to sign legal waivers in advance, attempting to avoid liability for such outcomes. The groups often warn that people who are currently undergoing mental-health treatment or who have taken psychiatric medications should not attend, according to Carol Giambalvo, an expert in LGATs at the American Family Foundation, a group that helps families and survivors of groups that use coercive persuasion techniques.

No such cautions are given about the WWASP seminars, even though their methods are virtually identical to those of LGATs. While the seminars for parents are less intense, both parent and teen versions use many of LifeSpring's exercises. WWASP admits that a significant proportion of the teens in its programs have taken or are currently taking psychiatric medications[17]—but nonetheless, all participants are required to complete the seminars or they cannot graduate and go home. And as with Straight, parents are told that if their children do not graduate, they will return to their prior bad behavior and almost inevitably die. WWASP accepts adolescents with depression, bipolar disorder, and attention-deficit disorder[18]—whereas LGATs, in an attempt to minimize legal problems related to psychological casualties, now often try to exclude adults who have had any psychiatric treatment, especially with medication.

Though the exact proportion of adults vulnerable to psychotic breaks or other psychological damage following participation in LGATs is not known, the phenomenon occurs regularly enough to be repeatedly documented among previously normal adults who attend such trainings, but who are free to leave at any time. The effects of these trainings on vulnerable, emotionally disturbed adolescents far from home, who have no such choice, are likely to be even worse, according to Richard Ofshe, professor emeritus of sociology at the University of California at Berkeley, who has studied both LGATs and Synanon extensively. Even normal teens typically have weaker psychological defenses than those of adults, and research shows that lack of control and choice worsens the impact of most psychological stress. Troubled children, of course, often have troubled parents—but they, too, are kept uninformed about the possible risks of the seminars.

The little research conducted on the outcomes of these seminars doesn't even find them effective at prompting positive change. Most participants find the experience profoundly moving—and many people believe that such an emotionally intense event must necessarily produce psychological improvement. Consequently, an overwhelming majority of participants, when surveyed afterward, say their lives were changed for the better. However, several studies (including one of Lifespring) have found that while participants say their LGAT experiences improve their lives, there was either no positive effect, or a small, short-lived one, on their actual psychological problems and behavior.[19] One study was conducted on an LGAT used in an attempt to reform prisoners. It was one of the few studies to use a control group for comparison, and it found that there was no difference in behavior between participants and controls studied both three months and twelve months afterward.[20]

KAREN AND KENDALL certainly had no idea at all what they were about to experience. They'd been told that the parent seminars would give them a taste of what Kyrsten was being taught at Tranquility Bay. They imagined seeing slides of the program, asking questions about its therapeutic processes. Karen says, "I entered the seminar with an open mind, eager to learn and share. . . . My daughter had written to me expressing her feelings of joy and significance after completion of her Discovery Seminar. I expected my experience to be worthy of the same sentiments."[21] But what happened at the Livermore hotel shocked and unnerved her. She and her husband arrived the night before the seminar was to begin. To orient herself, Karen walked around the hotel, passing the room in which the seminar was to be held.

"When I looked inside," she said, "I saw about twenty people busily engaged in setting up. . . . Posters with slogans like BASED ON THE RESULTS, YOU HAVE EXACTLY WHAT YOU INTENDED were on the walls. There was a feeling of underlying excitement in the activity of the staff members."[22] But Karen sensed that she was unwelcome, so she left.

The next morning, the sessions were scheduled to start at nine A.M. Written instructions repeatedly stressed being on time, obeying the seminar staff, and the importance of completing the entire seminar. They even said that in the event of a "physiological emergency," like the need to go to the bathroom, participants should ask permission before leaving the room. But at nine, the staff hadn't appeared. The couple now suspects that their lateness was a deliberate attempt to keep participants off-balance. At least half an hour later, the room was opened, and about ninety parents and other relatives of program participants were admitted. Karen says the conference room was set up with "military" precision, with masking tape ensuring that the rows of chairs were absolutely even. There was no way to see out or in: even the windows on the doors from the conference room to the hallway were papered over. Karen described what happened next:

> When everyone was seated and the doors to the outside hallway were closed, a 6'4" muscular man in a suit strode purposefully towards the front of the room. His presence commanded our attention. . . . He asked us to put all of our personal belongings at the side of the room and not to record or take notes. . . . There was a flurry of movement as everyone obeyed.[23]

Karen noted that the speaker, an African American man, spent a long time discussing his personal experiences but made no mention of any psychological training. He said he knew their children well because he'd done their seminars. She described how he made fun of them for posing as gangsters, saying that because he'd been in a gang himself in East L.A., he knew what a real gangster's posture was. He demonstrated this aggressive stance for the group. Karen continued to listen, waiting to hear more about his credentials. Eventually, she realized that he believed that his own turnaround from gangster to college graduate was all that he felt was required to make him an expert in helping troubled youth. Karen didn't agree, but she noted that everyone else seemed to accept his authority.

Both Karen and Kendall found themselves oddly compelled by his authoritative and dynamic speaking style. However, they rapidly began to find the content of his presentation disturbing. First, he drew a bull's-eye on a large white pad. The central circle, he said, represented each person's "magical inner child." The outer circles were the person's "fixed beliefs," "fixed behaviors," and "fixed emotions." The goal of the seminar was "to penetrate all these outer circles to reach the magical child." This "magical child" was supposed to be spontaneous and always intuitively right—what adults had learned since childhood (including, presumably, rational thought) was what prevented them from being good parents.

Having had extensive experience with therapy, Karen was put off by the trainer's assumptions of his audience's ignorance. He acted like he offered profound and original insights, and as though these were unquestionably the absolute truth for everyone. But what came next was even more distressing. Karen wrote:

> He then began to talk about concepts of right and wrong. To illustrate his point, he singled me out. . . . He stood so close to me, I was very uncomfortable. I had feelings of intimidation. I didn't want to act on those feelings, so I stood up and faced him squarely and said, "You are in my space." I had put my hand on my hip when I said that. Instead of stepping out of my space, he put his hand on his hip and mocked me with his expression and gesture and leaned closer . . .
>
> Suddenly, he changed from a mocking behavior to the aggressive stance he had described earlier as gangster posture. He pointed his finger at my face, about ½ inch away. . . . He said forcefully, "I could

rob you." He paused, looking me straight in the eyes with menace; "I could take away your womanhood." He paused for a response and when I gave none, he said, "I could kill you."

I looked back at him and felt the full force of his words. I knew that this facilitator knew nothing about my history. Others had confronted me before [genuinely intending to do me serious harm]. . . . I stood my ground, but I was shaken to the core. He had changed his behavior so quickly, I had had no warning and I was frozen in a state of shock. There were 90 other people in the room watching and no one said a word. He shook his finger at me and leaned closer, raising his voice to say, "And could I say I was right?" I was convinced that he could indeed believe that he was right in doing these things. . . . I answered softly, but with firmness, "Yes, you could." He stared at me for a few more minutes in silence. I stared back.

Then he broke the tension by laughing. He dropped his aggressive stance and leaned closer, saying, "You are welcome in my space anytime," in a slightly suggestive manner. I was shocked at his uninvited familiarity and said nothing, neither did I laugh or move back.[24]

The speaker stalked back to the front of the room. Kendall describes what happened next, as he later put it into context:

From the very beginning of the seminar, efforts were made to undermine our current belief systems and values. We were told early in the game that our current belief system was what was causing our problems in life. [After the trainer had confronted Karen, he said,] "There is no right or wrong, only what works and what doesn't work. . . ." In a carefully planned way, we were being taken for a ride, but so cleverly and subtly that we were hardly aware our values were being attacked.

And in a way, it made sense. Didn't we always have arguments with our teenage children about what was right and wrong? Wouldn't it be easier to just talk about what worked and what didn't?

But we weren't given a lot of time to think. If we had, we might have realized, as I later did, that by extension, no right or wrong means no truth or falsehood, no good or evil, and, ultimately, no working or not working. Because who's to decide? The trainer? If there's no right or wrong, how can he be *right* . . . ? How can he discredit us for giving a *wrong* answer? . . . But they didn't bother to address these issues.[25]

"No right and wrong, just what works and what doesn't" also conveys an additional troubling message: that the end justifies the means. By this logic, if a program's staff think something "works," they're justified in doing it no matter what the authorities say. Karen and Kendall soon began to believe that this philosophy allowed Teen Help to think itself above the law. So long as it "worked" to make a child obedient, they ultimately recognized, Teen Help would do whatever it wanted, no matter how risky. The Seed, Challenger, Straight, and North Star relied on similar reasoning.

As Tranquility Bay director Jay Kay told the British newspaper the *Observer*, "The bottom line is, what's the end result you want? Getting there may be ugly, but at least with us you're going to get there."[26] In other words, whatever I do to make your kid malleable and submissive is fine.

The seminar poster that read BASED ON THE RESULTS, YOU HAVE EXACTLY WHAT YOU INTENDED also fed into this philosophy. The idea here is that individuals control everything that happens to them in life. If you are raped, if you die in a plane crash, if you get a fatal illness: none of this happens if it wasn't what you "intended," according to the WWASP seminar philosophy. This ideology is pushed as a method of empowerment, as a way to avoid blaming others for one's problems.

Many people can certainly benefit from taking personal responsibility and from understanding that how they perceive the world can shape their relationships, of course. But that's a far cry from believing that your perceptions are the only reality—and that you are omnipotent. As psychologist Janice Haaken noted in a paper called "Pathology as Personal

Growth" (based on her observations of LifeSpring), what this does is promote an infantile belief in one's own Godlike powers—not a healthy respect for what an individual can and cannot control.[27] Perhaps for this reason, the extreme implications of these ideas are not introduced until late in the proceedings, after people have been broken down and have come to look to the seminar leader for "the answer."

As this philosophy was gradually revealed through lectures and exercises, the conflicts between the seminar's ideology and the couple's Mormon religious beliefs and personal values escalated. After several hours of lectures, the staff gave testimonials about how the seminars had turned their lives around. Most included weepy tales of teen terror, followed by joyous relief at how WWASP had helped. Karen noted that most of the parents had children who were still in the program, so they obviously had not yet seen whether the changes would stick. But two teen staffers who had recently graduated also gave glowing testimony.

Now the leader asked the group to stand and take a silent vow of commitment to complete the entire seminar and scrupulously obey its rules. Karen found herself rising—but simultaneously wondering why she was taking this vow when she felt so uncomfortable about what had already occurred. And this split in her thinking between wanting to comply and wanting to resist continued to gnaw at her. She says, "I hadn't known everyone else's actions would affect me so deeply."[28]

The silent vow, she later recognized, was also a way for the seminar leader to stifle dissent. Those who left early or refused to participate in any exercise would be said to be lacking in "integrity" because they had broken their word. They could be belittled and dismissed as quitters who couldn't be trusted.

Karen also felt compelled to go along because she felt that she'd already put her reputation on the line for the program. Just before the seminar, Karen had spoken with a newspaper reporter, who asked how she felt about a court decision that kept a child in Tranquility Bay against his will. Karen was quoted as supporting parents' rights to send unwilling kids to programs, saying that this was sometimes necessary and had been for her daughter.

Now, however, she began to question herself. Did she really know how her daughter was doing? Was Kyrsten being exposed to these same disturbing and coercive tactics in Jamaica? What did she really know about this program? But each time she started to question, she found herself thinking up reasons to comply instead. For one, she had already referred three other parents—taking advantage of a policy that gave parents who did so a free month for their child in the program or $1,000 if the child had already graduated. At the time, she hadn't felt uncomfortable about this because she had disclosed the fact that she'd been paid. But now she believes that such a system is unethical, even with disclosure (which most parents giving referrals do not provide, anyway).

As the seminar continued, Karen felt her self split even further between defending the seminar and considering her own doubts.

> I was protecting those who were hurting me. It became so much easier to take all the responsibility for what was happening, because if I did not, I would have to start dwelling on the implications of how what I was experiencing might relate to my daughter's safety. . . .
>
> The period of time without breaks was long. We never knew when our meals were going to be and we were not supposed to even go to the bathroom without permission. After a while, I found myself regressing in my age behavior and noticed that other people were doing the same. We were becoming a group of children following [the leader]. . . . There was continual emphasis on the fact that there was no "right" or "wrong." But, in practice, it was apparent that there were certain types of behavior that would be supported by the group and [the trainer] and other types of behavior that would be confronted. . . . I was not consciously aware that my behavior was being modified by peer pressure, but it was.[29]

One exercise involved breaking into small groups. Each person would be "given feedback" in turn. The trainer demonstrated how this should be done. Karen says he selected a woman and stood her up, saying he was going to show her "the kind of feedback that makes you feel slimed and dirty," the kind that he claimed indicated that someone was lying. He then praised and complimented the woman. To demonstrate what he called the "best kind" of feedback, "the kind you want," the trainer attacked her, saying what he thought her problems were. When the woman said she didn't agree, the trainer said, "You don't have to. But if fifteen or more people tell you the same thing, you will find yourself changing your mind."[30] He said that the appropriate response to feedback was not to disagree, but to say thank you.

Both Karen and Kendall were completely horrified. Kendall says:

At least where I come from, what we were being asked to do was presumptuous. You don't just meet a person . . . and then give them intimate assessments about their life and problems. . . .

Upon my expressing the difficulties I was having with this exercise, one of the other participants, who had been studying me, suddenly drew herself up with an aha!-type look, as if she had just made a tremendous discovery, and said "I know what your problem is! You're *in your head*!"

. . . I had heard of being "out of your head," but I had never before been accused of being "in my head." I was later to learn that this was part of the seminar "jargon." Being "in your head" is used in a derogatory way. It means that you think too much. . . . The term is designed to put you in your place.[31]

But it was the "trust exercise" that would prove the breaking point for Kendall. It occurred about twelve or thirteen hours into the seminar, when everyone seemed completely exhausted. On paper, the exercise sounds banal. What participants do is approach people, look them in the eye and say one of four things: "I trust you," "I don't know if I trust you," "I don't care to say whether I trust you," or "I don't trust you." As the exercise proceeds, participants are asked to say whether they'd trust each other with more and more intimate secrets or tasks, like taking a loved one to the hospital. Actually doing this with real people is daunting. As Kendall put it:

We were effectually being asked to choose between two inscrutable evils: To tell a person we didn't know and who may have merited our trust that we didn't trust them, or to tell a person who may not have merited our trust and whom we didn't know that we trusted them. . . . So basically, I went around and told everyone I met that I trusted them. The exercise seemed in many ways hypnotic . . . I felt my mind going to sleep.[32]

Next, Karen says, the trainer asked participants "to think of our deepest and darkest secret, something we would be ashamed to tell even our dearest friend for fear they would reject and shun us." They were asked first to say whether they trusted the person in front of them with this secret—then to disclose the secret itself. Suddenly, Kendall interrupted the proceedings. He says:

I objected to what [the trainer] was asking us to do because I considered it an invasion of personal privacy. He countered by asserting that I was still being "in my head," reminding me, in the tone of voice a parent might use with an errant child, that "we talked about this before . . ."

What he was doing was not, from what I could see, an attempt to try and understand my objections. It was, to me, a deliberately designed strategy to make what I consider honorable behavior, the act of standing up for what you believe are your rights, seem dishonorable. He also accused me of practicing avoidance behavior. . . . I didn't think that being the lone person standing up in opposition to ninety other people was what should be termed "seeking my comfort zone."[33]

Kendall left the seminar that night, with Karen staying until the next day, leaving when she began to feel that further participation might be emotionally devastating to her. She says of the period just before she left, "I hadn't slept for almost forty-eight hours. It was about 3:30 P.M. and we hadn't had a meal break since breakfast . . . I started to lose focus. I felt as though my skin had been peeled off with a can opener and I had no defenses left."[34]

Feeling that they had a duty to warn other parents who might not have felt able to speak out, both Karen and Kendall returned for the last day, to hand out a letter stating their objections. They were attacked by many of the remaining parents, who told them over and over that had they stayed, they would have been transformed. One letter they later received summed up the WWASP supporters' positions:

When you walked out of that room, you walked out on your daughter. No one EVER said the training would be comfortable, easy, or that you had to believe and agree with everything presented . . . the choice was yours. However, you made a commitment to be there and an oral agreement to abide by the rules as stated. . . . You showed yourselves untrustworthy when you broke your word and left. Is your word only good if it is convenient and comfortable and if you feel like it? Would that be acceptable for your daughter . . . ? When you walked out those doors, you stepped squarely in the path of your child. DON'T get in the way of mine.[35]

While a few parents quietly took them aside and said that they agreed and some wrote appreciative letters, most seemed to toe the party line. Karen says:

This was such a powerfully persuasive experience; it altered my reality and way of looking at things against my will. Although I had moments of lucidity for the next three weeks, I frequently would find my logical thought processes interrupted. I wasn't able to work for more than an hour a day. . . . For the first week, I was extremely vulnerable to outside stimulus. I couldn't listen to music or watch movies without feeling I had no boundaries to protect myself in case of objectionable content.[36]

Kendall, too, found his work disrupted and his mind filled with worries about his daughter. He said, "I was appalled by what I experienced in this seminar, and especially by what Karen told me she had experienced after I walked out. . . . [It] left me disillusioned and exhausted."[37] Two months later they went to Jamaica to give Kyrsten the chance to come home if she wanted to do so. They had been so shaken by the seminar that they had waited before acting, wanting to be sure that they weren't endangering her by acting impulsively.

But while they'd waited, Kyrsten had become ever more enmeshed in WWASP. She was glad to be off the streets. She was eating healthily—or at least much better than she had been as a runaway. She says she'd decided, "Well, I'm going to do something my parents said for once in my life," and she thought she was doing so by surrendering fully to the program. When her parents arrived in Jamaica, she was at first furious with them for sending such a mixed message.

Says Kendall, "She had gone through this excruciating rehab experience for us, and now it seemed to her that we were saying it wasn't a good thing." He says that when he first saw Kyrsten, "she was very thin, had lost a lot of weight, [and] was very sold on the program." She did, however, decide to return home.

Kyrsten describes herself as being extremely judgmental after leaving Tranquility Bay. "I didn't have very much tolerance or patience and I was just really, really strict on people. I thought I was this great reformed, healed person. My best friend wouldn't even come to me when she had an abortion."

While she still believes the program helped her, she says she would not recommend it for anyone else. And while Kyrsten herself hadn't found the seminars traumatic the way her parents had, this was not true for many other WWASP kids. The context in which the kids experience them adds to the intensity, as they know that if they do not "pass" each seminar or if they "choose out" (which means they are told to leave during the proceedings for noncompliance or other reasons), they will be staying in the program for at least another month.

As one boy, Adam*, seventeen, described it,

> This puts people in the mode that they'll do anything . . . the atmo-
> sphere is nerve-wracking. . . . Everybody is standing up blurting out
> what they think the facilitator wants to hear. The facilitator takes it
> and rolls with it. They want the child to give up some dirty secret,
> and all the children know that's what they want. The child tells
> them how they were raped, and is then asked to go into detail. Now,
> if the child merely made this thing up, they must really play the
> part, and sometimes, [they begin to] believe they were truly raped,
> beaten, etc.

This idea was confirmed by other teens, who told of either making up
or exaggerating stories or hearing others do so, just as had been done in
Straight. Says Jane, a seventeen-year-old who attended WWASP's Casa
by the Sea when she was fifteen,

> [The staff] always make you feel like you have to say something
> tragic happened to you or else you'll get in trouble. I told them it
> was hard for me to deal with it because my parents got divorced,
> and they said, "Dig deeper. Why are you being so shallow?" What
> am I supposed to say? That my parents died? That's not true.

The idea, once again, is that what the teens admit willingly is false, but
what has to be pulled out of them is true.

There are three "processes" that stand out in most of the accounts of
the seminars given by teens. One, the "parent process," is conducted very
similarly in the adult seminars. Before it starts, the teens are made to sit
in small semicircles and attack each other in turn. Fifteen-year-old Nina
describes it this way: "It was really, really painful because people would
just say the meanest things to you." Afterward, the teens were told they
had to "release" the anger that such an exercise provokes by beating the
floor with towels and imagining situations in which their parents had
upset or abused them.

Adam says, "In my first seminar, I was forced to bang my towel on the ground for over ninety minutes. It's more aerobic than you would ever know. If you stop banging it, you'll get chosen out. You keep going after your last breath. The girls are screaming like banshees." Says Nina, "It physically hurt, a lot. My knuckles were bloody and torn up."

The exercise ends with the facilitator saying that the hatred they now feel so viscerally for their parents is actually self-hatred. But research has found that "anger management" techniques that are supposed to "un-leash" anger through beating inanimate objects actually escalate fury, not decrease it.[38] Such therapies backfire, making angry people angrier. And there's no evidence to support the notion that all hatred felt by teens for their parents is self-hate.

Another process that disturbed many teens was the "lifeboat process." In this, kids are asked to imagine that they are lost at sea, with a limited number of seats in the available lifeboats. They are given three "live" votes—and told to choose the teens they think most worthy of being saved. They are not told whether they can select themselves. They must approach each person and say how they voted, shouting either "You live" or "You die" while looking into their eyes.

Nina actually "won" this game, which is essentially a popularity con-test. But because she didn't give one of her own votes to herself, she was told that she would "die." "It was really terrible," she says. "Everybody broke down. . . . I had to say, 'Nina, you die.' It really hurt, I felt like I just wanted to crawl into a corner."

Of course, for her, the exercise was in many ways ultimately an af-firming experience, with the facilitator pointing out how many people thought she was worthy of life and using the experience to illustrate that she shouldn't constantly place the needs of others in front of her own. For the majority of kids, however, who were repeatedly told "You die" by their peers, it was awful. "I could see pain in a lot of people's eyes," Nina says. And the lesson is a strange one, even for the winner: Altruism, self-lessness, and heroism are "wrong"—if you put others first in this game, you "die."

But probably the most difficult and certainly the most controversial seminar "processes" are those in which the kids are instructed to act out their worst characteristics, to put themselves in their "old images" and become "accountable" for them. In the case of many of the girls, this meant dressing as prostitutes and being publicly humiliated.

Adam says that the facilitators used "foul and degrading" language to refer to the kids. "They would call the girls 'little sluts,' and 'daddy's little whore,'" he reports, adding that they also frequently used words like "bitch" and "cunt." He says, "I was called a spoiled asshole who didn't deserve to stand with the rest of the other kids, because I told [the seminar leader] that I once had sex with a girl when we were really drunk. [The facilitator] told me I did this because I hated myself and never felt love from my parents."

To emphasize Adam's alleged misogyny and self-hatred, the facilitator made him wipe his feet on girls who were made to lie prone on the floor. "They had to lie on their stomachs while I used them as 'doormats,'" he says. "Even though I didn't want to do it, afterwards I was told by everybody how sick I was, and how disgusting it made them feel on the inside. They talked about how cold and shallow I was."

Another time, a seminar leader at WWASP's Spring Creek Lodge program in Montana took the sexual humiliation even further. Sixteen-year-old Doreen*, who, according to her mother, had been sexually abused by several men as a child, was made to wear a nametag reading SHAMEFUL SLUT. She was dressed in revealing clothes, and SLUT, 25 CENTS was written on her in lipstick. When she tried to hide, the facilitator, a man in his forties, confronted her. She says he told her to get on the ground and spread her legs, and then later, that he "asked whether I gave 'blow jobs,'" and made her get on her knees in front of him. "I can't tell you how ashamed I felt," she says. "Afterwards, you were supposed to rip up the nametag and feel better, but it didn't work."

BUT DESPITE THE CLOSING of several of its facilities and the growing number of abuse complaints, which it continues to claim are all unfounded, WWASP has grown almost exponentially over the last decade. In 2001, one WWASP program director, Dace Goulding, told Lou Kilzer, who had written a series of exposés for the *Rocky Mountain News*, "Because of the work that you do, [my program] is thriving. I was going to send you a thank-you letter for that."[39] Goulding ran Casa by the Sea, which had opened in 1998 in Mexico. That year, WWASP told *48 Hours* that it had 1,000 teens enrolled in its programs[40]; by 2003, it was saying the number was 2,400.[41]

In the fall of 2001, WWASP opened another new facility, this one near Orotina, Costa Rica, some fifty miles from San José, the nation's capital. The story of that facility, Dundee Ranch Academy, offers unique insights into WWASP's operations. Its third director, Amberly Knight—the only woman ever to run a WWASP program solo—quit in distress when she realized she was never going to be able to make the changes she thought the site needed. She later reported her findings and experience to Costa Rican authorities. While WWASP and its fellow tough love programs have often succeeded in discrediting teens' accounts of abuses as "manipulation and lies," the story of a high-level employee is far more difficult to dismiss. Knight's account is backed up by the stories of other former program staffers, as well as by those of many teens and parents. Her tale of her four and a half months as a WWASP director also shows how easily decent, intelligent people can be drawn in by the false promises of tough love programs.[42]

AMBERLY KNIGHT was an optimistic but naive master's degree candidate at Brigham Young University when she first met Joe Atkin in 2000. Atkin is the son of J. Ralph Atkin, founder of SkyWest Airlines and attorney and financier for the WWASP group.[43] Then in her late twenties, Amberly had worked for a year as a chemistry teacher in Utah and wanted further education. Her father is a leading figure in sports medicine, a Ph.D.; her mother is a homemaker who raised eight children, of whom Amberly is the second. A Mormon, she grew up mainly in Indiana.

At BYU, Knight studied international relations. She met Atkin in an economics class. They became fast friends, though she says they were never romantically involved. From his father, Joe had learned of the tremendous profit potential in working with troubled youth. And as he got to know Amberly, she says, he told her that he dreamed of owning a similar residential school for troubled teens, but one that would be independent of WWASP. Amberly saw him as a well-intentioned entrepreneur who wanted to do well by doing good. She found such a project amenable to her own aspirations.

Joe constantly told her how wonderful WWASP's system was, how the group was the biggest and the best in the industry, and how he'd take their ideas and make them even better. His plan went through several different permutations and a number of different business partners—but when Atkin called Knight in early 2002 to ask her to work with him at a school he'd helped start in Costa Rica, she jumped at the chance.

As she learned more, she found out that Atkin had given up on going out on his own. The facility was a WWASP affiliate, run by Bob Lichfield's brother Narvin. Atkin was assistant director, in charge of finances. Amberly would direct the educational programming. "I was very trusting and naive," she says. She'd told Atkin that she'd had only one class in working with "at risk" kids, but explains that he said that her teaching background qualified her.

The program opened in October 2001, and Amberly arrived early in 2002. Like most of WWASP's foreign affiliates, Dundee Ranch Academy was located in an isolated former resort. "The facility is beautiful," she says of the former ecotourism hotel. The site is surrounded by hilly tropical rainforest, teeming with wildlife and exotic birds like parrots. It has a lovely, irregularly shaped pool and burbling stone fountains. When Amberly arrived, there were eighty kids enrolled, a number that would soon rise to 200. Ten to twelve girls or boys would ultimately share what had been designed as single hotel rooms, sleeping on triple bunk beds.

"I felt like the kids were a bit crowded, but they have an answer to everything," Amberly says. In this case, she recalls, she was told, "These kids are all rich, they're spoiled, they don't deserve anything because they've taken advantage of their parents. . . . They need to learn how to live a rough life, basically." Because she had no prior knowledge of treatment for troubled youth, she took it on authority that WWASP, the "experts," the "leaders in the field," knew what they were doing. She assumed that there were sound reasons for their policies. She spent her first several months trying to fix the educational program.

"It was horrible!" she says. As an educator, she found it appalling. It's not an education program." The kids would simply read a textbook, then take the test for each chapter over and over until they received at least a B. To parents of teens who had been failing school, who didn't know how the grades were achieved, the results looked spectacular. "The parents were thrilled," Amberly says. "And I just wanted to say, 'Well, they've learned a lot less than they would have if they'd gotten a D in a regular school.'

"I tried to get real teachers down there. I did get real teachers for a while, then they would get fed up with the conditions and leave," she says, explaining that teachers were paid only the equivalent of $500 a month, and that even these meager paychecks would rarely arrive on time or in the right amount. Other staff—the people who spent the most time with the kids—were paid just $300 per month or $3,600 annually, essentially minimum wage in Costa Rica. Many were former hotel workers—maids, janitors, and receptionists—who had been kept on after the program bought the facility.

In a letter that Knight sent to Costa Rican child-welfare authorities after she resigned, she described the program's executive style:

> I feel that Dundee Ranch Academy should not be allowed to operate because it is poorly managed, takes financial advantage of parents in crisis, and puts teens in physical and emotional risk. . . . [Owner Narvin] Lichfield did not care and the children could not complain to outside authorities. The children were imprisoned in deplorable conditions that we would not tolerate for adult death row inmates in America. The parents were manipulated and misled by this organization.[44]

Part of the reason Knight stayed as long as she did was that she believed at first that the program was unlike the other WWASP facilities, that it wasn't following proper procedures either because it was so new or because the particular people involved weren't as competent as other program workers. "For two years I had heard from Joe how amazing and wonderful this program was and I had trusted him," she says. "I didn't realize that the problem was systemic." Since she was completely unfamiliar with the research in the field, she accepted Atkin's rationale for what was done at Dundee. "They would say, 'Well, we're the best in the business, this is the program, trust the program, it works.' So I kind of closed my eyes."

She thought, in essence, that she was seeing poor implementation of an appropriate treatment modality—she didn't realize that the program was intended to be as harsh and humiliating as it was. "A lot of things didn't sit right with me," she says, when asked about the conditions. "But I thought I was changing things little by little and I thought, okay, whatever doesn't sit right, I'll eventually get to it and be able to change it . . . I didn't realize that it was this way on purpose."

Amberly became director after the two previous holders of the post had either quit or been fired. It was March 2002; she'd been there for about two months. She moved quickly to rein in what she saw as the most egregious abuses. Though she did not know that psychiatric ethics bars the use of restraint for punishment, when she heard that a teen had gotten his shoulder dislocated in the process, she put a stop to it based on her own common sense. "They were no longer allowed to restrain people for punishment, intimidation," she says. "If somebody was literally out of control they were allowed to restrain the teen, but they weren't allowed to do it like they were, every day just for fun."

Amberly was also bothered by the use of extremely lengthy, handwritten "essays" as a punishment. These could run up to 150,000 words. As she wrote to Costa Rican authorities, "Students were required to sit in a dark room without proper back support, and write . . . until they finished the required number of words." The essays didn't need to be coherent, as staffers were often not fluent in English, so smart kids would just write pages of the shortest words they knew. Amberly writes, "Often, staff members, for no apparent reason, would rip up the essays and make students start over. Students were required to write for eight hours a day until their words were completed."

But the worst punishment, as in most WWASP facilities, was OP. Amberly described it this way: "In this, students were required to stand, kneel, sit or lay on a cement floor without moving for thirty minutes at a time. They had to do this for eight hours a day until they had 'served their time.'" The floor was uneven, making positions like kneeling especially painful. Teens in OP were also sometimes made to run hundreds of laps around the pool in the tropical heat, Amberly says. And noncompliance, at least when Amberly wasn't there or wasn't aware of the situation, often led to restraint.

Other former employees—as well as numerous teens—back up Amberly's account. One ex-employee told the local English-language newspaper, the *Tico Times*, "If you put a spy camera in Dundee for a day, you would find abuse and an ill-trained staff."[45]

At the time, Knight didn't realize just how out-of-line OP and the use of restraint as punishment were. Because of her lack of training, she says, she "didn't recognize [them] as abuse." But when she returned to the U.S., she saw a newscast that woke her up. "There was this woman and her husband who had been put in jail for putting their kid in a closet. They wouldn't let him go to school, kind of deprived him of food, and that was their punishment to the kid. And I was shocked. I thought, 'Oh my gosh, that's what WWASP does every single day. And if that is considered abuse, [if] a private parent can't do that and gets put in jail, well, why can this corporation make millions of dollars doing this?'"

When she heard about the "stress positions" used on Iraqi prisoners by Americans at Abu Ghraib prison, she says, "I [was] just horrified that that's what they do [at WWASP] every single day and I just put up with it without realizing it for that long." She also noted with outrage, given her own initial good intentions in signing on to work for the program:

The purpose of Dundee Ranch is not to help teens in crisis or their families. It is to make millions of dollars for the owner. Although the profit margins are essentially 50–75%, Mr. Lichfield is unsatisfied. He continues to try to squeeze out every penny he can. This is achieved by hiring unqualified, untrained staff, providing the bare minimum of food and living essentials.

By the time she wrote her letter, Amberly had recognized that the lack of qualifications extended as far as her own position, writing,

> I am the first to admit that I was not even qualified to be there. . . . As an employee, the only training I received was on how to manipulate parents. I was told many times that "there is no reason for a student to return home before 'graduating' the program. . . ." There were many students who had psychological, medical or special education needs that we could not meet.

But, she says, when she suggested that such students be sent elsewhere, she was told to keep quiet. "If there were students who would be better off going home or entering another program, I was not allowed to suggest this to the parent," she wrote. "Ironically, if the parents had concerns about what was going on, we were told to tell [them] that their children were 'just manipulating them.'"[46]

She recalls meeting with a teen who'd been sent to the program after a suicide attempt. He'd jumped out of a second-story window back home; his injuries were still healing. "I went in and he was just sobbing, sobbing, sobbing," she says. She learned that he hadn't been given his medications. "He should have been somewhere where they could have gotten proper treatment for him," she says sorrowfully.

Amberly's complaint to authorities also expressed concern about an affiliated facility, called High Impact, that was being built nearby. When construction started, she says, she knew that the compound was being built to replace a similar facility with the same name in Mexico that had been shut by local authorities. Parents who sent their children to Casa by the Sea in Mexico say that those who did not fall in line with the WWASP regimen there were often recommended for placement at High Impact. Though WWASP officials denied making referrals and refused to admit that High Impact was an affiliate, bills for High Impact and other WWASP facilities were handled at the same mailing address by R&B Billing. At least at the time, R&B was owned by WWASP founder Bob Lichfield.[47]

Mexico's High Impact had produced some of the most shocking abuses in the WWASP system. When Mexican police raided the site in December of 2001, they found conditions "deplorable," according to the *Rocky Mountain News.*[48] A spokesperson for the U.S. consulate in Tijuana told the paper that teens there "were all extremely dirty. . . . Some of the kids had calluses and blisters on their feet from being made to do a lot of laps around the place without wearing proper shoes."[49]

But that was not the worst of it: Mexican investigators videotaped teens kept in dog cages—footage that would later air on *Inside Edition*. A father from California, Chris Goodwin, later testified in court that his son had been locked in a dog cage there for a solid week. He told a reporter that the boy had been made to lie prone outdoors in his underwear with his chin on the ground for three nights and threatened with a cattle prod when he tried to remove fire ants that had crawled on him.[50]

As she continued to be frustrated in her attempts to change the Dundee program, Amberly says she typically worked twelve-to-eighteen-hour days. "There were some times I wouldn't go to bed at all because I had to get everything done," she says. She'd told herself she was tolerating the difficult conditions in order to help kids—but she now found herself snapping at them. "I realized that I just couldn't handle it any more. My personal boundaries were being crossed too often," she says.

By August 2002, she had decided to quit. Since she still didn't realize the problem was systemic, she discussed working for another WWASP program with the group's management in Utah. But while she was waiting for her replacement to take over, a horrifying incident occurred that made her reconsider that idea.

One of her last attempts to fix the Dundee program had been to hire a number of WWASP graduates from other affiliates as staffers. She'd thought that if she hired people who'd been through a better-managed program, they'd be able to guide Dundee's staff toward improvements. She chose students recommended by top WWASP officials and flew them to Costa Rica.

But one night, an adult staffer, in contravention of program rules, took several of these underage employees out drinking, according to Amberly. She says that after the group returned to their living quarters, an argument occurred. A young man slammed a young female staffer's head against the wall several times, causing severe head injury. Apparently, he also later raped her while her consciousness was still impaired by both the alcohol and the injury. In her letter to Costa Rican authorities, Amberly wrote, "While I was in the process of resigning from Dundee Ranch . . . an American male staff member assaulted and raped a female staff member at a location of about 100 meters from where all the students are housed."[51]

Amberly was not at the site at the time; in anticipation of leaving, she'd taken the weekend off. When she returned on Monday, she was not told of the incident. On Tuesday, the girl was brought in to see her and Amberly was told that she had hit her head in a fall. She took one look at the young woman and had her sent to the hospital. And soon the hospital called: they needed permission to do emergency brain surgery. Amberly OK'd it and called the victim's mother, who immediately flew to Costa Rica. The next day, Amberly visited the hospital. Now awake, the victim told her what really happened. Knight tried unsuccessfully to bring the perpetrator to justice. Fortunately, the young woman recovered, but Amberly says that the doctors told her that if she had not had the surgery when she did, brain swelling would have killed her. The *Tico Times* reported that medical records confirm that the woman was treated for a brain hemorrhage at San José's CIMA Hospital, but Atkin denied to the paper that a rape or an assault had occurred and "dismissed the incident as 'a non-issue.'"[52]

WHEN AMBERLY LEFT Costa Rica, it took her months to regroup. She had rejected the idea of working at another WWASP program, not wanting to live in another isolated location. After she went public with her account of what had happened at Dundee, Ken Kay tried to use this fact to discredit her, saying that she left not because of abuse, but because she was "a 30 year old woman" who "wanted to be transferred to the United States in order to enhance her chances of getting married."[53] WWASP officials also described her to the press as a woman spurned by Joe Atkin.[54]

Despite the smears, Amberly's marital prospects were far from bleak. After leaving Costa Rica, she soon became engaged. When a plan to create a nonprofit teen program in Hawaii fell through, she took a job at a university instead.

Now married and with enjoyable work, Amberly began to reevaluate WWASP. Even at the end, she hadn't quite been able to bring herself to see how abusive some of the disciplinary practices were. But as she looked back, she became more and more appalled by what she'd been a part of, and she realized that she had to do something to help the kids who were still at Dundee. At first, she was afraid to speak out because she'd signed a non-disclosure agreement. But when a desperate mother contacted her for help in removing her daughter, whom her husband had placed in the program without her knowledge, she decided to write to Costa Rican authorities.

Her letter, and an earlier visit by a mother of twin boys trying to pull them from Dundee after their father had placed them there without her permission, brought the program to the attention of both local authorities and local U.S. State Department officials. The State Department had taken its usual hands-off approach while Amberly had been director, despite the High Impact raid in Mexico and its knowledge of the connections between the WWASP programs.

But with some prodding from the press and local government, U.S.

and Costa Rican officials began an official investigation in early 2003. Costa Rican child-welfare authorities first cited Dundee for fifteen unacceptable practices.[55] These included holding teens in the program against their will, which is illegal in Costa Rica; providing "no privacy"; overly restricting communication with parents; and "inadequate food and meal portions." The investigators further said that staff were "unqualified to attend to needs of children" and that "some punishments qualify as physical and psychological abuse."[56]

While Costa Rica's child-welfare agency had planned to move slowly, as did the U.S. embassy, a local prosecutor, Fernando Vargas, decided that more immediate action was needed. He raided the facility on May 20, 2003. About 200 teens were there at the time. When Vargas announced what the youths' rights were under Costa Rican law, chaos erupted. Seventeen-year-old Hugh Maxwell told the *New York Times*, "They told us you have the right to speak, you have the right to speak to your parents, you have the right to leave if you feel you have been mistreated . . . kids heard that and they started running for the door. There was elation, cheering and clapping and chaos. People were crying."[57]

About thirty to fifty teens left on foot, heading for the beach or the nearest town. According to a witness quoted in the *Times*, staff "started kicking, hitting and choking children to [try to] stop them from leaving."[58] Although child-welfare officials urged the kids to accompany them in vehicles they'd brought for this purpose, most refused, apparently fearing they'd be placed in a dangerous homeless shelter. Staffers tried to make the remaining kids sign a statement saying that they'd been treated well at the school and would stay voluntarily, but some refused this as well. Most signed, however, convinced by staff that they would be sent to the tougher Tranquility Bay if they didn't.

Over the next several days, the facility swung between periods of calm and utter chaos. Some girls lit a fire in their dorm. Teens trashed staffers' cars and hit vehicles and buildings with sticks. They rampaged through the facility, destroying property, breaking whatever they could. Torn textbooks and papers flew everywhere. Child-welfare officials tried to take control at some times—at others, Dundee staff tried to reestablish order.

After the raid, Lichfield was arrested and charged with human rights violations, some of which carry a ten-to-fifteen-year prison term for each count.[59] Speaking about Dundee's disciplinary tactics, prosecutor Fernando Vargas told the press, "In Costa Rica, we don't even allow that kind of punishment for our prison inmates. We are conducting a criminal investigation for systematic violations of human rights."[60]

Lichfield has denied all of Amberly Knight's claims and says he knew of no abuse. He told the *Tico Times* in May 2003, "I am scared crapless. I am afraid because they are going to try and make me the poster child for rights abuses that didn't happen."[61] By September, he was telling the same reporter, "What did we do wrong? I am still confused about this. . . . I never worked with kids, so how could I abuse them? I heard rumors about what staff did, but I can't say because I wasn't there. . . . In Narvin's world, we will have a facility set up where [child welfare officials have] oversight and if the staff goes on its own and abuses kids, the government will prosecute the individual and not hold the facility guilty."[62]

Costa Rica banned him from leaving the country for six months, pending legal proceedings. It corroborated the accounts of abuse from former staffers and teen participants. The investigation also found that Dundee was distributing psychiatric medications without a license and that most of the staff were unqualified.

Narvin Lichfield owns another WWASP program, Carolina Springs Academy in South Carolina, that has been under close scrutiny from regulators there for a familiar litany of violations: overcrowding, accepting teens it is not equipped to serve, allowing students to discipline and restrain each other, failure to report child abuse and fire-code violations.[63] When he was charged with human rights violations in Costa Rica, South Carolina regulators barred him from Carolina Springs until the case was resolved. As of October 2004, he was still barred from involvement in day-to-day operations of the program and from having contacts with the teenage residents.[64]

IN LATE 2003, I went to Cross Creek Manor to interview two principals in WWASP: Ken Kay, President of WWASP, and Karr Farnsworth, who runs Cross Creek Manor, their most expensive residential treatment center and the only one to employ licensed therapists for the primary care of the teens. I wanted to see and hear for myself the other side of the story.

If they had just given me a tour of the facility and allowed me to interview the staff therapists they'd hand-selected, as originally planned, I would have come away with a much more positive impression than I'd ever have thought possible. But instead, they confronted me for several hours—making me turn off the tape recorder, so that I cannot quote some of their responses precisely. Throughout this section of the book, I've tried to present their point of view through statements they've given to other media; I cannot present it more directly, as they refused to comment further once they'd ended the official interview.

Cross Creek Manor is located in La Verkin, Utah, which is a tiny village of some 3,400 souls in the red rock country of southwest Utah. Most locals are Mormon. According to *Peterson's Guide to Secondary Schools*, Cross Creek enrolled 375 students in 2004,[65] making it a significant contributor to the local economy.

Cross Creek's low-slung main white building is unmarked, and most of the facility is not visible from the road. From the outside, it is impossible to see in at all; visible windows are blocked. As I entered the parking lot, Ken Kay and several other people arrived in what appeared to be a brand-new Hummer SUV. I went in and was taken to a small waiting room. Motivational posters hung on the wall.

Kay told me about his previous employment as a police officer and later as a night security guard at Brightway Adolescent Hospital. He noted that Brightway had been accredited by JCAHO, the private organization that rates hospitals, with commendation, which is its highest rank. JCAHO also accredited several Straight Incorporated facilities that allowed patients to restrain other patients in violation of their standards, so the value of these accreditations is questionable. Nonetheless, as Kay said, only 2 percent of health-care facilities get accredited with commendation by JCAHO. He told me that the "State of Utah Department of Health didn't like Brightway," and that rising costs and lowered rates of insurance coverage, not problems with regulators, were what led to the shutdown of that program.

I asked him about the influences on the development of the program's groups and its seminars. He said, "I think that you took a little bit of what Synanon [did], maybe LifeSpring, Tony Robbins, Carnegie, all of these and you kind of bring a little bit of everything together and then you have to adapt it to what you want your results to be." He said that seminar leaders never made girls dress in revealing clothes, and that demeaning and sexually humiliating language was never used.

He said that observation placement was no longer used in any of the programs, and then added, seemingly angered by my questions, "I will tell you right now that if this is the direction that your book is going to take, that this is no more than a long newspaper article, because the questions you're asking are media-related." He told me to turn off the tape recorder and then called Karr Farnsworth and two others—a woman and her adult son who'd been through the program—into the room. All the men were wearing bright Hawaiian shirts. Because the tape was off, the following relies only on my notes and memory.

Kay charged me with being sensationalistic and misleading, while Farnsworth was more amiable, occasionally agreeing with my arguments that outcomes data would be more convincing than anecdotes. The woman said that parents of troubled teens were desperate, and that her son would have died if she'd been exposed to the negative media reports about WWASP and hadn't sent him there. The mother said that if she were taking her child to an emergency room, she wouldn't waste time asking about the doctors' qualifications; she'd demand treatment. When I asked whether she'd want to know if any of the doctors treating her child had committed malpractice, she changed the subject and continued to insist that without WWASP, she's absolutely sure that her son would have been dead.

That son, a graduate of Paradise Cove, then spoke up. He said Paradise

Cove was wonderful and nothing like it had been portrayed in the media. He agreed that it had saved his life and said that it had taught him things he would never have learned otherwise. He berated me for comparing WWASP with Straight—but didn't respond when I asked him to discuss the differences.

Kay said that there was no point in letting me see the facility, but Farnsworth suggested that there might be some value in it. The Paradise Cove graduate sided with Kay, saying it was "bullshit" because I'd already made up my mind. Eventually, they decided it was OK for me to interview two Cross Creek therapists, as long as Farnsworth could observe while I did so.

For some reason, they would not give me their full names, nor signed permission to quote them, so I will have to use pseudonyms. I do, however, have them on tape. The therapists selected to speak with me worked with Cross Creek's girls. Both seemed well qualified and familiar with the research in the area. Once I started speaking with them, I could not understand why Farnsworth and Kay had not just skipped the attack and simply handed me over to these therapists: had they done so, I would have been highly impressed and would have believed that at Cross Creek, the treatment philosophy, at least outside the seminars, is in line with what experts say are the best approaches for dealing with troubled kids.

In fact, the first therapist I spoke with, Jim*, immediately cited William Miller, one of the most highly respected researchers in the addictions field. Miller's work, indeed, has probably done more than that of any other researcher to discredit the idea that confrontation is helpful in dealing with alcohol and other drug problems. For example, in one study he found that counselors who are aggressively confrontational—who use approaches like those used at the WWASP seminars, attacking people and telling them their flaws and what they should do about them—had more alcoholic patients who dropped out and more patients who drank than did counselors who used an empathetic approach.[66] He's also done major scientific reviews of other research in the field, which yielded similar conclusions about how harsh confrontation is not only ineffective, but also actually harmful in treatment of alcohol and other drug problems. In another study, worse outcomes among heavy drinkers who'd been subject to non-empathetic counseling styles were still evident a year later: the more the counselor confronted, the more the patient drank.[67]

Miller and his colleagues developed a counseling style, based on this work, called "motivational interviewing." In it, counselors do not tell patients why they should change their behavior; nor do they "confront denial" or try to break people down. Instead, they listen and learn what the patients think the problem is—and help them to discover on their own why, for example, shooting heroin might not be such a good idea or why one's parents might be upset by certain behaviors and why it might be to one's own advantage, not just theirs, to change. Motivational interviewing is based on empathy and respect for the patient's strengths, not on tearing people down for their weaknesses. The approach is about as far from the confrontational style used in tough love programs as it is humanly possible to get.

"Something I really like is motivational interviewing," Jim told me, "and we use that quite a bit." He then went on to list several other evidence-based therapies, none of which relies on confrontation, and said he used these as well with the girls he sees at Cross Creek.

Regarding confrontation, he said, after agreeing that motivational interviewing is essentially an opposite approach, "I think to some extent it can be effective when used properly. It's just like anything else. Too much of it, going after somebody, no, I'm not for that."

I asked about the seminars. "You know what? I've had very good results with what they do," he said. "I've gone in there and observed some things, and it raises the intensity with the kids, but that's OK. What you've got to think about is to what extent would they learn these lessons at home? What would have to be done . . . for these kids to learn these things? And frankly, my experience has been any confrontation that's done here is far milder than what these kids experience at home, you know, in their own lives. So I think at times it's OK to raise the intensity with the kids. I think again, there needs to be a reason for it. So the old seventies stuff, beat 'em down, the research indicates that that isn't as effective as some of the other things like the motivational interviewing." The second therapist I interviewed pretty much echoed the first.

I wasn't able to confront them—even kindly and empathetically—with the many examples I'd heard from kids about "old '70s beat-'em-down stuff" occurring at many seminars, including those at Cross Creek. Because Farnsworth would have ended the interview, I couldn't ask about the stories I'd heard myself from Cross Creek girls. One had told me she'd seen her therapist make a girl who'd had an abortion dress up as though she was pregnant. A lesbian had told me she was regularly made to dress in heels and skirts in an attempt to "cure" her sexual orientation. And I'd heard many other such stories.

Afterward, Farnsworth took me on a perfunctory, high-speed tour of the facility. Inside, I saw tidy dorm rooms with bunk beds, a decent-smelling school cafeteria serving hamburgers, a basketball court with a few kids playing, and a library with computers. The teens I hurriedly passed looked fine—though I could see them only from a distance. I was not shown the isolation rooms, which had been photographed by the *Rocky Mountain News* and seemed similar to those at the other facilities. WWASP's account of its practices and accounts I'd heard from its critics—including those in State Department documents and those from regulators—remained diametrically opposed.[68]

SEVEN

Tough Love on Trial

Despite the controversy, WWASP has continued to grow. It had $80 million in revenues in 2003.[1] The *New York Times* began to look into it, writing critical articles about Tranquility Bay and covering the riots at Dundee Ranch. The *Times* quoted the harsh criticism from former Dundee director Amberly Knight in its coverage. It included parents' concerns as well as the accounts of numerous teens who said they'd been seriously abused. The stories also contained negative comments from experts. But as is standard for reporting on this topic, the *Times* balanced all of this with WWASP's anecdotal claims of success and the accounts of satisfied teens and parents. It did not note the history of failed outcomes for similar programs or how all of them initially generated reports of miracle cures, were then labeled "controversial," and then ultimately were abandoned as abusive.[2] Other coverage of the story was similar, tending to ignore the complete lack of any evidence for the success of tough love residential care that would meet even the most basic scientific standards.

While this played itself out in the media, I attended one of the most spectacular trials ever related to the use of tough love on teenagers.[3] Lulu Corter had been held in a New Jersey Straight-descendant program called KIDS for thirteen years: from age thirteen to age twenty-six. She had lost not only her adolescence to it, but her early adulthood as well. She represents the worst-case scenario (short of death) of what can happen when such programs are not held to account—and for what happens when they believe they have the right to hold adults indefinitely. The Corter case would also reveal what had become of many former participants decades after their treatment. In the absence of follow-up studies, it was one of the few existing windows on these outcomes, and they proved to be shocking.

Lulu's tale begins when Straight's national clinical director, Miller Newton, left Florida and opened his own virtually identical program in New Jersey, KIDS of Bergen County, in the early '80s. The only major difference between KIDS and Straight was that KIDS added eating disorders and "compulsive behavior disorders" (including "sex addiction") to the conditions it believed it could treat—just as twelve-step programs had started with alcohol and had come to be seen as treatments for other compulsive and addictive disorders. (Note: Some identifying details regarding witnesses and their relatives in this section have been changed to protect their privacy.)

LULU CORTER WANTED a pleather outfit. In the fall of 1984, like most seventh-grade girls, she listened to pop stars like Madonna and wanted to look like them, too. Lulu was thirteen, living in Wanaque, New Jersey, a rural town of some 10,000 people. She wanted, above all, to fit in. The black fake-leather outfit was the closest the daughter of a single mom of four who worked in electronics factories was going to get to dressing like an '80s icon. She and her best friend found identical black pleather vests at the mall. Lulu also bought black pleather pants to match, her friend purchased a skirt of the same material, and they planned to wear Capezio shoes, skinny ties, and white shirts to complete their look. Lulu was tall for her age, chunky, big-boned, and blue-eyed, with feathered light-brown hair.

She wanted to impress some of her older brother Sam's* friends, who were hanging out a short time later, joking in the Corters' living room. Lulu was just starting to be interested in boys. She told her mom, Virginia, loudly enough for the other teens to hear, that she wanted to wear her hair in a tail: that whisper-thin braid of just a few longer strands worn with short hair which Boy George had popularized. Lulu added, to sound even more daring, that she wanted to bleach just the back of her hair blond.

But that fall, Virginia had been scrutinizing Lulu's every move for potential signs of "druggie" behavior. Sam, sixteen, was then spending his days at a strict teen rehab called KIDS of Bergen County because his pot-smoking, drinking, and back talk had gotten out of hand. Virginia had been terribly worried about him: he'd only gotten worse when she sent him to military school. The KIDS program seemed to be straightening him out. Virginia had been told, however, that if Lulu exhibited any aberrant behavior, this could interfere with her brother's recovery as well as being a sign that she, too, was headed in the wrong direction and needed treatment. Wearing black, wanting trendy hairstyles or fashions, and disobedience were all considered big, blinking "warning signs."

And so when Lulu wore her black pleather to a meeting for siblings of KIDS patients after being told not to do so, Virginia Corter thought her worst fears had been confirmed. Her daughter was becoming a "druggie." Her "druggie image" was developing before her mother's eyes. She, too, would soon be staying out late, getting wasted, and facing arrests. Like her brother, she would need perhaps several months away from the family and at least six months of daily, intensive (and expensive) treatment. After a coercive evaluation done just as it had been for Richard Bradbury at Straight, thirteen-year-old Lulu Corter was admitted to KIDS on October 27, 1984.

Lulu Corter was the youngest child ever to enter KIDS. She would sit on a blue plastic chair, twelve hours a day, frantically waving her arms and head, surrounded by dozens of other teens behaving similarly, seeking to get called on by the staffers up front. If she didn't "motivate," or didn't get called on, she had to sit with her back straight, her hands on her knees, silent. Just as at Straight, KIDS participants lived in "host homes," and weren't permitted reading, radio, TV, music, school, or privacy.

And if Lulu slouched, if she didn't "motivate" hard enough, if she crossed her legs, if she didn't appear to be paying attention, she would be poked and prodded by people around her. If she didn't immediately comply then, Lulu would be thrown to the floor and restrained by fellow participants, often for hours. She would ultimately be restrained not hundreds, but thousands of times.

She had never even tried marijuana, let alone any harder drugs.

ON A SPRING DAY IN 2000, Phil Elberg was working in his Newark, New Jersey, office. A medical malpractice attorney for more than thirty years, he had heard a great deal about Lulu Corter. Elberg had always wanted to be a lawyer, and his passion is evident whenever he speaks about his work. "I wanted to represent the good guys against the bad guys. Not very complicated," he says. Elberg and his partner, Alan Medvin, started their own firm in 1983. At fifty-six, Elberg has three sons and looks like Richard Gere, with twinkling eyes and graying brown hair.

Elberg had won a $4.5 million judgment against KIDS in 1999 for a woman named Rebecca Ehrlich. Ever since she left the program, Ehrlich has shuttled between various psychiatric hospitals and her parents' home. KIDS had failed to recognize or diagnose her bipolar disorder—seeing drugs as her problem, even though it would turn out that, like Lulu, she wasn't a drug user. The program had also diagnosed Rebecca with an "eating disorder," punishing her by lengthening her treatment if she so much as ate one cookie, because sugar was forbidden under the program's "meal plan." The jury believed that her seven years of "treatment" at KIDS had only worsened her psychiatric problems and had awarded the high dollar settlement—the largest ever in a tough love case at the time—accordingly.

While working on the Ehrlich case, Phil Elberg talked to dozens of KIDS graduates and dropouts and heard hundreds of horrifying stories about what had taken place there. He couldn't believe that the program had been allowed to stay open from 1984 until 1998. He didn't understand why state regulators and lawmakers had allowed this, despite numerous investigations, several of them criminal. It stunned and angered him to know that similar places were still operating, still restraining kids, still having them "motivate" or perform other strange behaviors to show their obedience to program rules. And all this, despite the fact that the only evidence that these programs worked was a few anecdotal stories!

But he'd never heard anything worse than what he'd been told had happened to Lulu. He told all of the former KIDS participants he interviewed to have her contact him if they ever heard from her, but no one knew where she was.

While the $4.5 million judgment in the Ehrlich case didn't make national news when it was settled in late 1999, it did eventually get major play in New Jersey. Lulu's grandmother—who was instrumental in finally ending her stay in KIDS—saw the page-one story in the *Bergen Record* on April 9, 2000. Lulu was living in a trailer at the time, working various low-level jobs and seeing a therapist for post-traumatic stress disorder. She had been hospitalized for major depression and suicidal thoughts related to KIDS six times since she had left the program. "My grandmother called and said, 'Get down here, there's an article about the KIDS Program—some big picture on the front of this girl, she did a lawsuit,'" says Lulu.

Lulu's grandmother urged her to sue as well. She hated the program and what it had done to her granddaughter. She hated how it had splintered her family for more than a decade during her daughter's involvement with it, for years keeping her daughter and grandchildren out of contact with her and, at many points, apart from one another. Lulu de-

murred at first, worried about relapsing into depression and about getting rejected by the attorney if she did get up the courage to call. She
wanted just to get on with her life. Her grandmother insisted, however,
and Lulu agreed to at least try to contact Elberg.

But she didn't know how to find him: she'd had virtually no education
since sixth grade and had no computer skills or knowledge of things like
state bar associations. In the newspaper article, however, she did notice
the name of a KIDS patient that she remembered. She was a bit afraid
to call her, for fear that the woman might still take the program's side
and dislike her for having left it, but she eventually made herself phone.

And when Lulu finally reached her friend and identified herself, the
friend's first response was, "Oh God, we've been looking for you." Lulu
felt enormous relief. She was told that Elberg was located in Newark,
and she found his office number and nervously dialed. When she said her
name, Elberg's assistant immediately put her through. Soon, Medvin and
Elberg were developing another KIDS case. Unlike the Ehrlich case,
which was settled out of court, the Corter case would go to trial and reveal just how devastating tough love had been to many of the families
who'd sought help at KIDS for their teenagers.

Elberg's work as a medical-malpractice specialist had uniquely qualified him to take on tough love. Unlike many others who have tried to sue
these organizations, he recognized it as a malpractice case, not a case of
simple injury. He knew the standards of medical evidence and what was
required to prove that something was an accepted medical treatment.
This perspective allowed him to see what others before him who had
opposed tough love treatment had missed. What his predecessors hadn't
grasped was that it doesn't matter whether or not people "believe in"
tough love or not. As WWASP had put it in a very different context, it
didn't matter whether it was right or wrong—but whether, by accepted
medical standards, it works. Elberg had found the programs' Achilles'
heel: they were simply bad medicine. In Lulu's case, he would put tough
love treatment itself on trial, illustrating in court that it did not meet
professional standards of care for diagnosis, for ongoing evaluation, for
patient care, or for evidence of efficacy.

He would show that what really counts is whether tough love programs like KIDS can prove themselves as medicine—nothing more. If they couldn't produce positive results by empirical standards of evidence, no matter what claims its former patients, parents, self-proclaimed experts, and others tried to make, they shouldn't be allowed to be sold to desperate parents as medical or psychological treatment. As a malpractice attorney, Elberg knew quackery when he saw it. He would demonstrate that when these programs are held to medical standards—and they do pitch themselves as treatments for accepted medical diagnoses like addictions, depression, bipolar disorder, attention-deficit disorder, eating disorders, conduct disorder, and oppositional-defiant disorder—they do not fare well in a court of law.

Elberg would also be the first to force Miller Newton—who had spent nearly three decades imposing the Straight model on thousands of teenagers—to explain what he'd done and why he'd done it. In the Corter trial, he would tell Lulu's story, illustrate how to beat tough love in court, and call Newton to account for his actions.

CORTER V. KIDS opened on a dreary June day in 2003. The trial was presided over by Maurice Gallipoli, presiding judge of the civil division of the Supreme Court of New Jersey for the Hudson vicinage. Gallipoli is a distinguished-looking man who wields firm control over the courtroom. He takes few cases himself, but he selected this one.

Lulu came to hear the opening statements, accompanied by her therapist, and looking extremely nervous. At thirty-two, she could still pass for the teenager she was for most of her time at KIDS. Her hair was now a streaked honey-blond. Her weight, which would become an issue during the trial because KIDS claimed she was being treated for compulsive overeating, was normal.

There were six jurors and three alternates: the foreman was a bearded Latino man in his thirties or forties whom the plaintiff's team nicknamed "Shakespeare" for his thoughtful manner and resemblance to the popular image of the playwright. There were three other working-age

Latino males, a white female retiree with red hair, a kind-looking and heavyset black woman, and three Latinas. All of those selected had said they had no prior experience with tough love programs.

Elberg's opening was brief. "In 1984, Dr. Miller Newton and his wife Ruth Newton moved to New Jersey," he began.

> The literature that KIDS distributed described Dr. Newton as one of the nation's foremost authorities in the treatment of compulsive behavior disorders in adolescents.
>
> [Newton's] audience and target were parents, frightened about their children's behavior. Scared parents. His message was very clear. "Your children are in trouble. If they continue along the path that they are on, they're going to wind up in mental institutions, in jails, dead on the street." Unless, of course, you enroll them with us.

Elberg described Newton's charisma, his lack of qualifications, and the even slighter educational background of his wife. Newton had a degree in anthropology and administration when he founded KIDS—he wasn't a medical doctor or even a psychologist, though he insisted on being called "doctor" in what seemed like a medical setting. The attorney described how the KIDS program was presented as tough love treatment, but that just as the Newtons looked impressive on the surface, their program, too, did not have the kind of evidence in its favor that one would expect from medical care. Elberg went on:

> The real effect of KIDS was not to cure adolescent drug abuse or behavior disorders—it was to create mindless discipline and a new family, in which Miller Newton was the father and Ruth Newton was the mother. This is a case of how the Newtons and the KIDS program did that to one particularly vulnerable thirteen-year-old girl.
>
> They tortured Lulu. They arranged for her to be physically assaulted, psychologically abused on a daily basis. They arranged for her to be watched on the toilet. They came in on the most private

of acts. And when that wasn't enough, they decided how many times she could wipe herself.

As he said this, Lulu was visibly shaking in her seat in the front row on the right-hand side of the courtroom and the jurors looked incredulous.

I know that I'm using strong words. I know that it sounds crazy. Torture, thirteen years. Kept out of school. Robbed of her adolescence, assaulted. And we live in a society in which exaggeration is common and in which the most trivial disputes seem to end up in court. It is enough to make us all cynical about our system of justice.

How could it happen? If what I just told you was true, where were the police? Where were the schools? Where was the family? It doesn't make any sense. I tell you now in my opening statement we're going to prove it all. And in the end, I believe, based on the evidence you hear, you will agree that this is the kind of wrong our justice system was created to right.

Sitting on the left side of the courtroom listening to the opening statements were the Newtons themselves. Miller Newton is tall, with a receding white hairline and a trim beard and moustache. In his sixties, he seemed fit, and was wearing a dark suit. He looks like a college psychology professor, not the kind of fiend Elberg was describing. Ruth Ann Newton had a helmet of dirty-blond hair, not one out of place. Her facial expression was sour. It curdled further as the trial continued. Several former KIDS patients sat with the couple, still seeing the Newtons as saviors, not sadists.

On the plaintiff's side almost every day were Harryet and Stewart Ehrlich, the parents of Rebecca, who'd won the previous settlement, and a varying group of other former KIDS and Straight participants and parents who supported Lulu.

Elberg sketched out Lulu's family situation when she entered KIDS. He noted that Lulu was not doing well in school, but that she did not cause trouble. She had never used alcohol or drugs. Indeed, he said, she did not have her first drink until she sipped champagne on the eve of the new millennium.

But her older brother Sam "was starting to use drugs, and Mrs. Corter was having problems controlling him." She entered him in the KIDS program. "It was described as a 'tough love' treatment center. Mrs. Corter certainly understood that," said Elberg.

He then described the events that led to up to Lulu's entry, how her normal adolescent desire to be fashionable had been seen as incipient addiction. Elberg told how Lulu was strip-searched upon entering the program. As he did, Lulu began to sob silently. The attorney noted, with outrage obvious in his voice, that KIDS had not kept records (as required by state law) to show Lulu's initial diagnosis and why they believed she needed treatment. Over time, they would decide she had both a sexual addiction—despite the fact that she was a virgin—and an eating disorder.

Elberg showed a video clip of KIDS participants "motivating." He said that the frantic arm waving was required, and told how days were spent in the blue chairs confessing bad behavior and hoping to be deemed "honest" enough to progress. But what if you had nothing to confess? What if, in fact, you were a victim, not a perpetrator?

The attorney now revealed that as a young child, Lulu had been sexually abused by a male relative—one who was already a patient at KIDS when she was admitted. The Newtons knew that this young man would have contact with Lulu if she entered KIDS—in fact, they would make her confront him. And for much of the thirteen years she spent at KIDS, Elberg said, "Lulu was pushed to 'take responsibility for her part in being sexually abused.'" At this, the red-haired juror's jaw dropped.

"Why didn't Lulu leave?" Elberg asked, again anticipating the jurors' thoughts.

At some point in this process, she gets to be eighteen. When you're eighteen, you can walk out the door. Why didn't she just take off and go? It doesn't make any sense. You can't hold people against their will. Yes, you can. We will prove to you that KIDS operated, essentially, as a private jail.

Lulu was in KIDS 'til she was twenty-six. She graduated every once in a while. Every once in a while she came back. All in all, she spent more than six years in that first and second phase of treatment where reading was prohibited, or having a newspaper, or a radio, or a television.

Elberg again listed Newton's qualifications, and how he had managed to hoodwink the New Jersey licensing authorities. He noted that Newton had written books published by major presses. He'd been praised by politicians and the media. The *New York Times Magazine* had even run a complimentary feature, which didn't mention the dubious backgrounds of both Newton and his program. "If all these other people were fooled, what chance did Lulu and her mother have?" he asked.

Elberg wrapped up, saying,

I make no apology for the fact that at the end of this case we're going to ask you to bring back a money verdict. This is a civil case. If we could ask you for the thirteen years that Lulu lost, we would do that. . . . At the end of this case, Lulu Corter is going to ask you for only one thing. The one thing that only the nine of you can give her in exchange for the thirteen years that were stolen from her. What Lulu Corter wants you to give her is justice.

MILLER AND RUTH ANN NEWTON were represented by John O'Farrell, who had also defended them in the Ehrlich case. A tall, courtly man with the air of a southern gentleman, O'Farrell is a former U.S. attorney. He began by saying that he was proud to represent Miller Newton and KIDS. He said that as he listened to Elberg, "I was struck by the irony of the situation. Nineteen years ago, Miller Newton and KIDS were the people to whom Mrs. Corter turned when she became concerned about her daughter's behavior. . . . Newton and KIDS were the people who attempted to help her come to terms with and overcome her compulsive behavior disorders, which included compulsive overeating and a compulsive preoccupation with sex." He explained,

[Lulu's compulsive behavior was] precipitated in no small part by the fact that from age seven to thirteen, she had been repeatedly molested and sexually abused. . . . This experience left her scarred for life, and the KIDS group were the people who never, ever gave up on Lulu Corter, despite her stubborn refusal at times to honor the program's rules, despite her repeated relapses and her compulsive, occasionally self-destructive behavior. . . . Newton and the KIDS staff were the ones who always stood ready and willing to try to help her, even when she was unwilling to help herself, even when others, including her own family, would not take her in.

You can say what you want about the KIDS program, but one thing you cannot say. Undisputed evidence in this case will show as long as Lulu Corter was in the program from the day she entered until the day she left, she was getting safer. And she was never again, while on their watch, subject to the devastating sexual abuse that had been a regular part of her life for six years prior to her entering the KIDS program.

With outrage in his voice, O'Farrell continued:

Today, Ms. Corter thanks the Newtons for their steadfast loyalty and efforts to improve her lot in life by hauling them into court and accusing them of being fakes, liars, and torturers and demanding that they be held liable to her in a money judgment. In this case, we will present for your consideration, the other side.

The plaintiff's first witness was Jeffery Stallings, who testified via videotape. He had only an undergraduate degree when he supervised admissions at KIDS. These were done as they'd been done at Straight: by patients. Elberg used Stallings's testimony to quickly establish an important element of malpractice: that the need for and appropriateness of treatment was being determined by unqualified staff and only later rubber-stamped by doctors who essentially rented out their licensure. The four psychiatrists who served as KIDS' "medical directors" over the course of Lulu's stay were also defendants in the case. Three had already settled. One would testify later in the trial before Elberg would agree to settle with him as well.

Stallings's testimony established that there was no oversight; that if a child was wrongly admitted, there were no procedures to double-check the appropriateness of the treatment. If a participant didn't think he belonged, he had essentially three choices, Stallings said: "One, to sit and do nothing; number two, act out and fight the process; number three, lie." Unlike in ordinary medical care, there were no "second opinions," and no ongoing evaluation to determine whether therapy was still appropriate and whether it was working. As the tape was played, Miller Newton's face increasingly reddened: after a while, he looked as though he'd had a bad sunburn.

Ruth Ann Newton came next. From her deposition, Elberg knew that she was unable to provide plausible explanations for the way teens were treated in their program the way Miller Newton could. He deliberately chose to have her testify early, so that by the time her charismatic husband tried to fool the jury with therapeutic jargon, they would see through it.

And she didn't disappoint. She angered the judge by claiming to be an expert in treating eating disorders—despite having signed an admission statement prior to trial saying that she wasn't. She couldn't explain why Lulu had been admitted, making vague claims that she had been "aggressively acting out" at home and saying that Lulu's mother was "extremely concerned about her behavior." She gave the example of an incident in which Lulu had allegedly grabbed the steering wheel while her sister was driving, in order to force her to get her some fast food.

But since she hadn't brought this up when asked the same question during her deposition, Elberg challenged her.

"What are you implying?" she asked haughtily.

"That you made it up."

"I know I did not do that. I don't lie. And I certainly wouldn't lie under oath."

After a series of evasive answers to his questions about how patients were assessed and whether certain conditions were ruled in or out during this process, Elberg asked, "Do you know what differential diagnosis is?"

"No," she replied. That is the process, Elberg explained to the court, by which doctors determine the cause of a problem by first making certain that other conditions with similar symptoms have been considered and rejected. To admit to not even knowing the term was practically an admission of malpractice by itself.

Elberg then asked whether Lulu had been made to admit she was "responsible" for being sexually abused at age seven. "Absolutely not," replied Ruth Ann emphatically.

But Elberg had evidence. He flashed an image of a handwritten document from KIDS records onto the screen, which read:

The main point of the rap [group session] was for the girls to recognize where they push off responsibilities for the actions they took. Everyone had a hard time understanding the rap. Lulu Corter, she went through a lot of feelings about her [relative] paying her to do sexual things when she was younger. She didn't want to admit that she had a part in the situation.

Elberg asked Ruth Ann again whether KIDS had suggested Lulu was responsible for being abused, but she remained steadfast in her denial of this.

His next questions would also provide devastating evidence of how and why Lulu had been kept for so long in KIDS and how tough love programs do not do the ongoing reassessment of patients and their conditions which is an essential part of good medicine. He tried to engage Mrs. Newton in a hypothetical discussion of what might happen if someone was wrongly admitted.

"I can't relate to that," Ruth Ann said.

Elberg tried a different tack.

"Mrs. Newton, I make mistakes all the time and I expect that everybody in the courtroom would acknowledge that they make mistakes all the time—"

The judge interrupted, smiling, saying, "Speak for yourself," and Elberg bowed his head and mock-sincerely apologized. But Mrs. Newton just couldn't bring herself to admit that KIDS had ever erred. In the rest of her testimony, she denied that KIDS had held patients over eighteen against their will and that the program had ever forcibly returned adult patients. She refused to admit that parents were often encouraged to enroll multiple siblings. She also denied that teens ever lied in order to progress.

At one point, Ruth Ann asked for a bathroom break, which was immediately granted. A buzz was heard from the plaintiff's side of the courtroom. Sitting there were several former patients with bitter experience of being denied bathroom privileges by KIDS to the point that they had wet and soiled their pants. Shortly after she returned she testified: "I frankly think I'm a really good counselor."

MRS. NEWTON had fallen right into Elberg's hands. If she hadn't denied that adolescents had been kept at KIDS past their eighteenth birthdays against their will, if she hadn't denied that multiple siblings were routinely recruited; if she had simply admitted that patients were sometimes kidnapped back into the program—then under the rules of evidence, Elberg couldn't introduce detailed testimony of victims to refute her. But because Mrs. Newton denied everything, he could put several KIDS victims on the stand. And that would provide vivid evidence of the lasting harm that tough love programs can do. It would demonstrate how far from medical practice KIDS really was and help Elberg explain why Lulu had really been admitted and why she didn't leave when she became an adult.

The first to appear was Ellen, sixty-one. Her testimony illustrated how KIDS recruited siblings just the way Straight had dragooned Richard

Bradbury and Fred Collins—and the horrific effects this had on her family. Unlike Lulu's mother, who had little education and a low income, Ellen was an upper-middle-class stay-at-home mom married to a vice president of a major corporation. She has three kids: Edward*, Bill*, and Amy*. Edward was the first admitted. At fifteen, he had a 145 IQ and was a promising athlete, but he'd become excessively angry, was drinking and smoking marijuana, and failed several prior attempts at treatment.

Before long, Ellen testified, the Newtons wanted his younger sister, Amy, in treatment as well. When Ellen and her husband resisted the idea, they were told, "If we didn't put her into the program, we would have to take Edward out." At the time, Amy's only experience with drugs or alcohol had been sneaking a drink with a girlfriend after a KIDS sibling meeting.

Ellen began to cry on the witness stand as she related her story. She said that she and her husband hadn't wanted to take Edward out because he seemed so much better. "It was almost like Edward was back to himself again. He started becoming the responsible, caring person that he was. Within the first two months, it was like, I had my son back," she told me.

KIDS also tried to have the couple admit their oldest child, Bill, who was just about to enter college. But they refused, and KIDS relented. "He's the only one of my children that is doing well," Ellen testified, deep sorrow evident in her voice. "He went on to college and he graduated and now has a family of his own and a normal life."

The same, unfortunately, is not true for Edward or Amy. Ellen later learned that Edward did not have a drug problem, but suffers bipolar disorder, a condition she believes he shares with his father. Edward's dad, however, has always functioned well, and Ellen is haunted by the idea that the stress of KIDS may have denied Edward this possibility. Ellen pays for a special 800 number for Edward to call home when he needs help. Both he and his sister are homeless now, and Edward refuses to take the medication that might allow him to hold a job or have a family, having been forcibly treated at KIDS and fearing the medical system as a result. Amy lives on the street: a heroin addict, she recently gave birth to a child.

ELBERG'S NEXT WITNESS was Donald*, now a banker, who would testify about how people over eighteen had been held against their will. This was critical to Lulu's case, because Elberg had to prove that she didn't choose to stay there once she was legally free to go. If she had voluntarily chosen the five years she spent in KIDS after age eighteen, it would be much harder to prove she deserved compensation for the harm she claimed the program had caused. Donald's testimony also illustrated the bizarre restraint practices taken from Straight. He said he himself had been restrained some three hundred times, and described what happened if he dared to ask to go to the bathroom during a restraint.

"My mouth would be covered so I wasn't able to complete the sentence and I would be forced to urinate or defecate on myself," he said, and went on to describe how the same thing happened to others, including Lulu. The horror of the testimony contrasted with Donald's conservative businesslike demeanor, making the jury take notice.

Donald had never been suicidal prior to KIDS—but while inside, he made two serious attempts. The program had instilled him with fear about leaving, too: when he did manage to escape once after age eighteen, he returned voluntarily because he had panic attacks. He'd been told so often that running away would lead to suicide, overdose, or prison that he wasn't sure he could make it on his own. He has been diagnosed with post-traumatic stress disorder as a result of his KIDS experience.

He ended his testimony by describing Lulu's self-mutilation. "She was chewing a hole in her arm," he said, adding that she was treated like the "runt of the litter. . . . I think everybody was pretty much treated badly; I think she was treated worse."

MORE DRAMATIC TESTIMONY illustrating the coercive recruitment of siblings, the virtual incarceration of adults, and the negative impact of KIDS treatment came from Britta, a thirty-six-year-old former participant. Platinum-blond, dressed in pink, she was eight months pregnant with her second child at the time of the trial. She hadn't just been held in the program as a teen—she'd been kidnapped back into it, after she left as a legal adult who was supposedly an employee, not a patient. Elberg used her story to reinforce both why Lulu had legitimate fears that kept her from trying to leave once she became an adult and to demonstrate again that admission of siblings who didn't need treatment was common.

The kidnapping happened like this: after Britta had fled the program, her brother, who was still involved, tried to lure her back by claiming he had run away and saying he wanted to meet at a mall. A friend, who she'd been living with because her parents had cut her off, drove her to meet him. Afraid that she'd be taken by force, Britta told her brother she wouldn't leave the car to speak with him.

"And then out of nowhere, a bunch of people came out and proceeded to try to take me out of the car," she testified. "They ripped my friend out of the driver's side. And I held on to the steering wheel as long as I could. One of them had taken my arm and twisted it and it hurt really bad. I had to let go. They proceeded to take me by my legs and my arms and then stuffed me in the back of a car."

She later described one of the worst parts of the experience, saying, "I was physically being taken against my will and no bystander would come to my aid. It was broad daylight on a sunny afternoon. And I'm in the middle of a huge parking lot, with cars galore, people galore. I'll never forget it. I was screaming 'Help me! Help me!' But no one did anything. That was the part that took years to get over."

Elberg asked if anyone who'd abducted her was in the courtroom. She pointed to a man on the left-hand side of the courtroom who was sitting with the Newtons and identified him: "Drew Giganti." She also pointed out a woman sitting on the right with Lulu's supporters. Each was asked to stand in turn.

After being forced into the car, Britta was held in the basement of a "host home." Her own parents and others confronted her, saying she needed KIDS. She got free only because her friend's father had been told about the kidnapping when the friend had returned home without Britta. He threatened to call the police if Britta wasn't released.

Britta's father, however, disowned her when she refused to return to KIDS. It would be over ten years before she would reconcile with her parents. They didn't even attend her wedding.

In her testimony, Britta went on to describe a period of drug use she went through immediately after leaving KIDS. It was far more destructive than any of her prior use, which had been limited to college drinking and marijuana-smoking. After KIDS, she began heavy cocaine use. She drank excessively. But with the help of Alcoholics Anonymous meetings, she straightened out. "I've been sober for fifteen years," she said proudly.

The judge asked her why she hadn't returned to KIDS for help after she lost control of her cocaine use. She laughed at the idea that the program could deal with such problems, replying, "I was frightened by what I'd seen done to other people. . . . [Lulu Corter] was eating herself . . . she had put a hole in her wrist. . . . People were being restrained for hours at a clip, urinating on the floor. Violence, hitting constantly . . . on one level or another, there was abuse every day."

LULU'S MOTHER, Virginia, also provided vivid evidence of KIDS' coercive influence and its deviation from medical standards. Her testimony was heartbreaking. The family resemblance between mother and daughter is obvious. Unlike Lulu, Virginia looks older than her sixty-four years and is extremely thin. She shook noticeably as she took the stand. Elberg first took her through her circumstances at the time before Lulu was admitted. As she listed her four children, her voice broke when she got to Lulu's name. She described her work in a factory making circuit boards, which she would solder after they were assembled. To pay for the KIDS program at first (later Medicaid and disability payments covered it), she would take home extra boards, often working all night.

She told how she'd found the program through a newspaper ad and visited it with her sister to check it out as possible treatment for her drug-addicted son. Another relative had already been admitted. She said she had been led to believe that Miller Newton was a medical doctor, but what had really sold her on him was that he was also a minister.

Asked about Lulu's behavior, she said, "It was like a normal [child]." She testified that Lulu had no disciplinary problems and no arrest record. "I wanted better for my kids," she said, explaining why she'd taken the advice of those she believed to be professionals about KIDS. Throughout her testimony, she looked almost childishly eager to please, and it became apparent how easy it would have been for anyone without scruples to take advantage of her credulity. Her careworn face came to life when she smiled if she thought she gave an answer that pleased either of the attorneys or the judge.

Mrs. Corter detailed what had happened when Lulu wore her pleather outfit to the KIDS sibling group: "I was told she had a behavior problem." When Lulu said she wanted to bleach the back of her hair, "I thought, 'Oh my God, I got a second druggie.'" Virginia testified that at open meetings, Mrs. Newton repeatedly asked if she was ready to put Lulu in. "But I wasn't sure she was a druggie just because she wanted to bleach her hair. And then when we went in and Lulu did her intake—I'll never forget it—she wrote down that she did drugs. And I fell to pieces." Mrs. Corter didn't know about the pressure exerted on teens during the intake.

Elberg asked about Lulu's weight. "She was a little chunky, but I didn't worry about that," she replied, agreeing that she hadn't put Lulu in for an eating disorder. Elberg gently queried Virginia about whether she had worried when her daughter was away from home for so long during first phase.

"I didn't ask many questions, I just trusted," she said, spitting out the last word as though she'd admitted to a crime. O'Farrell cross-examined Mrs. Corter about her husband's history of domestic violence, trying to suggest that it was her negligence, not that of KIDS, that caused Lulu's problems, but he didn't gain much traction.

AND THEN, it was time to hear from Lulu herself. Elberg had left her for last, wanting to give her testimony the greatest impact and wanting the jury to have gotten some sense of what had been done to her before they met her. She walked into the courtroom with her therapist. She wore a red silk blouse and black slacks. As she was sworn in, her anxiety became obvious. Like her mother, she shook violently and her voice was unsteady. The Newtons and other KIDS supporters stared at her coldly.

With her right hand, after she'd finished the oath, Lulu picked up a palm-sized blue stress-relief ball that she'd brought with her. She squeezed it so violently and waved it around so frantically during the start of her testimony that it seemed as though, at any moment, she might accidentally bean a juror or the judge with it.

Elberg started with easy questions, asking her about where she'd gone to elementary school and what activities she'd done. She described being a Girl Scout, playing on a traveling soccer team, and marching with a band.

He asked about her history of sexual abuse, and she mentioned being molested by three perpetrators: two male relatives and a neighbor. "I was always friendly with everybody," she said, detailing how she'd come to be victimized by the neighbor. "Always a pretty good kid, friendly, laughing . . . he would say things and I didn't think anything of it. And then he would touch me." As she spoke, she was clearly near tears. During particularly upsetting parts of her testimony, her mouth turned down so sharply that it looked like an upside-down smile.

Elberg asked about other sexual abuse that she'd disclosed in the program and she said she'd lied about that. He asked a strange question: "Did you ever have sex with a dog?"

"No, I made that up."

"Prior to the time that you entered the KIDS program, did you ever have sexual intercourse with anyone?"

"No—[my relative] tried," she said. Her hand tightened around the ball.

Elberg asked about the events leading up to her admission. "My girlfriends that I started seventh grade with . . . they were going to buy a pleather skirt and jackets. And I always wanted to fit in because I was pretty lonely when I was a kid."

"How did those pleather pants get you in trouble?"

"I was told not to wear those clothes to [the sibling meetings] at the program and I didn't listen."

"Did you have any understanding of why you weren't supposed to wear those kinds of clothes to the program?"

"Because black is very image- and druggie-looking."

Her attorney asked about her weight before she entered the program and whether her mother had been worried about it. "No one was really concerned about it. I was a little overweight, yes I was, but nobody was telling me anything about it." Again, the stress ball was attacked.

Lulu next described how a family conference was held at KIDS because the relative who was already in the program had confessed to abusing her. This young man was asked to apologize to Lulu in this meeting, but he minimized what actually occurred and, as Lulu put it, "I just kind of listened, cried. But I was scared to say any more because he always threatened me. And I thought if I said any more, that if he got out of there that it would come true that he would hurt me." The corners of her mouth were down.

Elberg asked her to describe what had happened next, regarding her hairstyle. "I wanted attention from the guys . . . I yelled into the kitchen where the guys were . . . 'Hey Ma, I want my hair cut with a tail and I want a blond streak.' Because my girlfriends were really going to do it, but . . . I don't think I would have ever gone to that extreme," Lulu said. She added that if she'd really wanted to do it, she would have just done so without asking permission.

As a result of this request, however, Mrs. Corter became convinced that she had to bring "druggie" Lulu to KIDS for an intake interview. "I thought I was going to go help out with the siblings with the haunted house that they were making for Halloween," Lulu testified.

Instead, she got a real-life chamber of horrors. "They brought me into an intake room . . . I lied . . . I said I did drugs, and I never even did or knew what they even looked like . . . and Dr. Newton came in at the end and told me that I was there for a behavior problem."

Lulu began to calm down at this point, settling into her testimony and squeezing the stress ball less visibly. She said she wasn't told she was admitted for an eating disorder.

She described being strip-searched in the bathroom. "I had to take all my clothes off and give them to the oldcomer . . . and then I had to show my mouth, lift my arms up, bend down and turn in case there was anything on me that I could hurt anybody else with. They had to check all areas." As she described this, she shook slightly.

She said that she didn't know what to talk about in the program, "because I never hit anybody or anything." But because she was hungry between KIDS' rigidly scheduled meals, she began to talk about food. Consequently, after a few weeks, Mrs. Newton diagnosed her with an eating disorder and put her on the food plan.

"Why were you on the first phase of treatment for so long?"

"Because I didn't listen . . . I would get rebellious and act out and prevent myself from going home," she said, replying as though she'd been questioned by a member of the KIDS staff, not her own attorney.

Elberg asked her if she understood at the time what she had to do to get off first phase. She said she knew she had to talk about "things that were out of control, things that were bad that I did with food and how I felt about them. Which I didn't have a lot of . . . I really never sat down and actually binged on anything."

So Lulu—like so many others before her—began to make it up. "I constantly would talk about bingeing on this and bingeing on that and almost eating a whole pizza pie, which were all lies because I wanted to go home." She took her cues from others diagnosed with eating disorders, changing the details to suit her own taste in food.

Lulu also spoke of constantly being pressured to confess in greater detail. "Every time I got stuck, I would be confronted and told, 'There's more, there's more, there's more.' And if I said there wasn't, I'd be told, 'You're not going to move on until you own something else.' I would sit in my seat, think of another, and I would get up and lie . . . Because I kind of understood that if I kept getting honest and I cried, I would get help possibly."

Elberg asked her whether she'd made up the story about the fast food and the steering wheel. She said that the KIDS participants had been asked to describe an incident in which their addiction had brought them close to death.

"I had nothing, nothing whatsoever. I got up. I said I had nothing that caused me to almost die. I was told 'bull.'"

So Lulu made something up. She said she was with her sister, Cindy. "We pulled into a QuikChek and she bought a Suzy-Q. And I said I was mad because she didn't buy me one. And I said on the way out of the parking lot I punched her and grabbed the steering wheel and we almost ran into a truck that almost killed us."

"Did any of that happen?"

"No."

Lulu also described how she was also made to discuss the sexual abuse with the perpetrator. "I would remind him about things that he had done. And then he would remember and share how he felt with me, that he felt guilty and mad at himself." She noted that these discussions took place in front of the whole group of some hundred kids, and sometimes in front of hundreds of parents at open meetings.

Elberg next had Lulu discuss how she was kept alone in an intake room with no furniture, twelve hours a day or more, for months. A patient guarded the door and allowed her to draw pictures if she wrote satisfactory "moral inventories" first. At other times, she had to scrub the baseboards of the bathrooms with a toothbrush. Lulu said she was punished this way because her screams during her frequent restraints interrupted the group. She testified that Miller Newton had asked the others if they thought Lulu "deserved" to be in group and that they had voted unanimously to reject her.

Elberg asked why she mutilated herself. "Instead of hurting somebody else, I thought I would inflict it on myself," Lulu testified. "Plus I wanted people to think I was crazy and throw me out. That was my plan, but it never worked. I was just told, 'If you're going to hurt yourself, keep doing it.' . . . Sometimes I would sit there at an open meeting, and I would literally have a pile of blood in front of me."

During this testimony, Ruth Ann Newton's face looked gray and stony, and at one point, she put her arm around her husband.

Elberg moved on, chronologically taking Lulu through her first graduation from KIDS, three years after she'd first been admitted, in 1987. Within two months, her mother had sent her back for overeating.

At this point, the juror who the plaintiff's team had nicknamed "Shakespeare," a Latino man in his thirties, stood up and interrupted the testimony. He asked the judge if he could approach the bench. The judge agreed, seemingly bemused by the unorthodox request. The juror told him that people on the defendants' side of the courtroom were being blatantly disrespectful. He said they were laughing and smirking at Lulu, and that this was distracting him. He singled out one woman, who, it turned out, was a defense witness. The judge sent "Shakespeare" back to his seat and rejected a call by O'Farrell to remove him for this sign of "bias." Gallipoli admonished all the spectators that there should be "no visualization of agreement or disagreement" with the witness.

Lulu continued. "First I was told I was a victim of incest . . . but then somewhere in that line it became a sexual disorder . . . because I would be told and blamed for doing sexual things to myself."

"Was that true?" Elberg asked. Lulu replied rapidly, her voice full of anger and sadness:

No. People would say they heard things. And people would say because of the way I was sitting in group. Or, when I went to the bathroom, people started saying you're wiping yourself too long, you're doing sexual things to yourself. So every time people thought it, I would get confronted and blasted and told you're doing it, you're doing it, you're doing it. So I had no way out.

I would sit down at first and feel like, OK, how do I get out of this situation if I really didn't do it? So then I would lie and say I did it just so I could get help to move on. . . . I didn't think I had an actual compulsion.

Elberg asked what she meant about being accused of masturbating because of how she sat in her chair. As she responded, her mouth turned down and there were tears in her eyes. Her voice was full of raw pain.

When I motivated, sometimes in order to prevent myself banging into people, I would go off to the side of my chair and I would go up a little bit and I would bring myself forward. . . . And I was told that I was getting a good feeling off my chair. And I'd say, no, I wasn't. And I'd get blasted, so I'd own it when I really wasn't.

But just to get people not to yell at me and confront me, I said I did it. Because I didn't like when people got in my face, yelled and spit in my face and everything else . . . In order to get people not to do that, I owned lies."

Elberg asked if she'd tried to leave KIDS after she'd turned eighteen. "There were numerous amounts of times after I was eighteen that I tried to leave," Lulu said. She described how she'd try to follow the bureaucratic process that was supposed to allow people over eighteen to sign out, sending a note up the "chain of command" for permission. "Either a staff member or a graduate would come over and rip it up and say, 'You need to grow up. Stop acting immature. You're not going anywhere. You're here for the duration. . . . You're a lifer, you're part of the furniture . . . you need to take responsibility to go home.'"

Lulu later discussed how devastating those particular taunts had been. "I would get confronted on that by everyone," she said, her voice shaky. "'You'll never move on, your mother will never take you out of here, you're dreaming if you think you'll ever get out and have a normal life because you can *never* have a normal life, Lulu Corter.' That's what I was always told."

After walking her through a few more painful incidents of restraints and humiliation, Elberg asked Lulu how she finally did leave. She had advanced to staff trainee at that point. "One day, the thought hit me to call for help. . . . I called my grandmother and I said, 'Grandma, I want to ask you something, and if you're not willing to do it, don't report me because I don't want to get set back.'"

And her grandmother told her she'd been waiting years for such a call. It was two days before her birthday, and she told Lulu that her call was the best present ever. "She was happy as a lark. She had a whole plan set," Lulu told me later. Her uncle and grandmother came to pick her up from a remedial school she was then attending.

"I hid out," Lulu testified, and she described staying with her sister Cindy (who had also spent time at KIDS, but had fled), fearing being taken back by her mother or others who still believed in the program.

"Have you tried to complete your education?"

"Numerous times." She explained that she found she couldn't concentrate in a classroom setting because it brought back terrible memories of KIDS.

"Let's talk about your work history."

"I worked in Shop Rite at the fish department for one or two years. [I left] because I was having a hard time. I was crying a lot." She also said that she'd worked in a daycare center. "Working with children is fantastic, I love working with kids," she said, her face lighting up at the thought. But then, she continued, "I would get emotional," so she left rather than "put that" on a kid.

Elberg asked why she hadn't run away from KIDS after she turned eighteen. "Because I was worried more about my mother and her feelings for the longest time," she said. "Because she had already lost her son and my sister—and I always felt bad for her. [Mrs. Corter wasn't allowed to talk to Cindy or Sam, because they'd left KIDS on bad terms; otherwise, she would have had to remove Lulu.] So I kept the lies going to protect my mother. . . . She wanted the family back together. So for me to leave, I thought I would like totally break her heart and I didn't want to do that."

Now came the hardest part of Lulu's testimony: cross-examination. O'Farrell once again had a Herculean task. Because Lulu was such a sympathetic victim, if he was too rough, he'd be seen by the jury as a bully, which wouldn't gain anything for his side. On the other hand, if he didn't challenge her, he couldn't make his case. He spoke quietly and gently, his tone acknowledging that the questions might be difficult.

He started by complimenting her: "You look splendid," he said. Then he began his questions.

"Between ages seven and thirteen, you had been regularly abused?"

"Yes."

"The nature of [the main perpetrator's] abuse essentially consisted of attempting repeatedly to have intercourse with you?"

"Yes, he attempted a lot."

O'Farrell asked whether during this time Lulu had also been abused by a neighbor as well as the relative, and she said that she had been.

"And while you were in the KIDS program, certainly nobody there engaged in sexual conduct with you, did they?"

"No."

O'Farrell then questioned Lulu about her weight before and after KIDS. He complimented her again on her present weight, but said that she'd weighed 265 pounds when he'd taken her deposition in June of 2001. He questioned her closely about her flashbacks and their content—emphasizing that they were all related to sexual abuse, not to the KIDS program. Lulu agreed but rocked in her chair, seemingly in an attempt to comfort herself. She seemed to become a young, frightened child during this questioning, even becoming unable to answer a few questions because she appeared not to have heard them. At one point, she replied "Yes ma'am" to Mr. O'Farrell.

The defense attorney moved on, asking about her lies and dishonesty. She said that she'd been honest about the abuse by her male relatives. "I get very confused because there were a lot of lies and a lot of not-lies," she added. Though O'Farrell did his best to put the blame for her problems on the earlier sexual abuse, Lulu's openness and obvious pain came through just as clearly in her cross-examination as in Elberg's direct.

As in most medical-malpractice trials, expert testimony would play an important role in Lulu's case. The plaintiff's psychiatrist, Dr. Jay Kuris, had the relatively easy job of illustrating the many ways that the KIDS program failed to meet medical standards and pointing out the differences between psychiatric fraud and genuine treatment. The defense expert had a far more challenging task.

Direct examination of Kuris was conducted by Elberg's partner, Alan Medvin. Kuris had studied medicine at Tulane and served as a military psychiatrist in Vietnam. He taught clinical psychiatry for over twenty years at the University of Medicine and Dentistry–New Jersey and had also been the medical director for a psychiatric center. He has white hair and brown eyes, and he wore a gray suit with a red tie.

Kuris told the jurors that he'd reviewed the available records on Lulu and had also examined her. He said he could find no justification for her admission to KIDS, and that it had violated psychiatric standards because it was not conducted by professionals.

Medvin queried Kuris about whether it was appropriate to admit a survivor of childhood sex abuse to a program in which the perpetrator was already enrolled.

"In 1984, before that and to the present day, I cannot imagine any program that would have done such a thing," Kuris replied. "One of the basic tenets of the treatment of sex-abuse victims, particularly those who were vulnerable, younger, smaller, weaker, is that they should not be in the presence of the victimizer. No treatment for any kind of abuse can even begin when the person is put in that kind of setting."

Medvin inquired about KIDS' philosophy of treatment and whether it was in line with the standard of care. Kuris replied,

> The underlying philosophy of the KIDS program, in my opinion, was that people should be managed through the total control of their minds, of their thoughts, of their behaviors and of their bod-

ies . . . and that control was enforced by measures that would be considered harsh, inhumane and absolutely not permissible in any conventional psychiatric facility.

Medvin next asked a tremendously long question, which he displayed as an exhibit to aid the witness's memory. It was a hypothetical question that read like a litany, listing all of the restrictions of KIDS' first and second phases and the time Lulu spent under them. It also included items like restraint, sleep deprivation, removal from school, and being made to make false confessions. Assuming that Lulu was subjected to all of this, Medvin asked, was it a deviation from the standards of care?

"There were at least twenty deviations [in that list]," replied Kuris. He explained that psychiatric standards, even for the sickest patients, "require treating patients with a maximum of dignity and freedom." The expert went on to describe the specific violations and how each deviated from quality psychiatric care. He emphasized the incredibly bizarre way that patients were restrained.

"I have never, in all my years as a psychiatric expert and psychiatrist, known of a program that permitted other patients to restrain and hold down a fellow patient," he said. "It is generally assumed that such people do not have the authority, the training, or the knowledge to know when and how to apply restraints safely."

Kuris discussed the KIDS food plan, which barred sugar and punished patients who ate sugary foods with a setback to first phase. "The food restrictions have no medical [basis]. There is no medical evidence that sugar by itself contributes to mental disease or even obesity."

As he continued to describe the numerous ways that the program failed to meet psychiatric standards, he kept an even tone. But when he got to the part about the twelve-hour days in the blue chairs and the strict posture required, he made no attempt to hide his disgust and anger. "[That] is so far from the usual standard of care that it goes beyond, in my opinion, malpractice and into inhuman and physically torturous and oppressive behavior."

He added that one other thing particularly troubled him. When she reached second phase, "Ms. Corter had to become the keeper of newer patients. This, again, is below the standard of care in that she is not a trained individual. She presumably had no great expertise in the treatment of substance abuse. And she herself had only barely been allowed off the floor. But in that second phase, Ms. Corter had to actually become a person who took away the rights of others . . . [who] took away the independence and the actual physical safety of other patients. So she had to become a policeperson, when she, herself, was supposedly there for treatment."

In fact, during his examination of Lulu, Kuris wrote in his report that he had noticed her distress when she told him that "to advance, you have to become one of the confronters." He also wrote, "Ms. Corter expressed that she now greatly regrets what she did to other patients in the program. . . . She expressed great concern and guilt that she had become and acted like those individuals in the program that had, indeed, harmed her."

Medvin asked Kuris about the impact of this unnecessary treatment that Lulu had been forced to undergo. At this, the expert let out a deep, audible sigh before responding:

When Ms. Corter was admitted, and I do restate that I find there was no cause for her to be admitted, she was only thirteen years old. She was not an adult with perspective. . . . Although we can look now and say that there was nothing wrong with her . . . she was, in fact, told that there was a lot wrong with her . . . that she was so bad that she needed all these freedoms taken away from her . . . because she was such a bad person that inevitably she was going to become a drug addict or a compulsive this or that.

So the first level of harm that is done to her is that her innocence about herself was taken away. It is pounded into her, verbally and reinforced, if necessary by severe behavior, that she is not OK. That she does deserve to be in this program. And that she's a horrible and incompetent person.

Throughout the many, many days that she spends in this program, the healthier part of Ms. Corter struggles to figure out why she was there and what she did do wrong and why she should have to change. The less healthy part starts to try to go along with the program to gain some measure of safety, maybe even authority. . . . The damage done is that she was not able to develop any sense of who and what she is. Because, right from the beginning, she's pulled between the accusations and the punishments and whatever desire she might have to be a normal person.

I have treated patients in environments as severe as the hospital for the criminally insane down in Trenton, where it's a strongly locked-up unit. I have actually been the director of a secure, locked unit both in the military and at Princeton House [a psychiatric hospital] and I can say that the restrictions placed on Ms. Corter were much more severe and oppressive than the restrictions one would find in a psychiatric facility, even with the most disturbed people.

The criminally insane, even those who had murdered others, were under far fewer restrictions.

Medvin noted that Lulu spent seven and a half years on first and second phase, and asked why she might have turned to self-mutilation. Kuris said,

It appears that it generally arose out of frustration, desperation. She was not allowed to protest her confinement in any way, except that which she could express against herself. Somewhere along the seven years of captivity, she became so frustrated and angry and so desperate and . . . as she admitted to me, so hateful of herself for being there that she did bite herself and scratch herself and injure herself.

Studies have found, in fact, that self-mutilation is common in institutions where people have little control over their environment, such as prisons and prisoner-of-war camps. The less control one has over one's conditions of incarceration, the less knowledge one has about how long he or she will be forced to stay, the more likely it is to occur.

Medvin next told the jury that Lulu was diagnosed with post-traumatic stress disorder when she was hospitalized in St. Clare's in 1992. At that point, even KIDS had become concerned about her mental health, as she reported hallucinating scenes of her prior sexual abuse and appeared to be dissociating. Sent by KIDS, she was admitted four different times. Medvin asked Kuris to explain her diagnosis.

The expert began by stressing that post-traumatic stress disorder (PTSD) can occur when someone is confronted by "an overwhelmingly scary, actual real threat to life and limb, or to something as important as that, and in the face of that threat, [finds himself] helpless to do anything about it." The diagnosis was first introduced in relation to Vietnam veterans, some of whom had had terrifying combat or prisoner-of-war experiences that left them anxious, depressed, paranoid, overreactive to loud noises, and susceptible to vivid nightmares and flashbacks of the traumatic situation. Research shows that the longer that people feel helpless in frightening situations, and the less control they feel they have, the more likely they are to develop PTSD. In KIDS, of course, the whole program was deliberately designed to make participants feel powerless.

Medvin moved on to the period before Lulu was first admitted to St. Clare's. "What did the admitting psychiatrists attribute the PTSD to?"

"They attributed it to earlier sexual abuse. I can accept that as part of what was going on. But I think the admitting physicians only got part of the story. Their conclusion was based on the fact that when Ms. Corter was brought to them, very much in distress, she claimed she was hearing and seeing [her abuser threatening her]." Medvin said the staff was told by those who accompanied her that the sex abuse caused the problem.

"What the hospital did not know is that the patient had been experiencing a different kind of abuse for many years and that [she] had been forced to ruminate about [the sexual abuse] daily," Kuris continued.

He then described his findings from his psychiatric examination of Lulu. "When I interviewed Ms. Corter, it was several years after she left the program, and in many respects, she wasn't doing too badly. She herself brought the conversation, though, back to her experience at the program and the many ways in which she felt that she was still trying to recover. . . . She was very upset that she had been deprived of an education . . . she was very upset that she had been deprived of the chance to develop through anything close to a normal adolescence . . . she was very upset that she must constantly fight again and again for her own sense of self-esteem. She was haunted by constant echoes from the program: that she was no good, that she was worthless, and that she could never make it on her own."

Medvin asked Kuris what his diagnosis of Lulu was. He said that Lulu suffers from three psychiatric conditions. She has chronic post-traumatic stress disorder and major depression that was in partial remission due to medications and therapy at the time of her examination. She also suffers from something called an "adjustment reaction to adult life," which describes her difficulty in coping with things like having been deprived of an education and normal adolescent experiences.

"It's very clear that the PTSD comes from two sources. There's no question that one source was childhood sexual abuse. . . . There is also no question in my mind that she also suffers PTSD from the ordeal of trying to survive the KIDS program." With regard to the depression, Kuris said, "I do believe a large part of her depression is again due to the fact that she knows she lost out. Her adolescent years were stolen from her.

"The adjustment disorder was caused largely by the KIDS program . . . at thirteen, her life just took a turn into the Twilight Zone, and she didn't get back from that for many, many years."

ON CROSS-EXAMINATION, O'Farrell wanted to counter the notion that KIDS was completely out of line with medical standards of the time. He wanted to raise doubt that the program caused the PTSD and depression—and prove that those could have been due entirely to the childhood sex abuse. He also wanted to suggest that whatever the cause of Lulu's problems, they weren't so bad. O'Farrell was being paid by the Newtons' insurers, so limiting their liability was his main task.

First, he questioned Kuris about whether Lulu was indeed "normal" at thirteen. "How many normal thirteen-year-old girls do you know that have spent the prior six years of their lives, from ages seven to thirteen, being sexually abused?" he demanded.

"My answer is that the vast majority of girls who are sexually abused are normal."

"They are normal?" O'Farrell asked incredulously.

"They then become . . . normal people who had a rather bad experience . . . it doesn't affect the normality."

O'Farrell got the expert to agree that sexual abuse itself wasn't a normal experience, but beyond that, Kuris wouldn't budge. He hammered Kuris about St. Clare's, noting how many different professionals had seen Lulu during her four admissions. "None of them, not one of them, concluded that her PTSD was being caused by her treatment at KIDS, did they?" he asked rhetorically.

Then, he asked whether Lulu had ever been sexually abused in KIDS, implying that the program had protected her from further molestation at home. Kuris asked him to clarify what he meant by "sexually abused."

"Do you have any evidence whatsoever that for thirteen years while she was in KIDS, that she was subjected to sexual abuse by anybody?"

"I believe that there is a gray area in terms of intrusive sexual thinking, issues of toileting and wiping. There is a gray area as to what is abusive." The implication was that by keeping Lulu focused on her history of abuse through policies like restricting the number of times she could wipe herself, by demonizing masturbation, and by saying that she was sexually compulsive, the program itself was sexually abusive.

"In those thirteen years, no man or boy in that program ever laid his hands on her sexually, did he?" O'Farrell asked.

"Not to my knowledge."

THE DEFENSE EXPERT, Dr. Philip Torrance, had attended Johns Hopkins Medical School and served for twenty-one years as a psychiatrist for the Air Force. Torrance had been the medical director for the alcohol rehab program at Andrews Air Force Base and has treated both eating disorders and compulsive behavior problems. He is overweight, with gray hair. He wore a gray suit and lavender shirt.

"Was Lulu a normal child at the time she entered KIDS?" O'Farrell asked.

Torrance denied this, saying, "She had stated that she was depressed as a child and often lonely and wasn't able to connect to people. She had been engaged as a victim of sexual abuse by [her relative] over about six-seven years prior to her entry."

"Dr. Kuris said that the restrictions of first phase, being restrained, spending hours in group, having privileges denied based on peer compliance, that environment caused her PTSD and depression. Do you agree?"

Torrance disagreed again. It was impossible for St. Clare's hospital to have admitted her four different times, he claimed, and each time miss that the real cause of her problems was KIDS, not the sexual abuse. He noted that her hallucinations always related to the sex abuse, not KIDS.

O'Farrell then attempted to prove that KIDS itself was an acceptable treatment that met the standards of care in the early '80s. He was told that the five-phase concept was valid and widely used, and that the tight restrictions were valid "at the time." Torrance chose his words carefully to imply that things have changed. One of the key differences between the experts that the plaintiff and defense called was their level of immersion in, and focus, on substance-abuse treatment. Torrance was deeply committed to addiction care, and particularly to the twelve-step model, while Kuris focused more on psychiatry and its standards.

While psychiatric treatment and commitment have long been regulated and have been the subject of numerous scandalous exposés when abuses have been discovered, treatment for drug and alcohol problems has typically been held to much lower standards. For example, no one would dare argue that physical restraint, food and sleep deprivation, and attack therapy are appropriate "consequences" to help schizophrenics or people with dementia learn to behave better—but that case is still regularly made by those who promote tough love for treatment of addiction. Restraining Lulu and keeping her under restrictions more severe than even those for the worst convicted criminals was "to keep her safe." First phase was, as a defense witness would later put it "a respite," which some participants even called "a gift."

While Torrance's claims that KIDS did meet the standard for behavioral treatment seemed to the jurors too shocking to be true, the real horror is that, as a result of the lax standards of care and decency for substance-abuse treatment, such abuse has been permitted to be part of drug treatment for so long. Torrance wasn't lying about the loose standards: they just don't sound defensible as part of a modern medical treatment system. KIDS was out of the mainstream, to be sure: but one of the most horrifying things about the case was that, aside from the extremely lengthy periods spent in treatment, the differences are in degree, not in kind.

O'Farrell asked Torrance about Lulu's alleged eating disorder—specifically, whether the fact that she was overweight and reported trouble controlling her food intake was sufficient to make this diagnosis. Surprisingly, the expert said yes: giving an opinion that is decidedly unorthodox, both now and even in the '80s. For one thing, most doctors would want to rule out physical and hormonal problems. Second, psychiatric definitions of eating disorders require far more specific criteria to be met. Such loose criteria would mean that two-thirds of the U.S. population—possibly including Torrance himself—would qualify for such a diagnosis.

From this point on, Torrance's responses seemed to provoke increasing skepticism and even hostility from the jury—but none more so than his next claim: that treating both the abuser and the victim in the same program was OK. "There was quite strict supervision so no further abuse could take place," he said, adding that "perhaps it could help the victim and the abuser to try to develop if they wished a more reasonable . . . relationship." As Medvin put it, he was selling but the jury didn't seem to be buying. O'Farrell had noticeably steered clear of the issue of restraint.[4]

EIGHT

Miller Time

FOR THE KIDS AND STRAIGHT VICTIMS who attended the Corter trial, it was a rare opportunity to make at least one of the main perpetrators of their abuse, Miller Newton, face the pain he'd caused; to make him, at least briefly, answer to them. Because he'd declared bankruptcy, he couldn't be made to suffer much more financially, no matter how large a settlement the jury imposed. Because it was a civil trial, he could not be sent to prison for his crimes. The statute of limitations on them had run out. A large judgment against him, however, would at least blacken his name. It could also make malpractice insurers more reluctant to cover such programs, making it harder for them to do business. Activists like Laurie Berg and Richard Bradbury increasingly see such suits as an important part of reining them in.

The first three witnesses for the defense were like hors d'oeuvres for Elberg, who was anxious to get to the main course and cross-examine Newton. He'd waited years to get this man in a courtroom and confront him. Like Newton's victims, Elberg wanted to know why: what drives a man to do what he'd done? Why seek such absolute control over others? Why such emphasis on constant humiliation, constant submission? Did Newton really believe he was helping people who came to KIDS—or did he, somewhere, have to know that what was done to Lulu and others like her must be hurtful? Did he even care? And might his story suggest ways to keep similar people out of the treatment field?

Earlier testimony had vividly demonstrated how tough love's victims can become perpetrators, and how well-intentioned people who don't know better can come to believe in it. But what about people who carry on with it for decades, years and years after evidence of harm is all around them? What about those who devise and refine its cruelest tactics?

Direct examination by O'Farrell was first. The attorney began by having Newton detail his qualifications and educational history. Newton wore a black or dark navy suit, with a white shirt and black-and-white tie. He had already started to redden as he took the oath.

Virgil Miller Newton III was born in Florida in 1938. He was named for his father, a journalist who was the managing editor of the *Tampa Tribune* from 1943 to 1965. Newton's father was a prominent advocate of openness in government. His work played a significant role in the passage of the federal Freedom of Information Act in 1966 and in the enactment of similar state legislation in Florida—legislation that would ultimately help the media and attorneys reveal evidence of wrongdoing by his son.[1]

Newton's educational career began promisingly. He won acceptance to Princeton University. After a serious car accident kept him out of college for a year, he finished his undergraduate work back home at the University of Florida, earning a degree in history. He then returned to Princeton and completed a master's degree in divinity. After receiving his master's, Newton went to work for the Methodist church, serving as a pastor in an inner-city parish in Indianapolis. He worked with youth as well as homeless alcoholics and heroin addicts. This led to involvement in Lyndon Johnson's "war on poverty," in which he served as a director of a Job Corps site. His history here gives no hint of his future actions; it suggests someone with high academic aptitude, with a social conscience and liberal leanings.

Later, Newton was appointed by the governor of Florida to serve as the county clerk of Pasco County. This led to an unsuccessful run for Congress, apparently as a Democrat. After the setback, he decided to get a Ph.D., this time via an alternative correspondence school called the Union Institute.

While studying for his doctorate in urban anthropology and public administration, Newton served as a consultant for several government agencies, including a task force to plan alcoholism services for the Tampa Bay region. Soon, he became director of the Florida Alcohol Coalition, in 1977 or 1978. At around the same time, his son Mark started taking drugs. And here is where the first public evidence of deceptive behavior comes in. Newton presented himself to Straight as an addiction-treatment professional when he enrolled Mark in the program. Despite his having no professional credentials in treating addictions, he insisted on being called "Dr. Newton" as soon as he received his anthropology doctorate in 1981. He appears to have been so desperate to be seen as a physician or Ph.D. psychologist that he would literally correct letters from regulatory agencies that did not address him as "Doctor."

Partly as a result of people's assumptions that this meant he was an M.D. or Ph.D. psychologist, and partly as the result of his ability to talk a good game, he rapidly rose through the Straight organization.

So while in the late 1970s, Newton was just another Straight parent, by 1981, he had risen to the position of director of the St. Petersburg facility. And in July 1982, cofounder Mel Sembler announced proudly in a press release that Dr. Miller Newton was taking over as national clinical director. Only a month earlier, Newton had dragged Leigh Bright by the hair in front of hundreds, cursing and ordering sleep deprivation.

"Our son Mark had gotten in trouble with drugs and alcohol," he testified now. "We placed him in treatment shortly after his fifteenth birthday."

Newton said that his son was in Straight for "a year to the day" and was successful, explaining that he is now a regional director for a pharmaceutical company. "I'm very proud of him. . . . I have a great relationship

with him," he added emphatically, seemingly trying to make up for the
jury's impressions of earlier testimony that had included so many families broken up by KIDS.

O'Farrell asked how Newton had become more involved with Straight.

Like most parents who come and your kid—instead of being angry
and petulant—we had an episode where Mark got very angry with
me and tried to choke me. . . . And when the kid comes running
across the room on the night he's coming home and comes into
your arms and is loving and sharing and honest and really concerned
with the well-being of parents and the older brother and sister, your
heart gets filled and you want to help.

He described how he was trained by Straight's completely nonprofes-
sional staff in using their model. He helped spread it by setting up
Straight programs in Atlanta and Cincinnati; Sarasota, Florida; and Springfield, Virginia.

"I found something that was effective but lacked something of the
professional rationalization, that we expect in current times," he said,
suggesting that he took Straight's amateur treatment and made it into
professional mental-health care.

Newton also detailed how he had left Straight for KIDS. "The Straight
program had treated the child of a very wealthy CEO. . . . He started to
lean on me to consider leaving because there was nothing like this for
adolescents and young adults in the New York area, which is where
he lived. . . . And I resisted it for a year out of loyalty to the Straight
program."

What Newton left out here was that at that time in Florida, a grand jury
was getting ready to hand up a criminal indictment of Straight-Sarasota[2]
and that the Straight program had a decades-long history of the exact
same abuses of which he was now being accused. Ironically, Straight
would take over one KIDS expansion program in California shut down
by regulators there for abuse—but a year later, regulators shut Straight
there, too.[3]

"How did the program you designed for KIDS differ from Straight?"

"It was designed from the beginning to use addictive-treatment tech-nology with people with eating disorders," Newton testified. He said that it had eight steps, rather than the seven Straight used, which had been modified from AA's twelve, and that it required more intense family par-ticipation. He added, "We determined that we wanted more psychiatric involvement, to review all admissions . . . [We wanted] an in-house out-side expert to look over our shoulder for check and balance."

The jury had heard earlier from one of these psychiatrists, the one El-berg hadn't allowed to settle before trial. He'd said that he simply signed paperwork and had never questioned whether a patient had been inap-propriately admitted. The settlements by the others indicated that they, too, had provided no check on Newton's power.

O'Farrell then showed the jury a blue binder, larger than a Manhattan phone book, which he said was the clinical manual for KIDS. He asked Newton why he thought he was competent to treat eating disorders.

"The primary fact that gave me that idea was the fact that Overeaters Anonymous was becoming a place of refuge and help, not only for overeaters, but for anorexics and bulimics. They were finding help that they did not find in the psychiatric and medical system. . . ." Newton once again did not mention that only anecdotes, not medical research, suggested that OA was helpful for eating disorders.

O'Farrell asked about the admission process and the role that the psy-chiatrists played in it. Newton admitted that psychiatrists did not con-duct the initial examinations. "It was based on the paperwork," he said.

"Was there an active policy at KIDS to recruit siblings into the program?"

"No, we would prefer not to," Newton said. "If we had a person in the program and somebody else who was covertly using drugs or bingeing or vomiting or self-starving, we would say, you know, if the second person doesn't come in, we can't help the first one. And so we would say you've got a choice. I mean, there's no sense in us continuing to try to help the primary admission if you're supporting somebody else doing the same thing."

"Why the severity of the restrictions of phase one?" O'Farrell asked, specifically listing the belt-looping, removal from school and family, and refusal of music, TV, and phone calls.

"Let's take not living at home. I would say that when kids arrived at our program, over ninety percent of the families were in a high conflict situation. Slammed doors, things being broken, yelling and screaming, no control over the kid. . . . The young person needs a respite from that conflict to calm down . . . and begin to think and take a look at what's going on there. And that's why no living at home," he said, and he added that this allowed KIDS to "begin the process of reformatting how you communicate."

"What about school?"

"Most of the kids . . . were not functioning in school. . . . With the drug and alcohol kids, it was very simple, the stuff in their brain messed with their brain chemistry, and the first thing that's impaired is learning . . . they were failing. And the acting-out behavior was almost a way to compensate for failing in school. It was not universal, but it was overwhelmingly predominant. . . . We wanted a respite period so they would come to terms with their problem, allow the brain healing . . . so when they went back they had the potential of not failing and feeling humiliated."

O'Farrell asked how this applied to eating disorders, and Newton said that kids with eating disorders had "negative friends" with whom they would binge or purge and from whom they needed to be isolated.

"What about [disallowing] phone calls?"

Newton mentioned a KIDS patient who'd been in a facility that allowed calls who used them to arrange drugs to be brought to her.

And the belt-looping?

That was invented by an adolescent mental-health facility in Georgia. . . . It's always portrayed . . . as a horrendous control thing [but] it was really more symbolic, as a way to say, "Hey, when you were in charge of running your own life, to use AA language, when you were the higher power, you made a big mess. So we're going to keep you under supervision by somebody who's accepted their problem and doing better." And besides, when you're in treatment, you're going to go through horrendous things in terms of stuff you've done that you don't even want to think about that's causing a lot of guilt and shame in your soul. And when you do, somebody needs to be with you to understand, so that oldcomer's there.

Asked about the twelve-hour days in the blue chairs, Newton protested that there was a thirty-minute daily exercise break and said there were "mandatory bathroom breaks imposed on us by the medical people . . . and people went to the bathroom individually other times." The jury was left to wonder, not only about the contradictions between this testimony and that of other witnesses, but about why it would take a doctor to "impose" bathroom breaks and if this was an admission that, in fact, there were times when people weren't allowed to go.

"What about this 'motivation' thing?"

"I don't even want to talk about that. I never liked it . . . I tried to re-press it twice in the original Straight program and it kept coming back. And I fussed and growled with the staff about it because I think it looks weird. And I was told by the young people on staff, 'Hey, you sit in the blue chair a lot of the day and it helps really to move around a bit to get your energy up. And besides, when the new kids start to do it, we know they've stopped being cool.'" He added, "I think when you're running an adolescent program, you cannot control everything."

O'Farrell's strategy seemed to be to ask the tough questions first himself, in order to give his client the best chance of answering them calmly and coherently, before Elberg asked more probingly. He moved rapidly from one topic to the next, not getting into much detail. He'd leave that for Elberg, perhaps hoping that Newton's rationale for treatment would at least win over the two jurors needed in this situation to hang the case, or at least whittle down the settlement.

O'Farrell asked why KIDS participants had to spend so much time in group and was told that this was "healthy" and that it was "less cruel to have them involved in structured activities." "Less cruel than what?" remained an unasked and unanswered question.

"Why was it so important for the patients to be honest?"

"Self-disclosure is important in all kinds of therapies, rational emotive therapy, cognitive behavioral therapy, reality therapy, it's necessary to get an honest view of the problem. People with these kinds of problems have an enormous amount of guilt and shame. If they don't get all that stuff out, we hear, 'If you really knew how bad I was, you'd think I'm unhelpable.'"

"How did the peer counselors know how far was too far to push?"

"We put them through a twelve-to-sixteen-week course, and a big part of that was doing exercises in counseling."

"What was the purpose of a setback?"

"The primary purpose was to create a respite, to take the pressure off. It was often triggered by dishonesty or significant rule violations. It was never intended to be punitive. Sometimes young people took it that way, sometimes peer counselors, with their limits, used it that way." Newton, as he had done at Straight, tried to pin the excesses on the youths themselves.

O'Farrell asked about the restraints.

Newton testified that the KIDS procedure had been developed at Straight, implying that it had been designed in response to problems with other restraint procedures used at the time in Florida which had resulted, he said, in the deaths of "five to eight" kids in psychiatric hospitals. Straight's procedure "created maximum control with minimum possibility of injury," he claimed. Many Straight and KIDS patients would disagree with that assessment—there are numerous accounts of KIDS and Straight patients suffering serious injuries as the result of restraints—but it was true that because the procedure was done face-up, there was no risk of the accidental suffocation deaths associated with facedown restraints that have killed dozens of children in wilderness programs and psychiatric hospitals. The use of hands to pinch the mouth and nose closed, as had been done to both Lulu Corter and Leigh Bright, could have resulted in such deaths, of course, but fortunately, there is no evidence that this ever occurred.

Newton explained, "The clinical and support group staff were taught [restraint] in experiential situations." What this meant, essentially, was that they learned by doing it to others, by watching others who'd been trained by watching others who'd had no other training. He said that restraint "was never intended as a punishment," and that it was never done, in his knowledge, in reaction to a patient's not paying attention.

O'Farrell then delicately asked if people were permitted to use the bathroom while they were being restrained. "Absolutely," Newton said. "If someone needed to go to the bathroom, they were taken to the bathroom." The patients sitting on Lulu's side of the courtroom stared stonily. The judge also looked skeptical.

"Are you aware of any incidents in which restraint was applied inappropriately?"

"Yes. We had to take the privilege of restraint away from some people because they applied it too eagerly."

Newton's language choices were Orwellian: restraining others was "a privilege"; having no freedom of speech, movement, or activity was "a respite."

O'Farrell questioned him about the procedure that patients over eighteen were supposed to use if they wanted to leave. "We were not in the business of rushing people to the door," he said, with no hint of irony. "These were clearly troubled young people. We had a one-on-one and asked if they were willing to think about it for twenty-four hours. Then we had a family conference. Very few got beyond the family conference."

O'Farrell asked about "retrieving" patients over eighteen. "In the beginning, I would allow a staff member and a graduate to go, to get a kid out of a crackhouse or something. But we had several incidents where staff members did go [and physical force was used]. Somebody called me and outlined the situation [with Britta] and my blood pressure went through the ceiling. I said, 'She doesn't come back.'"

He asked why patients could not associate with family members who had left treatment. "If a kid in treatment knows from associating with someone who has walked out of sobriety or abstinence [that he is OK even though he left], he would ask, 'Why do I have to stay?'"

O'Farrell then asked about Jessica, a KIDS participant who had testified that she'd been made to bow down before Newton after she disagreed with him about the proper way to bow in the style of kung fu she practiced.

"[Jessica] testified that you humiliated her with respect to martial arts."

"She had a severe auditory processing impairment," Newton testified. "Jessica would get a distorted piece of information and would lock up and get arrogant—[so] I tried to use some other form of communication. Her particular form of kung fu martial arts had an Arabic [sort of bow] that the Shaolin monks did more humbly . . . the idea that she would bow to me at the end was something the group staff came up with, I would never ask someone to bow to me like that."

Why he accepted this suggestion, however, he didn't say.

Now O'Farrell began to question the witness about Lulu. Newton said he didn't know whether he'd known that Lulu had been abused by someone in the program prior to her admission.

"I saw no problem with admitting [both abuser and victim]," he said, causing expressions of shock among the jury and people on the right-hand side of the courtroom.

"Was Lulu told that she had to accept responsibility for being abused?"

"That's unconscionable," Newton responded, not exactly answering the question.

As soon as Elberg stood to begin his cross, Newton's face reddened. Elberg's first question seemed gentle, but it was in fact designed to undercut one of the defense's key arguments. He asked the witness how he felt when he discovered that his son had a drug problem.

"I thought my heart would break," Newton said. "I was scared, frightened, and I wanted to find someone who knows what to do."

Now Elberg began his surgery in earnest. "Did you trust that the people at Straight knew what they were doing?" he asked, implying that any parent—for example, Lulu's mother—would trust that those who claimed to be providing legitimate medical care were indeed skilled and expert at their work, and as a result, would follow their recommendations even if they seemed unusual.

"I don't think most of us have absolute trust," he replied, dodging.

Elberg parried back, saying that the Newtons had admitted in formal statements, prior to trial, that they were not experts in eating disorders and sexual disorders.

"Didn't you tell parents that you were experts?

"We claimed to be competent, not experts," he said, his face getting redder. Elberg knew that Newton hated to be wrong, hated to have to acknowledge that he was far from respected in his field, hated to be challenged. He knew that this would set up a conflict: tell the truth about his incompetence and perhaps minimize the legal consequences of his actions, or lie and save face in court.

Elberg asked a series of questions to play up this dilemma.

"Is it important to gather information before making a diagnosis?"

"Ideally."

"In theory, would it be ideal to talk to teachers, get records from the physician?"

"As much as you can," Newton conceded. But then he argued that most drug-treatment providers found such investigation impractical.

Elberg now held up a copy of Newton's book *Adolescence* (Norton, 1995), which was aimed at professionals. He showed that in the book, Newton said it was important to gather as much data as possible from as many sources as possible.

"Did you get Lulu's school records before you treated her?"

"I don't know."

"Did you get her records from her personal physician?"

"I don't know."

Elberg asked whether Newton knew why Lulu had been admitted, and the answer was the same. The attorney replayed a video he'd employed earlier: "Hey, turkey, you did it and did it and did it," said a younger Miller Newton.

He paused the tape. "You don't know what Lulu did and did—"

Newton on tape continued: "You've blown your right to be trusted by society and by your family. You're going to give up the right to live with your family and walk free on the street and go to school—"

"What gave you the right to take Lulu out of school?"

"I believe parents do have the right in most states to sign kids into programs that take them off the street. The parent made the decision.'"

Newton was now beet-red. Elberg continued, "At the time Lulu was admitted by a group of peer counselors—"

"No, a single peer counselor was assigned to admission, and two or more girls from group," Newton interrupted. He had a habit of adding irrelevant qualifications as if in hope that this would confuse the jury about the main point. But this seemed only to annoy them.

Elberg asked about the period before Lulu's admission, when her relative had been on a higher phase and therefore free to have contact with her in her neighborhood, despite having disclosed sexually abusing her. "Who was protecting Lulu when [this young man] comes home?"

"I assume her mother."

"Mrs. Corter had failed to protect her daughter [from the initial abuse]."

"First of all, it was Mrs. Corter's family and we were not in charge," said Newton, clearly annoyed.

Elberg shifted to a discussion of the possibility of people being wrongly admitted to the program.

"I think it was highly unlikely for someone to be admitted who did not have a compulsive behavior disorder. The program was too intense. People with mild problems wouldn't want to go through the trouble," he said, implying that the patients had a choice in the matter.

Elberg asked about siblings. "We did everything we could to avoid admitting siblings," Newton replied, offering no explanation for the fact that three of the four Corters, two of Ellen's three children, both Britta and her brother, and Jessica and her two siblings had all been admitted.

At this point, the judge couldn't resist jumping in. The glibness and obvious dishonesty of Newton's testimony was infuriating him. "Can you treat eating disorders on an outpatient basis?" he demanded.

"Yes."

"Was any attempt made to treat this child as an outpatient?"

"Yes, I know from memory—" Newton began, but the judge interrupted him, heading off what he knew would be another evasive answer about the KIDS sibling groups. He asked instead if she'd been treated by any other program for her overeating.

"I don't know," Newton replied.

"What outpatient treatment did she get from KIDS for her eating disorder?" Judge Gallipoli asked sharply.

"None."

"For behavior?"

"She was in sibling groups and I believe—"

At this point, O'Farrell objected. The judge immediately sent the jury out. O'Farrell said to him, "You're skeptical . . ."

"I am skeptical," Gallipoli responded sharply. "We're walking through fantasyland here, and there really comes a point when the court cannot sit here like a bump on a log and accept it."

AFTER A BREAK, the jury was brought back and Elberg continued his cross-examination. He showed a magnified image of a KIDS document. He asked Newton to read it out loud. "Lulu was sexually abused by an old man. She let him. She needs to . . ." here it was hard to tell whether the next word was "clear" or "clean" . . . "it up." Whatever the actual wording was, the meaning was quite obvious: it was documentary evidence that what Newton had called "unconscionable"—blaming a sexual-abuse victim for what had happened to her—was exactly what KIDS had done.

Elberg let that sink in, asking a few additional questions that suggested that Newton hadn't followed the state-mandated abuse-reporting laws after Lulu disclosed the names of various men she said had abused her.

Then he displayed an image of a document detailing how the relative who had admitted abusing Lulu was brought over to "help" Lulu in group. "He shouldn't have had contact with her," Newton responded.

Elberg began to press him about whether KIDS was an appropriate treatment for victims of sexual abuse. "If Lulu did not have a compulsive disorder and was a victim of sexual abuse before she attended KIDS, KIDS was not appropriate," Newton said, contradicting his own expert witness with the concession. "I could not have recommended admitting Lulu as a survivor of sexual abuse. I could have recommended it if she became sexually phobic or had begun to act in addictive ways, just like Sexaholics Anonymous and Sex and Love Addicts Anonymous."

"What methods did KIDS have for considering or evaluating a patient who is there and claimed they didn't have a behavior disorder?"

"Every intake was reviewed by semi-outside psychiatrists. That was an important check and balance," Newton said.

"Do you believe that a patient admitted to KIDS without a behavior disorder would perceive first phase as a gift?"

"Probably not," he said, showing annoyance. "I think that's common sense," he snapped.

ELBERG ASKED about the ten-year estrangement between Britta and her parents and whether they'd refused to attend her wedding because the Newtons had said Britta hadn't made sufficient amends for leaving the program.

"I don't think so," Newton said.

Elberg called on his assistant to display the next exhibit, almost weary of having to humiliate the witness again. It was a letter to Britta, on KIDS stationery, from Ruth Ann and Miller Newton, rejecting an attempt Britta had made to apologize. In twelve-step programs and in most religious groups that suggest the spiritual value of seeking forgiveness, what matters is not whether one's amends are accepted or rejected by others, but whether one tries to make them. It was hard to believe it was possible for Newton to turn an even more vivid crimson, but he did.

THERE WERE more than two dozen questions from the jurors (who are allowed to question witnesses themselves, if the queries are ruled acceptable by the judge, in New Jersey), including at least one that was inadmissible: "Why, if the program was so successful, did it close?"

The jury was allowed to ask about funding. Newton told them that his initial benefactor, the "wealthy CEO," had been Andrew McKelvey, who now owns the successful job-search site monster.com. The KIDS program had also accepted insurance and had a "sliding scale" for payment. From 1993 to 1998, Medicaid approved coverage of the program, allowing even the poorest to attend—which was part of what had allowed Lulu to stay for so long.

Another insightful question was why, if KIDS patients needed such intensive care, it was safe to keep them in host homes. "The patients we admitted were not really dangerous," Newton said. If this was true, of course, there was no reason at all for all the restraints.

The judge asked, "What percent of those who started graduated and what percent dropped out?"

"I have no idea," he said loudly, illustrating both his anger and his seeming disdain for those who had trusted him. By the end of his testimony, Newton seemed tired, wrung out, diminished. He looked older and seemed somehow smaller. He and his wife did not stick around to hear the closings or await the verdict.

O'FARRELL STARTED his closing with an air of humility, saying he wasn't going to rehash what the jury had already heard. He began:

> This has been a long, difficult and emotion-laden case. Even as I stand here, I don't really know what to make of it. It's so different from the type of case those who deal with medical malpractice frequently deal with, where patients have died or experienced permanent bodily damage, where patients experienced some sort of injury

that precludes them from functioning for the rest of their lives. Here, in contrast, we are dealing with a woman capable of living a normal life.

He described how Lulu was currently in a relationship that he hoped would work out. His air was exquisitely polite, expressing support for Lulu herself as he tried to undermine her case.

"That said, the claims she has advanced are nonetheless serious, claims which stirred our passions and incited much debate. The testimony we have heard has affected all of us, and I will not pretend otherwise," he continued, seeming by implication to have conceded much of the case.

But that was not what he had in mind. O'Farrell went on to emphasize the abuse Lulu had suffered before she was admitted to KIDS.

I hate the fact that she had a horrible childhood. I hate that she had an abusive alcoholic father who abused her mother. I hate the fact that she spent seven years being abused by three different men. I hate the fact that during those years her mother, who was herself a victim, did nothing.

I also hate the fact that once Lulu was in the program and discovered that it wasn't all fun and games, she got [frustrated]. When she discovered that the only way to progress [was to admit what she'd done wrong], she responded by acting out, by lying, by attempting to manipulate the staff and spent far more time in first and second phase.

They say that KIDS stole Lulu's adolescence . . . and even went so far as to have an expert psychiatrist offer the opinion that she was a "normal" thirteen-year-old who became abnormal by virtue of her treatment at KIDS.

How many normal thirteen-year-olds had a father who tried to smother their mother? How many normal thirteen-year-olds have been sexually abused by three men by age thirteen?

I conclude not only that Lulu Corter was not normal when she entered KIDS, but that she was already suffering from PTSD as a result of the trauma she had suffered before. I ask you, given the life she had, what type of adolescence would she have had if she had not enrolled in KIDS, how likely would it be that [the abuse would have continued]? When you consider whether KIDS "stole" Lulu's adolescence, what exactly did they steal?

Elberg sprang up to give his closing arguments. He poured scorn on O'Farrell's assertion that Lulu's adolescence was valueless and had already been ruined before she ever got to KIDS. He summarized the case succinctly, highlighting the critical facts. He described how Mrs. Corter, when she sought a medical doctor to help her son, had found instead "a predator," who, once he'd admitted one child in a family to his program, wanted more. He attacked O'Farrell's claims that Lulu had had an eating disorder, showing that again and again, the KIDS program provided the exact opposite of what someone like Lulu, a sexual-abuse victim, really needed.

"While the eating disorder was crazy, the sexual disorder part was outright cruel," he continued, and described how Ruth Ann Newton had taken a one-day class on sexual disorders just before Lulu's diagnosis. He said that Lulu became her guinea pig: "Lulu who never had a date, Lulu who had never had [consensual] sex."

Elberg went through the chronology of Lulu's thirteen years at KIDS, using charts to show the lengthy periods that she was on first and second phases. He dismissed O'Farrell's claims that St. Clare's Hospital correctly diagnosed the real source of Lulu's problems.

What nonsense! St. Clare's had no chance. For one, Lulu would have had to break the rules to tell. Second, if she told, would they have believed her? If you wrote her story as fiction, you couldn't sell it because no one would believe it, it's that incredible.

Why did it happen? The first victim was Mrs. Corter. In every case, what got people into KIDS was fear. These weren't parents trying to get rid of their kids—it was the opposite. These were parents looking for help.

Who were the Newtons? Why did they do it? What was their real
agenda?" It wasn't about treating drug abuse . . . it was about control.

Only a desire for absolute power could explain bizarre policies like
having to bow down to Miller Newton or prescribing the number of
times a person could wipe herself on the toilet, Elberg went on. Only a
need for total control could explain why paid staff could be made back
into patients who would then need replacement as well as free treatment, presumably at the cost of a loss of income for that treatment slot
and a loss of employee expertise for the program.

"It was clearly about the desire to control every aspect of their victims'
lives," Elberg said. "Is that brainwashing? I leave that for you to decide.
What it was, was a horror."

He then began to ask for compensation. Under New Jersey law, he
wasn't allowed to ask for a particular dollar amount—and the jury was
given no guidelines on how to determine what Lulu's settlement should
be other than that it be "fair, just, and reasonable."

"It seems strange now to talk about money," Elberg continued. He said
he felt as though he really should be in a criminal court, asking for incarceration of the perpetrators, but that civil justice was the only arena
now open to Lulu.

He began a rhythmic, almost hypnotic litany. In a strong, loud voice,
he said:

It's time to pay fair, just and reasonable compensation, it's time to
pay Lulu for every minute of every hour of every day that she sat in
those chairs.

It's time to pay Lulu for every minute of every hour of every day
she was restrained on the floor.

It's time to pay Lulu for every time she was made to restrain others, for every day spent in solitary confinement.

It's time to pay Lulu for the indignity of being watched in the
bathroom and every time told the number of times she could wipe.

It's time to pay Lulu for being deprived of an education, for being deprived of the prom, for being deprived of the first date, and for every step she took while belt-looped, and for each of the things you remember that I haven't mentioned.

We only get a few chances in life to do something important, and when you do something like that, it's important to do it with a sense of responsibility and honor. . . . A few years ago, Lulu came to me and asked me to tell her story. For the last three years I have tried to understand how anybody could have done to another human being what was done to Lulu.

Lulu began to sob quietly.

Over the three weeks of this trial, I had the responsibility to tell the truth. And that has been transferred gradually from me to you. I have done everything I could to tell Lulu's story. The responsibility for speaking clearly, loudly, and unmistakably for what's fair and just is now yours. I have no doubt you will do what's right.

The jurors all seemed eager to deliberate—some were actually squirming in their seats as the judge instructed them. They were asked to answer two main questions: first, whether the treatment Lulu had received was in accordance with accepted standards of medical care, and second, if they determined it was negligent, if it was the cause of her injuries. If the answers to both were yes, they were to decide on damages.

They were told that the program didn't have to be the sole cause of harm to the plaintiff; only that if it was deemed negligent, if the treatment provided could have been reasonably expected to do damage. The jury was precluded from imposing punitive damages because with Newton in bankruptcy, Elberg had decided not to pursue them.

The judge gave the jury some very broad guidelines on the life expectancy of a plaintiff Lulu's age and said they should consider the duration of the period in which she sustained the injury and her past, present, and future suffering that could result. He told them that the verdict didn't have to be unanimous: only seven had to agree for a verdict to be accepted. Then, they were sent off to deliberate, and the attorneys and Lulu and her supporters were left to pace the hallways.

Waiting is often the hardest part for attorneys—in many cases, there is nothing more that they can do for their clients, and they tend not to like this lack of control. But Medvin and Elberg had an additional dilemma as the jury began to deliberate: that morning, O'Farrell had upped his settlement offer. They were unsure whether the jury would top it or whether they should just accept the figure and make Lulu a very wealthy woman.

After a few hours, there was a stir from the courtroom. It turned out that the jury had asked the judge if they could go on to the second question without being unanimous on the first. This was a bizarre and illogical request: if KIDS hadn't been negligent, there was no reason for them to consider whether it had harmed her. Also, the judge had said that they didn't have to be unanimous, only that seven had to agree. He reminded them of both these facts and sent them back to their deliberations.

Now Medvin and Elberg became anxious. How could even one juror think that KIDS wasn't negligent? Maybe the case hadn't gone as well as they'd thought. Maybe they'd better accept the settlement.

Lulu, as was her nature, had come to trust Elberg completely, and this made him feel even more responsible for advising her well. The judge had cautioned him that he was clearly very personally involved in the case and that he needed to be sure he considered his client's needs first. Most civil cases do not go to trial: Elberg had ensured that this one would by refusing to give the defendants a number in advance of trial about what amount of damages he would accept. He'd done this to ensure that Lulu's story would be told in court, so that it would be put on the record. He told the defense attorneys that his number was so high he felt that they'd be insulted if he started out with that demand.

The juror question turned him around, and he decided not to gamble and to accept the considerable settlement. Moments later, the jury returned its verdict.

"Here's the reality," the judge said with a poker face to the two lawyers, "one person here is making a very big mistake."

It turned out that the jury verdict was $2.5 million, substantially less than the $6.5 million Lulu would eventually receive from O'Farrell's settlement offer and the psychiatrists' insurers. One of the jurors later told me that the $2.5 million figure was arrived at by calculating $100,000 per year for her life expectancy—however, that would actually come to $4.3 million if the math had been done correctly. The amount the jurors said they wanted to give to her, if their math had been right, turned out to be very close to what she received in the end. But if she'd accepted their verdict, error—or some other adjustment the jurors had made for unclear reasons—would have deprived her of some $2 million.

All but one of the jurors had agreed immediately that KIDS was negligent. The holdout blamed Lulu's mother for her problems. He was the one who'd prompted the question to the judge that made Elberg accept the settlement. But after some strong arguments from "Shakespeare" and others, he relented and agreed to discuss the cash settlement. During their deliberations, all the jurors ultimately agreed that KIDS was more a cult than a clinic—and that such treatment had no place in a health-care system.

Lulu cried as she agreed to accept the settlement. Elberg said to her giddily, "We did so good. We told your story and we won." Lulu looked delighted and Elberg reassured her that he'd protect her from those who might seek to take advantage of her again, this time to get her money.

But who will protect other teens from suffering Lulu's fate in today's programs? And why—although these organizations have paid out millions of dollars in damages for proven violent and sexual crimes against children and are continuing to do so as groups fade and reemerge under new names—are their former employees free to continue to work with youth? Why don't people like Miller Newton ever go to prison? Will we see similar trials targeting WWASP and today's other tough love programs in coming decades, as the damage done becomes more visible? What harm are we really doing to the kids who undergo such treatment—and what can be done to stop it? And how can those teens who really do need help get treatment, not torture?[4]

NINE

The End of
Tough Love?

SINCE SYNANON, tough love has dominated long-term residential programs for both misbehaving teenagers and for drug-addicted adults. And despite Lulu Corter's victory and Richard Bradbury's decades of anti-Straight activism, if Miller Newton wanted to open another teen program tomorrow, he could. WWASP still has at least seven programs operating (Academy at Ivy Ridge, Tranquility Bay, Midwest Academy, Carolina Springs Academy, Spring Creek Lodge, Cross Creek Programs, and Majestic Ranch Academy). It is the largest organization in the industry. There are literally hundreds of other abusive tough love organizations, including tough wilderness programs, boot camps, behavior modification, residential treatment, and emotional growth schools. Some still employ the people involved in boot camp deaths like that of Aaron Bacon. Others—including mainstream, licensed programs— employ ex-Straight program staff. At least six exact-replica Straight programs are up and running. Laurie Berg, Richard Bradbury, Cathy Sutton, and the other activists still have huge battles ahead of them.

The obvious, outward consequences of these programs' abuse can be seen throughout this book. Aaron Bacon, Michelle Sutton, Kristen Chase, and at least several dozen others lost their lives to it. Paul Richards was cut off from his family, as were Fred Collins, Britta, Lulu Corter, Jessica, and so many others. Some lost touch for many years; others became permanently estranged. Every single one of the teens whose stories were told here lost out on many aspects of normal adolescence.

Online, hundreds of unique posts with confirmed contact information detail abuses at WWASP, Straight, KIDS, North Star, and other programs like them—on websites varying from those put up by program opponents, to general news sites, to those run by educational consultants for parents looking to place kids. I personally contacted roughly a hundred former participants and parents who told stories similar to those I included in the book. I could have contacted hundreds more, and mainstream media accounts are full of yet more such stories. There are several other chains of programs, including a number of linked Christian schools, which have the same kinds of patterns of abuses I documented here and could fill an equally long book with equally disturbing accounts. But regardless of the pervasiveness of abuse in the industry, the fact that some of its biggest players have been documented for decades engaging in unethical and brutal practices means that greater oversight is clearly necessary.

University of California sociologist Elliott Currie called programs like WWASP "the tip of the iceberg" in his recent book on troubled middle class teens, *The Road to Whatever: Middle Class Culture and the Crisis of Adolescence* (Metropolitan Books, 2004). He interviewed dozens of troubled teens, including those involved in a large federal study of mainstream teen addiction treatment. He writes:

> The treatment programs my interviewees encountered often seemed to equate treatment with the enforcement of obedience. They were shot through with arbitrary and sometimes confusing rules and relied heavily on a variety of highly public, ritualized punishments. . . .

The operating principles—enforced silence instead of open and honest dialogue, exclusion rather than inclusion in time of need, isolation and shaming rather than understanding and firm guidance—appeared to be unquestioningly accepted in agency after agency. Indeed, the degree to which an emphasis on punishment dominated the inner culture of many "helping" programs bordered on bizarre . . . the discipline meted out in many of the agencies encountered by teenagers was often explicitly designed to demean and humiliate them.[1]

Anecdotes regarding positive experiences with tough love programs also abound, of course—but without controlled studies, one cannot know which experience is more common; whether positive changes have actually occurred or are just perceived, and whether such effects can be attributed to the program or to simple maturation. The acceptance of such stories as evidence of effectiveness does a great disservice to parents and children who need help with behavioral problems.

A large proportion of the former participants I spoke with for this book or read about during my research suffer post-traumatic stress disorder. PTSD is not a normal consequence of adolescent misbehavior. It does not occur in the absence of trauma, and few middle-class kids ever experience anything as likely to cause sustained trauma (aside from child abuse) as these programs are, even in the course of genuine addiction. The atmosphere in the programs—in which emotional attacks are unrelenting, privacy is nonexistent, sleep and food deprivation are common, and the person has little if any control over his environment—is exactly the type that research has found most likely to produce PTSD.

The more researchers learn, in fact, the greater the evidence becomes that being put in any kind of situation of total powerlessness for a significant length of time has the capacity to produce lasting damage to the brain's stress system, especially when it happens to a young person. This damage has been linked not only to PTSD, but to increased risk for depression, addiction, other mental illnesses, and even immune-system disorders and cancer[2]—not exactly the kind of results parents seek from treatment that is supposed to help kids with emotional problems. The more scientists study the brain, the more clear it becomes that such treatment is the exact opposite of what most troubled teens need.

Further, records obtained by Phil Elberg show that roughly 1,000 teens entered the KIDS program in New Jersey—but only between sixty and seventy graduated. Elberg says that the graduates, who spent the longest time in the program, almost universally did far worse afterward than those who'd spent a shorter time in KIDS. This was especially true for those like Lulu, who were diagnosed with nebulous "behavioral" problems and did not have a great deal of preprogram misbehavior to confess and show "progress" in overcoming. Dozens of former Straight and KIDS participants are known to have committed suicide; almost every participant I spoke with reported periods of serious depression. One woman told me she had a shotgun in her mouth before deciding she could not give Miller Newton "the satisfaction" of having driven her to suicide. Given the fact that the programs clearly admitted many people like Richard Bradbury, Paul Richards, Lulu Corter, and Fred Collins, who had neither diagnosable drug problems nor psychiatric disorders at intake, this appears to be disproportionate.

Other suggestions of harm come from the fact that many people entered KIDS without serious problems but went on after they left to participate in serious "binges" of the behavior for which they had supposedly been treated. Britta, for example, who was told she had a drug problem because of her marijuana use and college drinking, began using cocaine only after treatment and rapidly spun out of control. Lulu, who had been only slightly heavy when she entered KIDS, went up to 265 pounds for a time. Ellen's daughter Amy, who hadn't even tried drugs prior to KIDS, became a heroin addict afterward. A majority of the former participants from KIDS and the other programs whom I interviewed said they experienced at least one period of heavy drug use or compulsive behavior related to the disorder they'd been told they had after they left the program. Even Kyrsten Bean, who believes that Tranquility Bay was beneficial for her in some ways, had this experience.

Of course, one might argue that this suggests that they were properly diagnosed and then relapsed, as most addicts do at least once—but if they went into a program with no prior evidence of addiction or compulsive behavior, left it, and then engaged heavily in such activities for significant periods of time, the program certainly didn't help them. It either made preexisting conditions worse or exacerbated, possibly even caused, new disorders.

Real research would be helpful to determine the extent of this damage and how common it is, but there is enough data already to suggest that the risks of tough love programs outweigh any potential benefits, at least as long as it cannot be proven superior to other approaches, even for a particular subgroup. This is especially true given the well-documented tendency of most teenagers to outgrow their bad behavior, the research showing that there are effective alternatives—and the data suggesting that grouping troubled kids together makes them worse.

Further, just imagine being awakened by strangers at three A.M., taken from the place you see as your safest haven—the bedroom in your family home—and taken in handcuffs to an unknown, unfriendly, inescapable place. People who are kidnapped even for short periods of time can be severely traumatized. Young people are even more likely to be harmed by such abductions—and yet tough love programs seem to have no concern for how this method of transport alone might hurt kids. Certainly, no one has ever studied it. Kids report simply being thrown into the program's daily activities with no opportunity to process what has happened. Their perfectly rational anger, hurt, and desire to escape are framed as pathological "denial," which must be broken down until they reach "acceptance" and come to praise their captors and keepers.

These programs also produce more subtle damage in addition to overt problems like PTSD, estrangements, and suicide. By making love conditional, tough love undermines familial affection, removing the one refuge where people can ordinarily assume they are loved for who they are, not what they do. Love becomes a tool, used in an attempt to change someone else's behavior. Tough love providers may accuse their teenage participants of manipulation, but deliberately using love and the possibility of its withdrawal to control people seems to me to be the ultimate in manipulative behavior.

Tough love programs are also structured in a way that ignores the developmental challenges of adolescence. During the teen years, children are supposed to become more independent, to test limits. They are primed to begin to separate, and to question everything. Because of their stage of brain development, they do not have highly developed judgment and decision-making skills. Says Aaron White, an assistant research professor of psychiatry at Duke University,

> Adolescents should take risks and experiment. Every generation does things that adults think are too rebellious. By definition, that's what adolescents do. It's a transition from depending on caregivers to becoming a caregiver. Evolution has given us a whole set of wedges that very naturally separate us from our caregivers. They push away, we push away from them, and it gets them out into the rest of the world.

But tough love programs impose greater restrictions and limits than most parents would set for grade-schoolers. Such a developmentally mistimed intervention is unlikely to foster healthy familial connections and emotional growth, even if the child complies.

Moreover, the education that teenagers receive in tough love institutions, if they receive any at all, is far inferior to what's available in ordinary schools. In the Straight and Straight-descendant programs like KIDS, of course, teens receive no education at all for however long the program keeps them in first or second phase. Boot camp wilderness programs like North Star do not provide education or qualified teachers and often run for several months if not longer. Most of the WWASP programs—especially those located outside the U.S.—have few or no qualified teachers. Teens kept in isolation or "worksheets" punishment can be denied education indefinitely.

While WWASP's educational program is accredited by the Northwest

Association of Accredited Schools as a "special purpose school," accreditation by this group relies primarily on self-reporting by schools of their teachers' qualifications and school policies. New York State Education Department officials have already told the press that diplomas from WWASP's Academy at Ivy Ridge "are not New York State high school diplomas . . . [they are diplomas] without any sanction from the state."[3] Some parents report difficulty getting high schools and colleges to accept WWASP school program credits.

Further, in order to afford the programs' high costs, many parents spend their teens' college funds on tough love. A sickening irony is that research has found that having a college education reduces the odds of long-term addiction by reducing the odds of unemployment.[4] Putting college further out of reach is yet another way these programs can exacerbate the problems they are supposed to treat.

Also, for teens in these programs, there are no opportunities to begin to explore romantic relationships: contact with the opposite sex, let alone dating, is barely allowed. Friendships are impoverished by the constant pressure to "turn in" one's fellows for misbehavior, and the depth of the betrayal that can result when secrets disclosed in confidence are used to advance a "friend" at your expense. Tough love participants are left behind to play catch-up in almost every life area. They are also socialized to behave in ways that aren't conducive to relational health. For example, as Kyrsten Bean described it, the WWASP program made her so hard on her friends that they became afraid to turn to her when in crisis because she was so judgmental and blunt. In the outside world, most people don't believe that it is appropriate or helpful to prod people in their emotional sore spots—but tough love participants are taught that this is an act of love for which they should be thanked.

Years after Straight, KIDS, North Star, WWASP—even if kids were compliant with the rules of the programs, even if they believed at the time that they needed help—damage to relationships is sustained. Almost all of the former teen participants I interviewed still felt hurt by what had been done to them; many were still upset decades later. Even those who accepted that their parents didn't know about the abuse had this problem. Many, many families have still not reconciled and continue to refuse to have any contact with one another. Most have great difficulty restoring trust. Some cope by simply agreeing never to speak of it again, leaving lingering anger.

The staffing of these programs is another area of concern: institutions that serve children, by their very nature, will always attract pedophiles. Those which encourage parents to ignore claims of abuse, which do not do criminal background checks and are under little government oversight, are certain to be magnets for them. Regarding unregulated youth programs, Utah regulator Ken Stettler told a reporter, "If I were a child molester and wanted to get in a situation where I have access to kids, this is perfect."[5] Convicted sex offenders are known to have worked at Straight[6] and North Star.[7] One of Lulu's abusers was a participant at KIDS, and there have been reports of sexual abuse in the host homes at several Straight sites and those of many of its descendants.[8] A WWASP director was charged with sexual abuse in 2002 (the charges were dropped after the two girls involved recanted, but the prosecutor made the dismissal conditional on the director having no future contact with teens in his program).[9] KIDS,[10] Straight, WWASP,[11] and North Star[12] staffers have also been convicted of violent crimes (mainly assault) against teens in their care while on the job.

While there undoubtedly are some well-intentioned, idealistic, caring people who staff some tough love programs, the atmosphere of fear and the programs' very structure continually discourages genuine affection and truly therapeutic relationships. The setup inherently encourages abusive use of power because there is no oversight, because inflicting pain is viewed as "helping," and because the people at the top can never be wrong. As Philip Zimbardo found when he had volunteers play prisoners and guards in his famous Stanford prison experiment, those roles can become so powerful that they overcome individual values and common decency.

When love is commodified as it is in these programs, when it is treated as just another tool, it loses its essence. Though tough love providers claim to be fighting consumerism and modern decadence by putting kids through character-building ordeals, instrumentalizing love as a reward for the well-behaved instead reinforces a consumerist perspective. Here, love is something to be traded, something to be paid for, to be given for good performance. It becomes exchangeable, not something God-given or a blood tie that transcends immediate displeasure or conflict.

The extreme toughness of tough love also presents another major problem: its ideology is essentially antisocial. The message presented by every tough love program in this book is that hurting others "helps" them, and that empathy and sympathy are weaknesses. At Straight and KIDS, defending someone who was being confronted or comforting them afterward was "enabling" them to stay "in denial" about their problems. At North Star, sharing food with a starving person was allowing him to avoid the "natural consequences" of his actions.

Further, in online dialogues between teens who believe the programs have helped them and those who found them hurtful, program supporters invariably blame the opponents for bringing pain on themselves by not complying or for exaggerating their hurt. They are told to "get over it," and are dismissed as whiners, losers, and complainers, who couldn't cut it and now want to evade responsibility. The idea that some kids could be naturally more sensitive than others and thus at greater risk from confrontational approaches is rejected out of hand. If it didn't help, it wasn't the program's fault; it was the kids' fault. Individual differences are a problem to be solved with conformity, not something to celebrate or even accept.

Tough love's embrace of a philosophy of "total personal responsibility" is ironically used by the programs as a way to avoid their own culpability in their brutal treatment of participants. Groups like WWASP claim that people are responsible for everything that ever happens to them. By extension then, their teen victims have chosen to be in the program even if they were brought in and held by force. Whatever the program does to them is what they really wanted to happen. Every rape victim here is "asking for it"—and no perpetrator, conveniently, has any responsibility. In KIDS, Straight, and WWASP, rape victims and those who had been sexually abused were actually told that what happened to them was their fault.

And WWASP openly claims in its seminars that "there is no right or wrong, only what works and what doesn't." This is unquestionably a sociopathic ideology: it means that people are morally justified in doing whatever they believe "works" and that they aren't responsible for the harm this may cause to others, because those others' own choices put them in whatever situation they now find themselves. While many of the other programs are less obvious about presenting these ideas, they all teach that the ends justify the means and that altruism is foolish. This is not a lesson that most parents usually intend to impart.

The similarities between the exercises in sexual humiliation, food deprivation, sleep deprivation, and stress positions used by these programs and the American human rights abuses we are currently seeing in Iraq, Guantánamo Bay, and elsewhere are also not coincidental, I believe. They derive from the same kind of morality, the same desensitization to the suffering of others, and the same belief that there is no possibility of error when the "good guys" have positive goals. Of course, tough love programs don't usually go to anywhere near such extremes—but do we really want to train potentially antisocial kids to be less empathetic, to see altruism as despicable "enabling"? Do we really want to teach them how to find the emotional sore spots of others and poke them, "for their own good"? Can we really be surprised if people put through these kinds of ordeals grow up to believe that torture is an acceptable part of justice?

I BELIEVE that the ultimate tragedy here is that we already have far better treatment alternatives for most of the kids who wind up in tough love programs. For one, though again no real data is available, from the claims made by the schools themselves and from my interviews with numerous teens and parents, it is my impression that the vast majority of teens sent to these programs do not have problems serious enough to require residential care at all. It seems that more than half of those sent to these programs had either never used alcohol or other drugs at all, or had patterns of the kinds of nonhabitual drinking or marijuana-smoking that typically end without treatment. For example, Chaffin Pullan, associate director of WWASP's Spring Creek Lodge, told the *New York Times* that only 25 percent of the teens he sees are serious drug users, "about 70 percent are not hard core—they [just] cannot communicate at home."[13] WWASP claims it won't even admit intravenous drug users, for whom the best case can be made *for* residential treatment.[14]

Research shows that there are effective methods for coping with ordinary teen rebellion, marijuana use, and drinking without residential care. For one, the evidence is clear that with no professional intervention at all beyond simple parental care, most kids simply grow out of these behaviors. Even among the worst "stoners" and "burnouts," the majority become productive workers and family members by their mid-twenties. Those with less severe problems are even more likely to get better rapidly without invasive treatment. A supportive family, a middle-class socioeconomic status, and a college education are all linked to the best outcomes for people with any kind of drug involvement.

It's hard to comprehend just how oversold the need for tough love programs really is. But government statistics show that:

- Murders of teens ages fifteen to nineteen are down 47 percent since their peak in 1995.[15]
- Violent crime in schools dropped 50 percent between 1992 and 2002.[16]
- Suicides of youth ages fifteen to nineteen are down 29 percent since peaking in 1990.[17]
- Teen drug use peaked in 1981 when 52 percent of high school seniors reported having taken an illegal drug in the last year. In 2004, only 39 percent did so—a 25 percent drop.[18]
- Drunk-driving deaths among sixteen- and seventeen-year-olds are down 60 percent since 1982.[19]
- Teen pregnancy is down 25 percent since peaking in 1990.[20]
- The number of teens with more than four sexual partners dropped by 23 percent between 1991 and 2003, according to the federal Centers for Disease Control and Prevention.[21]
- Abortion rates for teens are down 40 percent since 1990.[22]

And the overall death rate among teens and those in their early twenties has fallen nearly 40 percent since 1950.[23] Given this, chances are good that most kids are all right without intervention. When young doctors first begin to see patients, one of the key advisories they are given is, "Don't just do something, *stand there!*" When interventions can harm, waiting and determining the best approach for the particular situation can save minds and lives. Doing the wrong thing is often far worse than doing nothing—especially when the natural tendency is toward recovery and the wrong approach can derail it by destructively labeling kids as lifelong deviants, grouping them together and blocking educational opportunities. Figuring that "it can't hurt" to intervene "before it gets worse," is an error that many parents who resort to tough love regret forever. Not sending a child away doesn't mean standing by and ignoring bad behavior, of course—it means doing what will be most likely to help with the least possibility of damage.

The vast majority of teens will benefit most from effective parental discipline and adding outpatient professional help as needed: genuine drug treatment for drug problems, counseling and family therapy for behavioral problems, and psychiatric care for depression and other serious mental illnesses. "Cognitive-behavioral therapy" (for the whole family or the individual teen), "motivational interviewing," and education in coping and relapse-prevention skills are effective for drug problems. "Multisystemic" and "functional" family therapy are effective for both drug and other behavioral problems. In only the most severe cases is inpatient treatment needed, and usually only for brief periods.

If you are a parent who suspects that your teen may be headed for trouble, or if you have a teen who already has serious problems, please see the Appendix for information and more details on effective alternatives for teens with drug problems, behavior disorders, and/or mental illness, and for questions to ask to find the best care for them.

Unfortunately, despite growing knowledge about what works and what doesn't, despite the existence of evidence-based alternatives, the best treatments for teens are incredibly hard to find—as the ongoing popularity of programs like WWASP might suggest. People who present themselves as experts often don't know the research, and those who should be calming parents down and helping them avoid undue panic often escalate their fears instead in order to sell their own programs. Medicine has long had a problem with teaching doctors to change techniques to reflect advances in science—but nowhere is this more extreme than in mental health. And in psychology and psychiatry, nowhere is this problem worse than in dealing with addictions and behavior problems.

There is a massive systemic problem in mental health care and behavioral treatments for young people: what works isn't what is sold, and what is sold isn't what works. There is no evidence to favor long-term residential programs of any kind for most teen problems—and yet they are a multibillion-dollar industry.

Simultaneously, there is a shortage of child psychiatrists so severe that there are only 6,300 in the entire United States—but an estimated 30,000 are needed.[24] Residential psychiatric care is so rare and so expensive that each night, according to a report prepared for Congress, some 2,000 teens with mental illness and severe behavior problems—neither charged with nor convicted of any crime—sit in juvenile prison awaiting treatment. These teens make up at least 7 percent of the juvenile prison population.[25] Some are homeless, some are from foster homes, but others have been deliberately turned over to the state by working families who cannot access treatment in any other way. A study by the National Alliance for the Mentally Ill found that 20 percent of families with seriously mentally ill children had been forced to give up custody to the state in order to access treatment.[26]

Further, approaches like multisystemic family therapy, motivational interviewing, and cognitive behavioral therapies (see the Appendix for details)—which are actually cheaper than long-term residential care and which have repeatedly been demonstrated to be effective and safe in the most severe cases—are largely unavailable. Worse, parents have no way of easily finding evidence-based treatments—or of even knowing that what providers offer isn't required to be proven safe or effective. It's hard to imagine that in a world of high-tech medical care, much of psychology and addiction treatment is based on little more than anecdote, but unfortunately, it's true. In fact, researchers have often found that the treatments most often provided are the most likely to be harmful and ineffective—and vice versa. While the situation is beginning to improve, the problem is still so bad that the NIH, the Robert Wood Johnson Foundation, and the Substance Abuse and Mental Health Services Administration are spending millions to attempt to encourage providers to use better tactics.

To complicate matters even further, some therapists claim to use evidence-based methods like "cognitive behavioral" and "motivational interviewing" treatments but don't actually practice them. Because there are so many seemingly different treatment options even among residential programs, and because there's no objective research to guide parents in making choices about them, an entire industry has sprung up that claims to offer professional guidance.

These "educational consultants" present an additional set of problems. Some are former (or even current!) employees of tough love programs and believe in their methods based on this work. Many have little training beyond their own experience as parents of troubled teens or as former program employees. Some take kickbacks from programs for referrals but do not disclose them to parents. Like many involved in running these programs, often these consultants are not licensed professionals of any kind. There's no regulatory oversight—anyone can call him- or herself an educational consultant. While some can be extremely helpful, and one group, the Independent Educational Consultants Association, has set up a code of ethics that it requires its members to follow, this is policed by the honor system.

Industry groups like the Outdoor Behavioral Health Industry Council (OBHIC) and the National Association of Therapeutic Schools and Programs (NATSAP) have also developed ethical standards and defend the practices of their members. But membership in these groups is voluntary (WWASP—the biggest player in the business—is not a member, for example), and supervision of compliance is based on the programs' self-reports.[27]

But beyond the lack of oversight and the lack of information about effective alternatives, there are even more reasons why these programs have thrived and remained underregulated. Some are practical: when a program calls itself a "school," for example, it is regulated differently from how a "residential treatment center" is regulated. A diagnosis isn't necessary to be sent to a boarding or military school. Another issue is that many programs are located outside the U.S. but aimed at American parents and teens. The U.S. doesn't have jurisdiction over these. Wilderness programs pose special problems for regulators, too—even if legislation requires it, it's hard to do a surprise inspection if you have to first ask program operators where the kids will be. Like North Star, they might claim to be kind and gentle but turn out to be anything but.

In addition to these practical issues, there are larger cultural reasons for the persistence of tough love. Tough love programs have played to parents' concerns about the medicalization of bad behavior, dismissing the complexity of the debate and offering a one-size-fits-all solution. By lumping all teen problems together as problems of discipline that can be sorted out only by such rigid tactics, tough love programs deny the multiplicity of teen problems and the need for a variety of solutions. Not all "bratty" kids have oppositional-defiant disorder—but not all oppositional-defiant disorder is just "brattiness." Just because depression, attention-deficit disorder, and bipolar disorder are overdiagnosed by some psychiatrists doesn't mean that some teens don't genuinely suffer from them. Applying the same treatment to someone who mouths off to Mom and someone who stays up for days manically shouting is just as wrongheaded as seeing all teen rebellion as mental illness. Yet this is exactly what these programs do.

We have made the attachment of a medical label to a problem a condition of having modern science study and find effective treatments for it; certainly this is true if we want insurance to cover it. But alternatives that forgo diagnostic "labels," like tough love programs, carry all the risks that medical treatment does—and more. These include undertreatment of severe problems and overtreatment of mild ones. They include the use of harmful and ineffective methods. They even include the problem of labeling—because sending a child to a program that sees all of its participants as manipulative, selfish liars labels her as much as saying she's "oppositional defiant" does. It does so either implicitly, by the repeated reinforcement of the idea that she belongs there and deserves the punishment meted out to her, or explicitly, by calling her names and using tactics like making her wear demeaning signs and outfits.

In contrast, while psychiatry labels and pathologizes, its basis in science at least limits use of harmful and ineffective approaches. Diagnosis and evaluation at least limit under- and overtreatment; the very existence of these processes also make it explicit that one size doesn't fit all. Medicine at least attempts to treat its participants with dignity and respect; it at least recognizes the problem of stigma. "Poor bedside manner"—i.e., treating people arrogantly, high-handedly, and without regard for their feelings—is seen as a problem, not a solution, for people who are ill. Practicing medicine that harms patients leaves the practitioner vulnerable to expensive malpractice judgments—and medical practitioners must be licensed. Their licensure can be withdrawn if they do not meet required standards. All of this provides serious checks that tough love treatments just don't have.

To bring about the strict regulation that would make treatment programs safer and more effective, however, parents need to build a political constituency on both the left and right to support better behavioral health and mental health care for kids. Groups like the International Survivors Action Committee (www.isaccorp.org), which was started by former Straight participants and provides information online about problem programs and help for parents, are beginning to raise awareness, but they need more funding and more support. Concerned parents and activists also need to build coalitions with larger groups like the National Alliance for the Mentally Ill and the Children's Defense Fund in order to get the issue on the map. Traditional advocates for youth have typically focused on state institutions or private ones used by the state for poor children; traditional advocates for the mentally ill have focused on improving licensed mental health care. Human rights advocates have also tended to highlight abuses in state-run or state-financed institutions, not private ones—and have focused on state and political use of torture on adults. Although recently, advocates for the mentally ill have begun to include people with addictions under their umbrella, in the past, they have tried to distance themselves from drug issues for fear of being even further stigmatized. Tough love programs and the kids they harm have been allowed to fall through the cracks as a result—not only by states and the federal government, but by the advocacy groups that would normally have spoken up for them.

Fighting for better insurance coverage of mental health care isn't enough: some of the worst abuses in psychiatric care have occurred when there was too much insurance coverage, not too little. Research has found a near-perfect correlation between length of stay in teen mental health treatment and the maximum of the child's insurance coverage— a correlation that holds regardless of the severity of the diagnosed condition.[28] In other words, no matter how sick or healthy a teen is, his insurance, not his symptoms, determines how much inpatient care he will get. What troubled kids need is effective, evidence-based care—not insurance coverage for unproven programs. So advocates need to tell the industry that they will support more funding if, and only if, the industry provides care it can scientifically demonstrate to be safe and effective. Otherwise, the industry will simply become bigger and better-funded— not more helpful.

I believe—and I think the evidence in this book supports the necessity of this—that the federal government should mandate that behavioral treatments for kids be proven safe and effective before they can be sold. Research shouldn't come after the fact—it should be done first. If a technique is strong enough to do good, it's strong enough to do harm—so we need to know, before it's widely practiced, how to minimize potentially negative outcomes. Just as drugs have to pass the FDA before being marketed, children's programs should have to be approved by an independent research-based agency that would determine that the tactics used are, at the very least, not damaging before they can be widely adopted. Then the programs should be monitored by the states and regulated like other medical facilities.

Such an agency could also help to inform parents about what research finds effective and what it doesn't support. This alone certainly wouldn't stamp out abuse—which continues to reappear from time to time even in psychiatric facilities and other institutions that explicitly bar most abusive tactics. At least, however, when people know about what the data supports and what it doesn't, providers can't justify abuse as a treatment method. Well-intentioned professionals like Amberly Chirolla (née Knight) couldn't be as easily misled about what methods are and are not appropriate. Treatment seekers, professionals, and people who worked in the field would have no excuse for not knowing that attack therapy is both potentially harmful and demonstrably less effective than empathetic approaches. And by its very existence, the agency would show that as in the rest of medicine, anecdotes are not enough to prove that something works.

A federal law that might face less opposition would be one that requires an evaluation by an independent, non-program-affiliated, licensed professional before residential placement is allowed. These professionals would determine whether residential treatment was appropriate based on diagnosis, evaluation of the family situation, and whether all other options had first been exhausted. Just as in other areas of medicine, less-intensive procedures would have to be tried before risky, invasive approaches would even be considered, except in the most extreme cases. This law could also include the requirement that teens must be able to appeal indefinite commitments, and such appeals could be reviewed by the same independent professionals on a regular basis.

Right now, the Interstate Compact on the Placement of Children (ICPC) regulates program placements in which a child is moved from one state to another. It is supposed to apply even when parents choose to place a child out of state themselves—not just when government agencies do so. Requirements vary from state to state, and enforcement seems rare. In practice, all it seems to do is add to the paperwork load of parents, programs, and bureaucrats. Certainly, none of the parents I interviewed who placed kids in harmful, unlicensed out-of-state programs reported any obstacles to placement imposed by ICPC. The compact is

currently being rewritten—but the recommendations for changes include suggestions to loosen the control over placements by parents, not
tighten them. And, as a compact, it is not federal law.

A federal law should replace this and require independent evaluation
of any teen being placed in any lockdown residential program, with significant and onerous penalties imposed on programs that don't comply.
Another crucial reform would be a federal mandate that kids in all residential programs must have unmonitored access to an abuse hotline that
would trigger immediate investigation. Tougher enforcement of existing
state regulations—and state oversight of all programs aimed at "troubled
teens" no matter what they are called—would also help. Definitions
of these programs must be strictly written into the regulations so that
programs cannot avoid oversight by labeling themselves as "schools." If
they advertise as residential "programs" for troubled teens, have a rigid
behavior-modification system, and require participation in "emotional
growth" groups or seminars, they should be at least as regulated as
psychiatry.

Further, the use of restraint and isolation should be eliminated in all
programs which do not have qualified, on-site 24/7 psychiatric staff, and
even then must be tightly regulated. Even the toughest addiction treatment programs like Phoenix House and Daytop, which were both originally based on Synanon and are now the largest addiction treatment
providers for both adults and adolescents in the U.S., do not use restraint
or isolation. And this is despite the fact that the population they serve is
made up of far more violent, state-subsidized and court-mandated teens
than those admitted to general tough love programs like Straight, KIDS,
and WWASP. If teens run from Phoenix House or Daytop, these programs call the police; if someone becomes so disturbed as to need restraint or isolation, he's transferred to a psychiatric facility. If the tough
cases that these programs manage can be handled without restraint and
isolation, the use of such tactics is unwarranted in easier cases—and if a
child cannot be managed without these extreme measures, he belongs in
a psychiatric facility, period.

The court system could also be a force for change, since many teens are placed in tough residential facilities as an alternative to incarceration. The *Milonas v. Williams* case against Provo Canyon School barred abusive practices performed "under the color of state law"—which means that teens sent into programs by courts should have the right to appeal their confinement if they believe they are being abused. Unfortunately, kids are rarely aware of these rights, and judges rarely enforce them or know much at all about the programs to which teens are sent. Courts should require than any treatment program that accepts court-mandated clients—whether the state or the parents are paying for the program—allow juveniles the right to call their attorneys or guardians ad litem (lawyers appointed to represent kids in certain proceedings) if they believe that a program's practices are harming them. They should require that programs approved as alternatives to incarceration be evidence-based—or at least be working toward becoming so.

Schools can also do their part. Some school systems pay to place teens in tough love programs under the federal IDEA act for treatment of learning disabilities and behavioral problems, but they should not agree to placements in behavioral programs that are not licensed, don't have certified teachers, and don't use techniques proven effective in controlled studies. Students should have a way of appealing their confinement in these programs to their original school district if they believe they are being abused.

The best way to accomplish this would be an amendment of the IDEA act. Guidance counselors and school psychologists also need to be educated about the dangers associated with tough love and the teen treatment industry in general—so that they don't feed kids into abusive programs as alternatives to suspension or expulsion.

The "escort" services that parents hire to take kids from their beds in the middle of the night in handcuffs should also be regulated—if not eliminated entirely. At the very least, federal regulations should require criminal background checks and bar admitted violent criminals and sex offenders (one has already been found to work for a service linked with WWASP).[29] Regulations should specify what types of techniques can be used for restraint and how teens can complain of maltreatment and of being falsely seized. These services' employees should require training and licensing as well.

In addition to these legal changes, the medical malpractice and personal injury lawyers could also do great work here. Though it's hard to find a "perfect victim" like Phil Elberg found in Lulu Corter, who could not be discredited with claims about her own drug use, there are others out there. And even without a perfect victim, I've come across dozens of kids in my research who were demonstrably victims of abuse and medical neglect and who received treatments that cannot be justified as medical care, despite their own prior drug use and misbehavior. For example, one teenage girl is currently suing WWASP because her jaw was broken during a restraint at Tranquility Bay—and treatment was delayed for so long that her face is now misshapen.[30] Another girl suffered a lung infection at Casa by the Sea that was also neglected and required surgery and, potentially, a lifetime of additional treatment. Aside from abuse and medical malpractice, fraudulent advertising should be attacked in both civil and criminal cases. Nothing gets an industry's attention like the possibility of having to pay out large financial settlements.

WWASP will increasingly be a target here, it seems—and while the one lawyer who tried to take them on in at least half a dozen cases over the years was unable to make his charges stick, the group recently appears to have made a major legal mistake. Under the Lanham Act, which prevents business competitors from publicly making false claims that can ruin their rivals, WWASP sued a woman named Sue Scheff. She had posted online accounts of problems at the program under various pseudonyms. Scheff was considered a competitor because she runs a business called PURE Inc. that refers teens to other residential programs and is paid by some of those programs for referrals. But because Scheff was able to demonstrate that her claims were based on information from reliable sources, WWASP lost.[31] It may be the first chink in WWASP's previously impenetrable armor.

As I write, Representative George Miller (D-California), who has so far unsuccessfully called on the U.S. attorney general to investigate WWASP, has introduced federal legislation that would put its foreign

programs under federal jurisdiction and would fund greater state oversight of the industry. The bill would also establish federal criminal and
civil penalties for institutional child abuse and require the State Department to report on abuse in foreign programs like WWASP's.[32] It would
be a good start. As of yet, however, Miller does not have any Republican
cosponsors, who would be needed if the bill is to have any chance of
passage.

UNFORTUNATELY, I feel, tough love will be with us in some form or
another as long as we see mental disorders like addictions and depression
as moral defects, and as long as we pathologize adolescence and expect
teenagers to behave like perfect adults. It will persist if we insist on leaving mental health treatment underfunded, uncoordinated, and with little support for evidence-based practice. Our kids deserve much better.
We need a society that allows them room for error, rather than com-
pounding one or two mistaken judgments with "zero tolerance" policies
that magnify them into potential disasters. We need caring, compassionate responses to the normal teenage desire to take risks, fall in love,
rebel—not programs that try to extinguish those tendencies. We need
programs that strengthen families, not split them. Parents' impulses to
protect their kids from negative consequences of their dumb decisions
about drugs and bad behavior should be celebrated—not demonized.
Rather than becoming more punitive, schools should look for ways to involve kids in educational and extracurricular activities—not cut those
things off or send kids away if they try drugs or relapse a few times.

As I was finishing this chapter, I was contacted by Cynthia Clark,
whose daughter, then fifteen, died in 2002 at the Catherine Freer Wilderness Program. Catherine Freer has one of the best reputations in the industry. It is supposed to be gentle and supportive, was involved in an
industry effort to do outcomes research, and was profiled glowingly by
Primetime Live.[33] That show, however, ominously included a segment in
which teens were denied water until one member of the group, who was
struggling with her pack, agreed to stand up and move forward. Under

no circumstances should people be denied water while hiking in the desert, of course. This denial does not suggest a truly gentle program.

Harvey died in the high desert—of dehydration and heatstroke complicated by methamphetamine intoxication, according to the coroner's report. After she collapsed, she was apparently left on the ground for forty-five minutes, because the counselors believed she was trying to manipulate them with her behavior. The statements given to police by the other kids in Erica's group illustrate that she'd complained for several hours and had collapsed repeatedly on the trail before she died. Once again, the kids knew there was something wrong, but the counselors refused to believe it. One counselor told police that participants "often feign injury to get out of doing something."[34] But Harvey was known by the program to be a recent methamphetamine user—and this should have precluded hiking in the desert heat because it increases the risk of heatstroke and dehydration. At the very least, it should have prompted special attention to any complaints suggesting dehydration or overheating.

Harvey had been plagued by mood disorders, variously diagnosed as depression and bipolar disorder. Before she plunged into serious depression in the eighth grade, she'd been an A student, with numerous friends and a seemingly limitless future. Her parents sought help from various counselors and psychiatrists, once hospitalizing her briefly when she had been weeping for nights and refusing to get out of bed to go to school. After this, while they were trying various mental health professionals and medications, she began using drugs and skipping school. She also engaged in self-mutilation. But eventually, her doctors seemed to find a combination of medications that worked. At the time that her parents sent her to the wilderness, Erica's mood was stable, she was attending school, and, by almost all objective measures, she had dramatically improved.

She was, however, continuing to test positive for drugs, including methamphetamine, on the tests her parents had been advised to give her at random. The counselor she saw and her psychiatrist both recommended more intensive drug treatment—despite the improvements in other areas. Following their advice, Clark and her husband, Michael Harvey, decided on Catherine Freer because Erica had so hated the psychiatric hospital.

Like the Bacons, Cynthia Clark and Michael Harvey had done everything right—just like them, they'd sought nurturing and professional treatment and thought they'd found it. They'd turned to a wilderness program with its restrictive measures only when prompted by professionals. And those measures, because of the punitive culture that pervades the teen treatment business, can become dangerous if they occur in circumstances that in themselves carry risks. Why did teen participants in nearly every boot camp and wilderness death see the health problems in the victim that the counselors just couldn't recognize? Why do they always assume teens are "faking"? When a teen admits drug use that can raise body temperature dangerously even in the absence of exertion or high external temperatures, why is she still sent into the desert?

I believe this occurs because tough love desensitizes its perpetrators and dehumanizes its victims. The adolescents, as Clark put it, "saw each other as human beings"—they didn't see them as "resistant brats." They didn't view Erica's every action as a symptom of "bad behavior" marked by "manipulation"—they saw a fellow human in pain.

Working with teens who may indeed often be manipulative may in itself desensitize counselors over time—but this is a tendency that needs to be fought against, not codified. "Better safe than sorry," not "Assume they're faking until they can't possibly be," should be the watchword. The idea that teens will automatically hate and rebel against treatment comes from the fact that the treatment itself is harsh and punitive; rebellion is often a function of the environment that the providers create, not one solely caused by the teens' inherent resistance. No one wants to be depressed, for example, so if you make clear that you are offering teens relief, not trying to control them, they usually recognize this and accept help. But if you frame treatment as punishment, and make conditions difficult for no apparent reason other than to be punitive, it's hardly surprising that teens resist.

Until we reconfigure our ways of dealing with adolescents until the methods are genuinely nurturing, not only will we cause unnecessary trauma, but we won't improve teens' lives and chances for a brighter future. Kids in trouble do need boundaries and structure—but not rules so rigid and elaborate that even those without behavior problems can't help but occasionally violate them. The evidence shows repeatedly that honey works better than vinegar, that love works better than fear. Making love contingent on perfection only adds to the problem. If we err on any side of the balance, it should be toward love, not toughness.[35]

Epilogue

RICHARD BRADBURY has never given up in his battle to reclaim the spoils of Straight for its victims. Part of this battle involved his making routine searches through the trash of Straight cofounder Mel Sembler. Sembler has never been charged with any crime in connection with Straight, and he has continued to defend the program's tactics against its many critics. In 1999, he told *Florida Trend* magazine, "People thought we were taking away children's rights. But we saw it just the opposite—giving them back their rights by helping them get off drugs."[1] He proudly notes in his official State Department biography that he and his wife founded the program, saying, "During its seventeen years of existence, STRAIGHT successfully graduated more than 12,000 young people nationwide from its remarkable program."[2]

On one of those searches through Sembler's trash, Bradbury found a penis pump (a pre-Viagra impotence treatment), which he put up for auction on eBay in 2003, saying that he would donate any profits to

Straight victims. Sembler sued him for intentional infliction of emotional distress and invasion of privacy—reacting exactly as Bradbury had wanted.

Bradbury hopes to find out what happened to Straight's money. For years, the group took in millions. Since it was a nonprofit organization and relied heavily on volunteer staff, it did not have high overhead. Facilities sent money beyond that needed for expenses to a charity called the Straight Foundation. After Straight closed, this became the Drug Free America Foundation, which fights against the liberalization of drug laws. Bradbury wants its money to go instead to Straight's victims. He wants Sembler, as well, to pay.

Bradbury says he has never had a romantic relationship, with a partner of either sex, in his life. He says that his sister, who was the first in his family to be sent to the program, is, as far as he knows, still an active drug addict.

WWASP FOUNDER BOB LICHFIELD has become one of the top contributors to the Republican Party in the state of Utah, following in Sembler's footsteps. He and his family members and associates have given more than $1 million since 2002.[3] Eyebrows were raised recently when Lichfield contributed $30,000 to the campaign of Utah House Speaker Marty Stephens, six days after Stephens killed a bill that would have more strictly regulated youth programs (including those that call themselves boarding schools) like WWASP's Majestic Ranch. Regulator Ken Stettler said he believed the votes were there to pass the legislation, but Stephens did not allow it to come up for consideration.[4] Donations from WWASP's Academy at Ivy Ridge to New York governor George Pataki have also come under scrutiny as part of a pool of money that may have illegally paid for a maid for his wife.[5]

KYRSTEN BEAN, the daughter of Karen Lile and Kendall Bean, recently got married. She met her husband-to-be, a hairdresser, in rehab. After she left Tranquility Bay, she started college at seventeen, but dropped out and relapsed. She says her experience at Tranquility Bay made it difficult for her to cope with genuine addiction treatment, but now, two rehabs and several relapses later, she's been sober for more than two years.

LULU CORTER is also a newlywed. Her husband, whom she began dating before her case went to trial, is a bus driver. On the night he proposed to her, they went out country line dancing. He had the DJ play Elvis Presley's "The Wonder of You." He then got down on his knees on the dance floor and proposed. Lulu was so startled that her first response was "No," but she soon clarified that yes, she did want to marry him. They were married on April 17, 2004, and she is now pregnant with her first child. Phil Elberg ensured that Corter has a professional money manager and a prenuptial agreement. Elberg is pursuing at least two more cases against KIDS.

THE KIDS PROGRAM lost its Medicaid funding and facility in 1998. But even after it officially closed, participants still stayed at "host homes" and were restrained if they tried to flee. One teen who attended Lulu Corter's trial as a spectator had entered the program as an alternative to prison and stayed on after its official closing, believing she had to serve out her sentence. She didn't leave until the terror attacks of September 11, 2001, jarred her and made her question the program's legitimacy.

MILLER NEWTON now calls himself Father Cassian and is fighting neighborhood opposition to a church he operates in Madeira Beach, Florida, where he lives. His bankruptcy case has been reopened because the church sits on property assessed at $300,000 but is probably worth far more in the current hot real estate market. The bankruptcy trustee has said the church is an "undisclosed asset" of the Newtons, which should be sold to pay off their creditors, such as the State of New Jersey. Numerous Straight and KIDS survivors have contacted local authorities, telling their stories and warning the neighbors and the bankruptcy court about Newton's history.[6]

For Parents of
Troubled Teens

I F THE STORIES of bad behavior by some of the teens in this book are all too familiar, or if you are simply worried about your teen's potential for drug and alcohol use to escalate out of control, I've included more details about better alternatives to tough love programs in this appendix. The following provides a brief overview of what the best data we have shows about how to deal with adolescent psychiatric, drug, and behavioral problems—as well as some information on what I've concluded from my research here.

TEEN MISBEHAVIOR AND DEFIANCE

Family values vary greatly—and parents have widely varying standards for acceptable behavior during adolescence. Consequently, it's very difficult to determine when professional help should be sought for teen problems, and such a decision will often rest on individual judgment. Most parents can expect a certain level of rebelliousness, rule-breaking, back talk, and moodiness—and most accept this as part of the normal course of adolescence.

Families that best ride out the roller-coaster teen years tend to have several things in common. The rules are clear and the kids know what they are. Because the rules are reasonable and not arbitrary or capricious, the kids accept their parents' limits (often with much grumbling), but generally abide by them. Communication is a two-way street, and parents adapt the rules to suit the teens' individual maturity levels and growing need for independence and responsibility.

If any of these factors is missing or breaks down, however, serious trouble is possible. If a child is punished harshly for his actions one week and then ignored when he does the same thing the next, the extreme inconsistency does not help him regulate himself and is perceived as confusing and unfair. If an adolescent has been behaving responsibly and feels the rules are too strict, minor rule-breaking can escalate into major rebellion and a battle of wills over seemingly trivial issues. Ordinary teen moodiness and irritability can escalate such conflicts, blowing things further out of proportion.

So when, in the absence of drug use, drinking, or symptoms of mental illness (see section below on mental illness for details), is teen bad behavior a sign of serious problems? First, if the bad behavior is a long-term problem that started before the teen years, this warrants professional evaluation: teens with histories of serious childhood behavioral problems are far less likely to outgrow their problems than those whose problems begin around puberty.[1] Second, if the behavior is affecting parents or other family members so much that it is interfering with work, school, or the ability to take any pleasure in family relations, help should be sought. In such cases, the child should have a full psychiatric evaluation and family therapy and/or individual counseling should be considered.

TEEN ALCOHOL AND OTHER DRUG USE: DISCIPLINE, ONE-ON-ONE COUNSELING, AND FAMILY THERAPY

If you suspect that your teen is using drugs or drinking and that this may be behind her bad behavior, it's always important to keep things in context: although since the "Just say no" era we've heard that any drinking or other drug use at all is a sign of serious trouble, in fact, most teens will try marijuana and drinking before they graduate high school. So it's one thing if your daughter stays out past curfew and comes home appearing drunk once or twice yet has high grades and a generally good attitude, but quite another if she stays out later and later each week and her grades are plummeting. If your teen appears to be drunk once every other month, it's a far different situation from his coming home wasted every day. It's also important to know that most of the time marijuana use and drinking by teens doesn't signal addiction.

Here's the bad news: in the United States, by the end of high school, more than half of all teens will have at least tried an illegal drug, and three-quarters will have tried alcohol. Sixty percent of high school seniors in 2004 report having been drunk at least once; 29 percent report having had five or more drinks at one event in the last two weeks, and nearly 25 percent used an illegal drug (primarily marijuana) within thirty days of being surveyed.[2] The numbers have bounced up and down during the three decades during which the government has been surveying such behavior—but they were actually far higher for today's adults. According to the best population survey of such conditions that we have, only roughly 4 percent of Americans will have a diagnosable level of problems with alcohol or other illegal drugs in any given year.[3]

The good news is that the statistics show that the majority of people who take drugs or drink alcohol in their teens will not become alcoholics or addicts. The American Psychiatric Association's diagnostic manual for psychiatric problems (*DSM*) defines two types of drug problems: substance abuse, which is less severe and tends to run a shorter course, and substance dependence (addiction), which is defined as compulsive use of a drug despite negative consequences and can last for decades. Most teens with substance problems suffer substance abuse, not dependence. But most teens who use drugs or alcohol never meet the criteria for either disorder.

Drug abuse is defined as risky use of substances (drinking and driving, for example) which is ongoing and may have had some negative consequences. However, unlike with dependence, desire for the substance has not taken over the person's life, quitting does not result in withdrawal symptoms, and use occurs, for example, on weekends, not daily. Setting aside the moral considerations about the appropriateness of substance use by young people, substance problems are defined medically as occurring when drugs interfere with school performance and with relationships with one's family and friends.

So what do you do, then, with a teen who you know or seriously suspect is drinking, smoking marijuana, or using other drugs? In all cases, at first, the best interventions are absolutely the least intensive. Start with firm, consistent, loving, and appropriate parental discipline: setting, elaborating, and enforcing family rules that encapsulate your values, and using punishment judiciously. Parents in this situation need to be sure to keep punishments for behavioral violations consistent, proportionate, and fair: grounding for a weekend or a month, not a year, for example. Continually escalating punishments, lengthy punishments, and those perceived as unfair or arbitrary tend only to worsen the problem. Family therapy can be helpful here to set ground rules on which everyone can agree, even if everyone isn't thrilled about them.

It is also absolutely critical to keep the lines of communication open. Teens who can communicate with their parents seek their help when they get in over their heads—those who feel they can't, won't. One obvious rule, for example, could be that if they find themselves in a situation in which they might feel forced to accept a ride with a driver who is drunk or high, they can and should always call you, no matter how late. If they know the consequences will be proportionate, that you don't condone the behavior but that their lives are obviously more important, they will be less inclined to take these kinds of risks, for fear that "my parents will kill me." You may also want to suggest to them that while you hope that they never, ever try drugs, if they do and immediately find the experience to be the "best thing that they ever felt," this is a serious warning sign of potential future problems, and you will not punish them if they come to you for help.

Of course, teens whose drug use occurs weekly or less frequently may see little need to stop because they feel (and often actually are, relatively speaking) in control of their behavior. Consequently, however, they may seem as though they are "in denial" of a bigger drug problem or simply rebelling against their parents' rules. Recognizing the need for change here often takes time, patience, and consistent parental responses, so those faced with uncertain or erratic behavior need to be sure not to give up too quickly. Parents needn't condone behavior that is morally unacceptable to them or that they fear is dangerous—however, they should be pragmatic about ensuring that the cure doesn't do more harm than the disease.

When you consider taking an action aimed at changing teens' behavior, always consider not only what will happen if they comply, but what will happen if they don't and whether those consequences are more likely to hinder or help them in the long run. For example, an arrest for drug possession may mean the denial of future federal college financial aid: if you are considering having your child arrested to teach a lesson, you may want to consider a lesson that is less likely to affect the youngster's ability to attend college. Having a college education, of course, is linked to a lower risk for addiction and for relapse among those who do get addicted. Your goal of getting your child through college is one of the best ways to reduce the odds of long-term addiction—even if it doesn't reduce the immediate risk of drug use or abuse.

Drug testing is often recommended to parents who suspect drug use, but this presents several problems as well. For one, it implies a breakdown of communication—it implicitly says that you don't believe that your child will tell you the truth. Even if you say you are doing it to give the youngster a reason to say no, many teens still see it as a sign of mistrust. Secondly, drug testing can only tell you if children have used a substance—it can't tell you whether they're substance abusers or addicts. Depending on the rules you set around it, it can also set up a cycle in which consequences escalate rapidly before the child has had enough time to change a specific behavior, even if he or she is trying hard. Drug testing, essentially, can lead to treatment before it's needed, and this can sometimes make matters worse, not better. That said, there can be families and circumstances in which it is valuable—but once again, it is not without the potential to do harm, and this is often not considered when it is recommended.

To get a sense of what your child faces in regard to drug use or drinking, consider the challenge of dieting and other major lifestyle changes. Almost no one moves immediately from all junk food to all health food—almost everyone slips and messes up and eats some extra cookies from time to time. Learning any new skill, including avoiding alcohol and other drugs, takes practice—and practice tends to mean trial and error. Consider, too, that the brain's self-control regions aren't fully developed until around age twenty-five. Parents here should look for progress, not perfection, as recovering alcoholics say, and recognize that teens face enormous pressures—both internal and external—to take risks and do things of which their parents don't approve. By recalling your own adolescence and how you needed time to understand that your parents were probably right when they did certain things that infuriated you at the time, you can often develop the patience needed to deal with what can be a maddening process. The main goal here is simply to keep the teen safe, connected to you, on track for college or other positive future plans, and working to improve as he or she matures. Given that so many teens almost immediately relapse after residential care (just as they do without it), if the teen is not frequently engaging in dangerous behavior like drinking and driving, it's better to work this out without resorting to such care.

IF DISCIPLINARY MEASURES and discussions fail and/or if a child is using harder drugs like methamphetamine, prescription opioids (OxyContin, Vicodin, Dilaudid, Percoset, etc.), heroin, or cocaine on an ongoing basis, start with one-on-one counseling for the teen and/or family therapy.

Again, any treatment should begin with a full psychiatric evaluation: more than half of teens who go on to develop the most serious drug problems have psychiatric problems like depression. Treating these problems is often critical to treating the drug problems: research finds that those who are treated simultaneously for their psychiatric disorders and their substance-misuse problems are 57 percent more likely to be abstinent six months after treatment than those who receive no psychiatric treatment.[4] Also, evaluation can help determine how serious the drug problem really is. It's important to stress to the teen that treatment and evaluation aren't punishment—teens are far more likely to be cooperative if you make sure that they understand that you want them to be happy, not to deprive them of pleasure, and that you are getting help in order to achieve this. Many parents worry that using antidepressants for depression and/or stimulants for attention-deficit disorder might incline teens to use drugs to solve their problems—in fact, the opposite is true. For example, teens treated with medications for attention-deficit disorder are half as likely to develop addiction problems as are those whose condition goes untreated.[5]

For counseling, research has found that certain techniques are especially helpful. "Motivational interviewing" and "cognitive behavioral" counseling styles have repeatedly been found to help reduce teen drug use—and they work for the entire spectrum of teen drug problems.[6] If a child has a substance-abuse problem, not dependence, however, it's a good idea to avoid group treatments and stick to one-on-one counseling—unless the group involves parents as well as teens.[7] Otherwise, the more severely addicted kids tend to teach the less troubled to get worse, often offering specific tips on avoiding parental detection and guidance on where to get drugs.

Family therapy can also be extremely useful.[8] One idea that tough love programs do get essentially right is the notion that many of the problems of teenagers are really family problems. Though it's hard to get any kind of exact figures, I was struck during my research for this book by how many times teens wound up in tough love programs in the midst or aftermath of a parental divorce. It is a time when parents are stressed and often guilt-ridden, and a time when even the best teens may begin to behave poorly. In such situations, family therapy, which addresses these problems and keeps the child at home, is a far more sensible solution than residential treatment—and one that is far more likely to effectively help not just the teen, but the family, in the long run.

FINDING GOOD COUNSELORS AND THERAPISTS

Finding the best help for these problems is hard: many mainstream family therapists and counselors use outdated techniques and recommend tough love or residential care almost reflexively if the teen doesn't change rapidly. There is also a serious shortage of psychiatrists who specialize in treating children and adolescents.

To find the best counseling and family therapy, parents should ask a lot of questions and get a number of referrals. Think about the problem as though it was any potentially serious illness: you want second opinions, and you want to do your homework and choose the approach demonstrated to help the most people in your situation. Research shows that it is, above all, the connection between the counselor and the client—and the empathy that the counselor shows for the client's situation—that produce positive results,[9] so if a teen doesn't like the counselor and doesn't find him or her compassionate and understanding, go elsewhere. It may help to have the teen choose from several counselors you've first identified as potential candidates: the more choice people are given about treatment, the better they tend to do in it.[10] For family therapy, everyone needs to feel at least some connection with or at least minimal respect for the therapist.

When considering a specific counselor or mental health care provider, ask specifically:

1. *What techniques does the practitioner use?*
You'd like to hear "cognitive-behavioral," "motivational interviewing," "brief intervention," or "interpersonal" for individual counseling, and

"functional," "behavioral," or "multisystemic" for family, although there are other types that may help. "Eclectic" may mean that the counselor draws on a number of approaches—or that he makes it up as he goes along, so ask further if this is the response you get. Research has found that what matters most is rapport between the client and the therapist and warmth and empathy from the therapist, so although specific techniques are helpful (especially for diagnosed conditions like depression), personal connection matters more. If you are not confident about the counselor's techniques and their basis in evidence, however, remain aware of this in relation to advice that is given and act accordingly.

2. *What evidence is there to support them?*

Ideally, the practitioner will have peer-reviewed published data to support the approach she prefers—if she doesn't seem to have high standards for evidence, she may not use good techniques. A good sign is if she supports "evidence-based" practice. A person who supports evidence-based practice is more likely to give good referrals and advice on additional treatment, if it is needed.

3. *How does the practitioner work with teens who don't have addictions but are using drugs dangerously and not necessarily inclined to stop immediately?*

The reply should involve helping the teen discover reasons of his own for not using, not "confrontation" or "breaking denial." The counselor should also not be focused on trying to get the teen to admit he is an addict or insistent that he attends twelve-step meetings (suggestions are fine, requirements problematic, especially if the teen is not substance-dependent). The counselor should be willing to "meet the teen where he's at," and work on increasing motivation for abstinence if he begins therapy unconvinced that it is necessary.

4. *What are the practitioner's qualifications, and is he or she licensed?*

You want someone with at least a master's degree. Also, check with the appropriate state agency about whether there have been disciplinary actions. Google them as well: you'd be amazed at what you can find out this way and what people don't disclose.

5. *Does the practitioner ever accept fees from programs for referrals?*
The answer should be no—this is an unethical practice.

IF KIDS REMAIN seriously resistant to change despite quite a few attempts at therapy (try several different counselors), and parents really feel there's a need for the teen to spend some time away from home (for example, if they need a respite from the conflict and a sense of a fresh start that they don't think outpatient counseling and/or discipline alone can provide), another option may be to send the child to live with relatives for a time. This can also remove a teen from a negative peer group and allow her to get a sense of perspective—and many teens who struggle against every parental rule behave very differently for Grandma or Auntie Sue. If there is a caring, willing relative or even a family friend, this tactic can be helpful, both to defuse acrimony and allow both the parents and teens to regroup and recover. It also carries few of the risks of sending a child to live with strangers, costs little, and can be done in conjunction with family therapy and other community-based treatments.

WHEN MORE HELP IS NEEDED

So how do you know when it's time to move up to more intensive treatment; when a child really is in danger? There are several key signs, which almost all experts agree indicate the need for a higher level of care than simply discipline and weekly counseling. One is injection drug use: this carries a high risk of infection with HIV and other potentially fatal illnesses, and of overdose. Another is daily use of almost any drug: if someone cannot manage to go a day without a non–medically indicated substance, a serious problem has usually developed. Depression that significantly affects schoolwork or socializing needs further attention, as does, for obvious reasons, suicidal behavior—particularly specific plans, giving away belongings, and any life-threatening attempts. Self-cutting without overt suicidal intent requires investigation as well: it might be done as a response to peer pressure (it is almost "fashionable" among some groups of kids) or may signify a major problem. Significant violence toward others, of course, and profound mood swings, especially with severe insomnia or excessive sleepiness, merit additional help—as does seemingly psychotic or delusional behavior. Running away, when it has gone beyond going to a friend's house for a night or two and especially when the teen is trying to live on the street, also clearly suggests the need for more intense help. Extreme weight loss can also indicate an eating disorder or a drug problem.

For the small, highly troubled group of kids who develop such problems, there are no easy answers—and the tough love industry prospers by preying on their parents and on the fears of other parents that their kids might become just as troubled without help. There are a variety of different treatments known to help kids with addictions, those who exhibit antisocial or criminal behavior, and those with mental illnesses, but the unfortunate thing most of them have in common is that they are not widely publicized or readily available.

For kids whose primary problem is alcohol or other drug addiction—who meet the diagnostic criteria for "substance dependence," not just "substance abuse"—there are a number of approaches known to be effective. Intensive outpatient counseling (such as a day rehab, in which people sleep at home but spend most of their waking hours at the program) using motivational interviewing and cognitive behavioral approaches has shown good results. There is little evidence that inpatient treatment is superior to outpatient care for all but the most severe drug problems,[11] but for kids whose drug problem is chronic and high-risk, such as drug injectors, it may be useful. In addition, by the time a teen has developed a disorder this severe, there is also little risk of worsening it through exposure to kids with worse problems or by labeling the child as an addict. For kids with substance dependence, twelve-step support groups like AA or NA may be helpful—especially if the teen enjoys them. However, they should be used with extreme caution or even avoided if the problem is abuse or use and not dependence. These are self-help programs with no professional supervision, after all. They encourage people to see themselves as having a lifelong relapsing disease and to label themselves as alcoholics or addicts: this can be a self-fulfilling prophecy or a limited way of viewing themselves for young people whose identities have not yet solidified. Such meetings can also lead kids to connect with those with more severe problems and develop new drug sources.

FINDING TEEN ADDICTION TREATMENT

For teens with genuine addictions, programs that focus on addiction are best, namely, those that take only addicts, not people with all manner of different and vaguely defined "behavior problems." General "tough love" does not teach the specific skills that addicts need to resist relapse and cope with craving; in fact, many such programs expressly forbid teens from any kind of discussion of drug use. Good programs address any co-existing mental illnesses either with talk therapy, medication, or, ideally in many cases, both. Since at least half of teens with the most severe addictions also suffer from other mental illnesses, it is critical that programs do ongoing and rigorous evaluations to be sure to identify and treat these conditions. And such evaluations should be done before placement, with a second opinion being obtained at that time as well, to prevent teens who are actually just experimenting and do not have addictions from being placed in inappropriate programs or kept there unnecessarily.

To find community-based addiction programs that are working with the National Institute on Drug Abuse to provide evidence-based care, check out NIDA's Clinical Trials Network, found at: http://www.nida.nih.gov/CTN/ctps.html. If your region is not served by any of these programs, try the Substance Abuse and Mental Health Services Administration's (SAMHSA) treatment facility locator at http://findtreatment.samhsa.gov/. This allows you to search for local licensed services, but not all of these are focused on evidence-based care and, consequently, some may use tough approaches. Most addiction programs use twelve-step groups as part of their treatment—if you can find one that suggests but does not require twelve-step support and that offers options for those who don't take to the twelve-step approach, you've probably found a good treatment center.

TEEN DEPRESSION: COGNITIVE BEHAVIORAL THERAPY AND MEDICATIONS

For mental illnesses like depression, both certain medications and cognitive behavioral therapies have been proven effective with teenagers—with a recent, large, government-funded study finding medication to have an edge over talk for depression treatment but that combined treatment with both was slightly better.[12] Though teens are at higher risk for medication-related suicide than are adults, during this age of massive prescribing of antidepressants, both teen and adult suicide rates have gone down significantly and studies have linked higher regional prescribing rates of drugs like Prozac with lower community suicide rates.[13] This doesn't mean that medications can't induce suicidal thoughts in some adolescents—just that for all but a tiny minority, the medications seem to be more helpful than harmful. Since bad reactions tend to occur primarily when people start or stop or change dosing of medications, careful monitoring at these times can probably dramatically reduce risk.

Because medications are often overprescribed, prescribed for the wrong conditions, or prescribed without adequate explanation or support for the teen regarding effects and side effects, it is critical for parents to be informed consumers. Psychiatric medications can be enormously helpful—but they can also be enormously harmful if used improperly. Find professionals who don't throw medication at everything—but who don't denigrate it, either.

Certainly, outpatient psychiatric care, whether using talk, medications, or ideally both, is a far more appropriate approach for a child over-come by sadness than taking her away from the people she loves and confronting her about her weaknesses and faults. Given that depressed people tend to be oversensitive to rejection and often filled with self-hatred, there are few people for whom tough love could possibly be more contraindicated. Since inescapable stress is now widely believed to help cause and/or exacerbate severe mental illness, putting a child in a program in which she faces daily emotional assault, is given no recovery time or privacy, and has no choice about participation seems far more likely to ultimately increase depression, not cure it (although short-term im-provements may be seen as teens try to appear positive to advance in the program and are distracted by the immediate fear and threat they face).

OTHER MENTAL ILLNESSES

For other mental illnesses in which complete loss of self-control can be part of the disease—schizophrenia, bipolar disorder, obsessive-compulsive disorder, etc.—tough love is just as bad as it is for depression, and psy-chiatry is a far better bet, even with the current system's flaws. When used on the severely mentally ill, tough love just repeatedly punishes them for behavior that they cannot stop. This demoralizes them, making them less likely to seek help or comply with future medical recommen-dations for fear of further harm. Psychiatry doesn't offer "guaranteed solutions"—but that's because the truth is that no one has them for these illnesses.

To find the best care for severe problems like these, you might start with a general search, using SAMHSA's mental-health services locator, found at http://www.mentalhealth.samhsa.gov/databases/default.asp. This includes tough love programs that have licenses for mental health treat-ment, so use this only as a starting point. Ask at local support groups like those of the National Alliance for the Mentally Ill (or on its website/mailing lists, http://www.nami.org/) and consulting organizations like the

United Way (which funds specific mental health and addiction programs and encourages high standards for them).

The National Institutes of Health's clinical trials network (Clinical Trials.gov) can help you locate researchers who are studying particular mental illnesses—as can local universities. Some of the highest-quality care available for the seriously mentally ill is in research settings. If there are no studies, referrals from academics who do research in the area are often helpful; they may know the local providers who are most interested in improving their care based on research from prior collaborations. Again, with any recommendation, try to get a second, objective opinion if at all possible, because there are so many questionable organizations that appear reputable but are not, and because even the most knowledgeable people can sometimes be taken in. Never even consider programs outside the U.S. that are linked to American organizations: they are located outside the country for one reason, and that is to avoid supervision.

Because of the disorganized, chaotic mental-health system, if your child does have severe psychiatric problems, you will need to act not only as your child's advocate, but as his case manager as well. Keep track of all treatment, medications, doses, etc., and try to plan in advance for all contingencies. For example, if inpatient treatment is needed, what kind of follow-up care will be provided? If the inpatient provider doesn't provide it, who will? Inpatient providers often don't even get the child's medical records and so may try medications that have previously failed—since no one coordinates care in the system, it is unfortunately up to parents to track this in order to maximize results.

QUESTIONS TO ASK OF ANY RESIDENTIAL TREATMENT PROVIDER

If a child is so ill as to require hospitalization or any form of residential care, these are the key questions to ask providers you are considering:

1. *How often may I contact my child, and how often may I visit?*

The program should encourage contact and visits. Excessive restrictions are a red flag—especially if they are rigid (for example, you should always be able to contact him or her in an emergency). A week or two without contact may be OK, but more than that is questionable. You should be able to talk privately with your child. You should never be told not to believe your child. You should be able to visit with little notice, within reason.

2. *What are the qualifications of the line staff who work directly with the teens?*

There should be someone of at least a master's level working with the kids most of the time; staff should have been subjected to criminal background checks, and the more educated the line staff, the better. Any kind of group should be led by a therapist of at least master's level—less than that (especially no degree required, trained only by the program itself) is a red flag.

3. *What is your policy on isolation and restraint?*

They should never be used in addiction treatment or for those without major psychiatric disorders. They should never be used for punishment. In psychiatric facilities, staff should be trained in specific restraint techniques, every restraint should be written up and analyzed by staff as to whether it was appropriate and how it could possibly have been avoided, and restraint should be used only by staff. Isolation should be extremely time-limited, and the person should be checked on frequently. Ask also about how often restraint is used—it should be very rare; once every six months, not daily, for example.

4. *What is your procedure for patient complaints?*

Ideally, there should be an ombudsman, whose sole job is to investigate patient complaints and solve such problems. At the very least, there should be a written procedure that allows a child to complain to someone at a higher level of authority than the person who makes the usual treatment decisions about him, without fear of retaliation. If you hear something like "the children are always lying and manipulating" in response to a question like this, you want a different provider. Also, ask if there are state hotlines to which the child has access for complaints.

5. *What are the rules of the program, and what are the consequences for breaking them?*

Again, ideally, you want to hear about clear, minimal rules and little emphasis on punishment. Trivial rules like not being permitted to look at a member of the opposite sex or not being able to look out a window are a red flag. If punishment is used, it should be short, reasonable, and not humiliating. It should almost never interfere with education. If there is any kind of "level" system, it should not punish kids for having "one bad day" with a "setback" that involves months of restrictions and/or withdrawal of privileges. There should be a complaint procedure if a teen believes she's being punished unfairly, and levels should not be determined solely (or even primarily) by peers. This can simply become a popularity contest and unfairly penalize kids with poor social skills.

6. *How do you deal with medical complaints?*

You want a program that seeks medical attention immediately, regardless of cost and regardless of the possibility that the child may be "faking." It should err on the side of believing the kid, basically.

7. *What is your philosophy on confrontation?*

You want to hear that empathetic, supportive approaches are more productive and that necessary confrontations are done with kindness and respect (i.e., "When you do X, I feel Y," and not "You're a selfish monster.")

8. *How long will my child need to be in treatment?*

Here, you want to get a sense that the philosophy is to minimize time away from home and that there are clear rules about length of stay.

9. *What is a typical day in treatment like?*

You want to hear about a very structured day, but one that includes at least some "down" time for reflection. You want to be sure that education is given enough time, if this is a long-term program.

10. *What are your policies about medication?*

Blanket policies against medication are a red flag—so are policies that don't have staff supervision of medication use (i.e., they have the teens keep and take their own meds, rather than have a nurse, counselor, or physician's assistant distribute them). Except in cases of uncomplicated addiction, teens disturbed enough to require long-term residential treatment typically need at least some medication. Skepticism about over-medication is good—but seeing medication as a "quick fix" which allows teens to avoid needed emotional pain may miss the complexity of their problems and often represents the kind of black-and-white thinking that is not indicative of the best care.

KEEP IN MIND, however, that even if you ask all the right questions and get all the right answers, this cannot guarantee that you have found a good program. As the Bacons and others found out to their great regret, program providers can mislead parents about their services, complaint procedures, and treatment philosophies. So, again, you need to be absolutely sure, first, that your child needs residential care—and if so, that the program is safe and appropriate. Search it thoroughly online—look at activist sites such as www.isaccorp.org, www.fornits.com/wwf/index.php?viewcat=1, www.teenliberty.org, www.nospank.net, and www.unmarriedamerica.org/emancipation/entry.htm for accounts of problems. Check with the Better Business Bureau and state licensing agencies as well. Search local media if possible, too. Google the name of the program and "abuse" or "investigation."

Be suspicious and ready to change track if the program you choose doesn't turn out to offer what it has claimed to offer. Trust your intuition—if something doesn't feel or seem right, it probably isn't. You know your child better than any expert does: sure, kids, like all humans, often try to find the easy way out, but most will not come up with extreme and specific tales of abuse unless it is occurring or something else is making them incredibly unhappy. Even if a child makes a false report, it's a sign that treatment isn't going well, and the incident needs to be properly investigated, not dismissed.

Recovering from addictions and mental illness is often far from pleasant—but good providers work to make it as easy and painless as possible, not the opposite. Kids may rebel against fair rules and appropriate structure, but most recognize the need for them and, though often grudgingly, agree to comply. Unfairness and unkind and arbitrary displays of power, however, are not good treatment—and you've raised an ethical child if she disagrees with such policies. If it doesn't seem appropriate, it probably isn't. If it seems too good to be true, it's bound to be a scam: avoid anyone promising "cures" or "guarantees."

EDUCATIONAL CONSULTANTS

As noted earlier, there are people called "educational consultants" who aim to help parents find the best programs and to sort out which providers are ethical and effective and which ones aren't. Unfortunately, here, too, there seem to be a number of bad apples—consultants who take kickbacks from programs without disclosing these payments, consultants who have no education or qualifications beyond having had a troubled child, consultants who are actually employees of programs but who pretend to be objective, and consultants who allow programs they know to be problematic to advertise on their free websites, but steer clients who pay for their services elsewhere. A group called the Independent Educational Consultants Association (IECA; www.iecaonline .com) has a code of ethics that bars most of these practices, but it does not police adherence. However, the group will expel members if ethics violations are reported and confirmed—so avoid nonmembers. If you can afford such services and can find one you can trust, it may help you find a good fit and can help coordinate ongoing care—but unfortunately, as with the rest of this industry, you will need to be very cautious and selective.

ANTISOCIAL BEHAVIOR AND VIOLENCE: MULTISYSTEMIC FAMILY THERAPY AND FUNCTIONAL FAMILY THERAPY

Finally, for antisocial and violent teens with or without drug problems and other mental illnesses, probably the best and most widely researched approach is multisystemic family therapy (MST). This approach was designed for the hardest cases: the kids who simply won't listen, who physically attack people, who have little empathy, and who often do genuinely try to manipulate others in order to get what they want. MST is one of the Justice Department's "exemplary" programs, the other best-researched treatment is also an outpatient family therapy called Functional Family Therapy.[14]

MST has been used on thousands of kids as an alternative to juvenile prison—and has shown its effectiveness by being tested on the chronic, violent offenders who have traditionally failed with all other approaches. Nine randomized controlled trials and one quasi-experimental trial that included nearly 1,000 families found that it reduces re-arrest by 25 to 70 percent compared to alternatives like juvenile incarceration, community drug-treatment services, and individual therapy. It also increased school attendance, reduced drug use, decreased psychiatric symptoms, and cut out-of-home placements like hospitalization and foster care by 47 to 64 percent.[15] Results are similar for Functional Family Therapy (FFT), though there have not been as many studies.[16]

Also, when compared directly to inpatient hospitalization, MST improved school attendance and cut placement in foster care or other treatment centers by 50 percent. One study, which compared MST with usual juvenile justice alternatives (including incarceration), found that a year later recidivism had decreased by 43 percent in the MST participants. Treatment completion rates are far higher than with usual therapies—in fact, in one study, MST dropouts actually did better than those who completed individual therapy.[17]

The therapy itself involves home visits by a therapist who uses positive encouragement to help families reestablish consistent discipline and help teens move away from negative peers. It helps parents set firm boundaries and enforce consequences for unacceptable behavior—but it makes them proportionate, consistent, and fair. It also helps the teen find alternative sources of pleasure and friendship that do not involve antisocial activities. Functional Family Therapy is similar, aiming particularly at reframing negative communication patterns in families in order to reduce conflict.

Scott Henggeler, a professor of psychiatry at the Medical University of South Carolina and director of the Family Services Research Center there, developed MST. He says bluntly that residential treatments don't work. The teenager will eventually have to cope with the snares and temptations of the outside world, so there's little point, except for brief periods necessary for health and safety reasons, to remove him from them, he says. This is congruent with research on drug treatment and boot camps, which largely finds that it is outpatient "aftercare" in the community, not residential treatment that makes the real difference.

Though MST is most commonly available to chronic juvenile offenders in the justice system, the website at http://www.mstservices.com/text/licensed_agencies.htm lists some agencies that are licensed to provide it. Parents whose kids have become involved in the juvenile courts can also ask for their children to be enrolled through the system: MST is now available in thirty states. FFT has been adopted by the New York State Office of Mental Health and is available in fourteen other states as well.

A NOTE ON WILDERNESS PROGRAMS

So what about wilderness programs—the ones that claim not to be boot camps, and that use qualified therapists, high quality camping and communications gear, and provide adequate nutrition? My research makes me highly ambivalent here: while I believe that a wilderness challenge may be incredibly healing for the right child at the right time, the same program might be unmitigated torture for another kid. Coerced survival training, even at its gentlest, also has many of the same problems as do teen military-style boot camps. As with those programs, you may bring home a more arrogant child who now knows he can survive almost anything, is in better physical shape than before, and is still furious with you and determined to do what he wants.

My main problem with recommending even the wilderness programs with the best reputations is what happened to Aaron Bacon and in several of the other wilderness deaths. The Bacons did everything a parent is supposed to do: asked questions, met the program's owners, were referred by a therapist. And yet they were still deceived, being told their son would receive tender loving care, when in fact he was starved and allowed to die a hideous death. It's true, now that Internet access is widespread, that parents in a similar situation would probably be able to find out about the program's owners' troubled history with a Google search. But that doesn't mean that bad programs can't still lie about their practices without discovery.

The story of Erica Harvey—who attended Catherine Freer in 2002, a program with a top-notch reputation—also suggests danger. Erica, who was known to be a methamphetamine user, was immediately taken into the high desert upon entry into the program. She died of dehydration and heatstroke—even though anyone trained in dealing with addiction knows that methamphetamine raises body temperature and water should never be withheld. As in the Bacon case, Harvey's problems were misread as "faking"; as in the Chase and Sutton deaths, communication failures led to delays in medical attention, Clark's lawsuit claims.

The combination of potentially deadly conditions and an attitude of "These kids are faking" is just too explosive for me to find justifiable—especially in light of the fact that wilderness programs have not been able to prove themselves superior to other treatments. There is a suggestion in recent studies that kids with attention-deficit disorder respond particularly well to being involved in outdoor activities, but before I would feel comfortable recommending any form of extended wilderness expedition aimed at troubled youth, I would have to see a lot more regulation and a lot better data. I do think that if a troubled child wants to take an Outward Bound course—one aimed at voluntary participants from all backgrounds who will not automatically be seen as malingerers—that may be helpful in some instances. If a teen is opposed to all other options and is seriously drug-involved, the teen loves the outdoors, and you've found a program that uses qualified counselors and allows significant communication, you may want to consider it, but be aware of the risks.

Wilderness proponents insist that downhill skiing is more risky than troubled teen wilderness programs based on the number of reported deaths and the number of reported participants—but downhill skiers can choose when they eat and drink and are not thought to be fakers by ski patrols if they claim injury. And the reported numbers of both deaths and of overall participation in teen wilderness programs may not be reliable. There is no one who keeps track of either, and there are deaths that have occurred in these programs without attracting media attention.[18]

I also think a family adventure trip of some sort—or a volunteer vacation in which families perform community service together—is a great idea to improve communication and increase empathy. But until there is better oversight of wilderness programs or until replicated, controlled studies are done that prove them so superior that the benefits justify the risks, I think other alternatives make more sense and carry less risk.

Acknowledgments

Writing a book like this is a deeply emotional experience and required the assistance of many people. Peter McDermott urged me to take on this difficult subject—I can't imagine having written it without his encouragement, inspired editing, and support. My editor, Megan Lynch, profoundly improved and enhanced the manuscript. My agent, Andrew Stuart, is, to me, the ideal of what an agent can be, and he helped at every stage of the process.

Thanks as well to Amy Hertz, who bought this book for Riverhead and got me started, and to Sean McDonald for his support. I am also grateful to Lisa Rae Coleman, my transcriber and great friend, who took care of me during the most difficult parts of the reporting. My intern, Judy Jackson, brought wonderful energy and intelligence to her work. Thanks, too, to Trevor Butterworth and stats.org for their support.

But my greatest appreciation must go to those whose story this book attempts to tell. Without their honesty and openness, it would not have been possible. For every account I included, there are thousands of others—and I wish I could have told the tale of each teen and parent who took the time to relive their trauma for me. Every one deserves to be heard.

Some I cannot thank by full name for various reasons, but I would like to at least acknowledge the teens (some now grown) who gave me insight into their experiences: Aimee, Alex, Allison, Amber, Andrew, Anthony, Garred and Geoffrey Bock, Brian, Leigh Bright, Britta, Christine, Danielle, Danny, David, Michelle Dellino, Denise, Donald, Shelby Earnshaw, Emily, Erica, Erica A., Aldo Fonticella, Greg, Marti Heath, Jessica, Kim, Aaron Kravig, Kristen, Lauren, Lindsay, Lindsey, Lyla, Paul M., Matt, Michael, Samantha Monroe, Nicole, Kathryn Ottersten, Paige, Michael Perry, Melissa Rein, Codi Rouvinen, Ryan, Andy Sakamoto, Scott, Nick Violante, and Zayne.

I would also like to thank, of course, Paul Richards, Kyrsten Bean, and Lulu Corter, who gave me a great deal of their time and assistance. Special thanks to Richard Bradbury for his research, openness, and activism. I hope I have done their stories justice.

The parents and other activists who fought back also deserve attention: Laurie Berg, Karen Lile and Kendall Bean, Sally and Bob Bacon, Cathy Sutton, Cynthia Clark, Donna Headrick, Shannon McCullough, Karen Burnett, Gini Farmer Remines, Barbe Stamps, Alexia Parks, Jeff Berryman, Jordan Riak, and many others. I'm grateful to Ginger Warbis for her brave website (www.fornits.com) and to Amberly Chirolla for her courage. My friends Anne Kornhauser, Sue Young Wilson, and Joanne Dwyer; siblings Kira Smith, Sarah Szalavitz, and Ari Szalavitz; and mom Nora Staffanell have also provided great help. Thanks to Carol Vozella for sharing her recollections of service on the Corter trial jury.

There are many journalists and authors without whom this book would not have been possible. They include Arnold Trebach, whose book *The Great Drug War* (Macmillan, 1987) was one of the first to detail the abuses of Straight Incorporated. A new edition was issued in 2005 by Unlimited Publishing LLC. Trebach should also be credited with funding and helping organize the first conferences for survivors of abusive treatment. Jon Krakauer, Joe Morganstern, and Christopher Smith exposed the true horror of Aaron Bacon's death for *Outside*, the *Los Angeles Times*, and the *Salt Lake Tribune*, respectively; Lou Kilzer did a brilliant series of exposés on WWASP for the Denver *Rocky Mountain News* that should have won him a second Pulitzer. I would also like to thank Tim Weiner of the *New York Times*, Tim Rogers of the *Tico Times*, Page Bierma, Ethan Watters, Kenneth Wooden, Richard Ofshe, David and Cathy Mitchell, and the producers of *48 Hours, Primetime Live*, and *Dateline NBC* for their work in this area. Though they all have sharply different perspectives, Carey Bock and Sue Scheff brought important information to light, and Bruce and Karen Richards graciously shared their correspondence with me.

Finally, I must credit Wes Fager's exhaustive research on Straight, and his help and support, which were critical. And I could not have written this or understood its complexity without the time, help, and kindness of Phil Elberg. I sincerely apologize to anyone whom I have inadvertently neglected—and of course, for any errors I may have included. Those are mine alone.

Notes

INTRODUCTION

[1] Rimer, Sara, "Desperate Measures—A special report," *New York Times*, 9/10/2001.

[2] Johnston, L. D., O'Malley, P. M., Bachman, J. G., and Schulenberg, J. E., *Monitoring the Future national survey results on drug use, 1975–2003: Volume II, College students and adults ages 19–45* (NIH Publication No. 04-5508). Bethesda, MD: National Institute on Drug Abuse, 2004, Fig 4-19A.

[3] Deaths: Final Data for 2002. NVSR, Volume 53, Number 5 (PHS), 2005–1120.

[4] National Center on Health Statistics, *Health, United States, 2003*, p. 51, http://www.cdc.gov/nchs/data/hus/hus03.pdf.

[5] U.S. Department of Health and Human Services, *Mental Health: A Report of the Surgeon General—Executive Summary*. Rockville, MD: U.S. Department of Health and Human Services, Substance Abuse and Mental Health Services Administration, Center for Mental Health Services, National Institutes of Health, National Institute of Mental Health, 1999.

6 Wilmshurst, L. A., "Treatment programs for youth with emotional and behavioral disorders: an outcome study of two alternate approaches," *Ment Health Serv Res*, 2002 Jun; 4 (2): 85–96.

7 Johnson et al., *Monitoring the Future*, table 4.5.

8 Chen, K., and Kandel, D. B., "The natural history of drug use from adolescence to the mid-thirties in a general population sample," *Am J Public Health*, 1995 Jan; 85 (1):41–47; Moffitt, T. E., "Adolescence-limited and life-course-persistent antisocial behavior: a developmental taxonomy," *Psychol Rev* 1993 Oct;100(4): 674–701.

9 Schulenberg, J. E., O'Malley, P. M., Bachman, J. G., Johnston, L. D., and Laetz, V. B., "How social role transitions from adolescence to adulthood relate to trajectories of well-being and substance use," *Monitoring the Future*, Occasional Paper No. 56.

10 Bates, Marsha E., and Labouvie, Erich W., "Adolescent risk factors and the prediction of persistent alcohol and drug use into adulthood," *Alcoholism: Clinical and Experimental Research* (1997) 21: 944–50.

11 Dishion, T. J., McCord, J., and Poulin, F., "When interventions harm: Peer groups and problem behavior," *American Psychologist* (1999) 54(9): 755–764. Poulin, F., Dishion, T. J., and Burraston, B., "3-year iatrogenic effects associated with aggregating high-risk adolescents in cognitive-behavioral preventive interventions," *Applied Development Science* (2001) 5(4): 214–224.

12 Sherman, Lawrence W., Gottfredson, Denise C., et al., "Preventing Crime: What Works, What Doesn't, What's Promising." Department of Justice, July 1998.

13 National Institutes of Health State-of-the-Science Conference Statement, "Preventing violence and related health-risking social behaviors in adolescents," October 13–15, 2004, Draft 10/15/04, http://consensus.nih.gov/ta/023/youthviolenceDRAFTstatement101504.pdf, p. 27.

14 Ibid., p. 13.

15 Additional sources for introduction: interviews with Elliott Currie, Ph.D., Richard Bradbury, Bob and Sally Bacon, and Bruce Perry, M.D., Ph.D. See also York, Phyllis, York, David, and Wachtel, Ted, *ToughLove*, Bantam, 1983, and *One Day at a Time in Al-Anon*, Al-Anon Family Group Headquarters, 25th Edition, 1990.

CHAPTER ONE

1 Villano, David, "Money Man," *Florida Trend*, May 1997.

2 Nemy, Enid, "Mrs. Reagan Deplores a Drug 'Epidemic,'" *New York Times*, 2/17/1982.

3 York, Phyllis, York, David, and Wachtel, Ted, *Tough Love*, p. 34.

4 Ibid.

5 Straight teen quiz, circa late '80s or early '90s.

6 KIDS quiz, 1990s.

7 This was on an apparently WWASP-linked website: www.teenbootcamps.us (accessed in 2005).

8 Baum, Dan, *Smoke and Mirrors: The War on Drugs and the Politics of Failure*, Little, Brown, 1996.

9 Substance Abuse and Mental Health Services Administration, http://oas.samhsa.gov/MJinitiation/chapter3.htm#3.2, table 3.1.

10 York, et al., *ToughLove*, p. 34.

11 Ibid.

12 Ibid., p. 12.

13 Baum, *Smoke and Mirrors*, p. 156.

14 Ervin, Sam J. and staff of subcommittee on constitutional rights, Judiciary Committee, 93rd Congress, "Individual Rights and the Federal Role in Behavior Modification," U.S. Government Printing Office, November 1974, p. III.

15 Ibid.

16 Ibid.

17 Ibid., p. 1.

18 Ibid., p. 15.

19 Lieberman, M., Yalom, I., and Miles M., *Encounter Groups: First Facts*, Basic Books, 1973, p. 174.

20 Ibid., p. 170.

21 Ibid., p. 194.

22 CBS News, *60 Minutes*, 1984 [exact airdate unavailable].

23 Gerstel, David U., *Paradise Incorporated*, Presidio Press, 1982.

24 Mitchell, Dave, Mitchell, Cathy, and Ofshe, Richard, *The Light on Synanon*, Wideview Books, 1980, pp. 144–45.

25 Ibid., pp. 62–63.

26 Ibid., p. 167.

27 Ibid., p. 84.

28 Janzen, Rod A., *The Rise and Fall of Synanon: A California Utopia*, Johns Hopkins University Press, 2001, p. 214.

29 Randolph, Eleanor, "Today the Seed, Tomorrow the World," *New Times*, 9/6/1974.

30 Zimbardo, Philip, et al., "A Pirandellian Prison," *New York Times Magazine*, 4/8/1973. For more on the experiment, see www.prisonexp.org.

31 Additional sources for Chapter One: interviews with Richard Bradbury, John Foley, Richard Ofshe, Ph.D., and others.

CHAPTER TWO

1 Trebach, Arnold, *Why We Are Losing the Great Drug War*, Macmillan, 1987.

2 Ibid., p. 45.

3 Additional sources on Collins's case and his story: Latimer, Leah, "False Imprisonment Ruling Upheld; Drug Program Ordered to Pay Virginia Man $220,000," *Washington Post*, 11/27/84; Zibart, Eve, "Three Testify Against Straight Inc.," *Washington Post*, 5/25/83; CBS News, *60 Minutes*, 1984 [exact date unknown]; Zibart, Eve, "Va. Jury Finds Drug Program Imprisoned Man," *Washington Post*, 5/13/1983; Anonymous, "Drug Rehab Center Loses Suit; Victim Loses Family Life," AP 6/8/1983; Burgess, John, "Held at Drug Center Against His Will, Fairfax Man Says," *Washington Post*, 5/10/83; Zibart, Eve, "Red Eyes Basis of Drug Diagnosis, Court Told," *Washington Post*, 5/11/1983.

4 Trebach, *Why We Are Losing*, p. 51.

5 Ibid., p. 52.

6 Ibid., p. 53.

7 Ibid., p. 56.

8 Letter from Miller Newton to Frankie S. Goldsby, Florida Dept of Health and Rehabilitative Services, dated 7/23/82.

9 Trebach, *Why We Are Losing*, pp. 60–61.

10 Ibid.

11 PR Newswire, 5/25/1983.

12 Clifton, Doug, "Seed's Effect Disputed," *Miami Herald*, 10/13/1972.

13 Ibid.

14 Randolph, Eleanor, "Today the Seed, Tomorrow the World," *New Times*, 9/6/74.

15 Ibid.

16 Villano, "Money Man."

17 Anonymous, "Report says Straight fulfills its purpose, urges more training," *St. Petersburg Times*, date unknown. See also, anonymous, "headlines unknown," *St. Petersburg Times*, 3/3/78, 3/19/78, 3/24/78 and 5/7/78. Also documented on the website of Wes Fager, a former Straight parent turned anti-Straight activist, www.thestraights.com.

18 Nottingham, William, "Drug Program Allegedly Used Coercive Tactics to Control Clients," *St. Petersburg Times*, 2/12/1978.

19 Finkel, David, "Going Straight," *St. Petersburg Times*, 5/3/1987; Rivera, Carla, "Parents Protest Straight's Fate," *Los Angeles Times*, 11/2/1990.

20 Moore, Molly, "'Straight' to Open Area Chapter," *Washington Post*, 7/28/1982.

21 Villano, "Money Man."

22 Journey, Mark, "Prosecutors Want Ex-counselor Jailed," *St. Petersburg Times*, 11/25/1988.

23 Hurst, John, "Drug Program's Tough Tactics Draw Fire," *Los Angeles Times*, 3/24/1990.

24 Barstow, David, "States Take a Hard Look at Straight," *St. Petersburg Times*, 7/31/91.

25 WFLA, "Eye on Tampa," exact broadcast dates unknown, two programs on Straight, January 1992.

26 Unsigned editorial, "A Persistent Foul Odor," *St. Petersburg Times*, 7/17/1993.

27 Baum, *Smoke and Mirrors*, p. 284.

28 Ibid.

29 Unsigned editorial, "A Persistent Foul Odor," *St. Petersburg Times*.

30 Letter from Ray Berry, district program supervisor for the Florida Department of Health and Rehabilitative Services to Loretta Parrish, executive director of SAFE, 10/25/1993.

31 WAMI-TV, "28 Daze," September 2000.

32 Links between Straight and each of these programs have been documented by Wes Fager. See www.thestraights.com. For Kids Helping Kids, see also Zibart, Eve, "Controversy Over Drug Program Extends to New Va. Clinic," *Washington Post*, 1/2/1983. For Phoenix Institute for Adolescents and Pathways Family Center, see Sarsfield, Annmarie, "Treatment Center Lives in Name Only," *Tampa Tribune*, 7/7/1993. For Growing Together and Possibilities Unlimited, see Aaronson, Trevor, "Suffering Together," *New Times Broward–Palm Beach*, 12/9/2004. I interviewed a former Turnabout/Stillwater partici-

pant who described the Straight method to me as being the treatment model
used at the program.

33 Butts, J. A., and Schwartz, I. M., "Access to insurance and length of psychiatric
stay among adolescents and young adults discharged from general hospitals,"
J Health Soc Policy, 1991; 3(1): 91–116.

34 Dorfman, Lori, and Schiraldi, Vincent, "Off Balance: Youth, Race and Crime
in the News," *Building Blocks for Youth*, April 2001, http://www.building
blocksforyouth.org/media/media.html.

35 Abbott, Karen, "With Teens, Whose Rights Count Most?" *Rocky Mountain
News*, 8/29/1999. Also, presentation by Gerard Glynn, J.D., executive director of Florida's Children First.

36 Room, R., and Greenfield, T., "Alcoholics Anonymous, other 12-step move-
ments and psychotherapy in the U.S. population, 1990," *Addiction*, 88(4):
555–562, 1993.

37 Church, Gene, and Carnes, Conrad, *The Pit: A Group Encounter Defiled*,
Pocket Books, 1973.

38 Singer, Margaret Thaler, et al., "Report of the APA Task Force on Deceptive
and Indirect Techniques of Persuasion and Control," American Psychological
Association, 11/1986.

39 Mathison, Dirk, "White Collar Cults, they want your mind," *Self* magazine,
February 1993.

40 Rushkoff, Douglas, *Persuasion: Why We Listen to What "They" Say*, Riverhead,
1999, pp. 212–13.

41 Myers, David G., *Social Psychology*, 2nd edition, McGraw-Hill, 1987, pp.
61–72.

42 Hassan, Steven, *Combatting Cult Mind Control*, Park Street Press, 1988, p. 72.

43 Macionis, John J., *Sociology: 6th Edition*, Simon & Schuster, 1997, pp. 178–79.

44 Schodolski, Vincent, and Haynes, V. D., "Captive Girl's Actions Hint at Brainwashing; Experts See Signs of Manipulation," *Chicago Tribune*, 3/16/2003.

45 Myers, David G., *Social Psychology*, pp. 522–23.

46 Lifton, Robert Jay, *Thought Reform and the Psychology of Totalism*, University
of North Carolina Press, 1989.

47 Keys, A., Brozek, J., Henschel, A., Mickelsen, O., and Taylor, H. L., *The Biol-
ogy of Human Starvation*, University of Minnesota Press, 1950.

48 CIA, Kubark Counterintelligence Interrogation, July 1963, p. 82.

49 Gudjonsson, Gisli, "Confession: After days of confinement and hostile ques-

tioning, people will say anything, true or false, to make it stop," *New Scientist*, 11/20/2004.

50 Lifton, *Thought Reform*.

51 Hare, Robert D., *Without Conscience: The Disturbing World of Psychopaths Amond Us*, Guilford Press, 1999, p. 199.

52 Additional sources for Chapter Two: Interviews with Richard Bradbury, John Foley, Leigh Bright, "Katy," former Straight board member "Walter," and Ira Schwartz, Ph.D. Interviews/presentations by youth rights experts: Paul De-Muro, consultant; Gerard Glynn, J.D., of Florida's Children First; Mark Soler, J.D., president, Youth Law Center; and Bruce Perry, M.D., Ph.D.

CHAPTER THREE

1 Krakauer, Jon, "Loving Them to Death," *Outside*, October 1995.

2 Morganstern, Joe, "A Death in the Desert," *Los Angeles Times Magazine*, 1/15/1995.

3 Krakauer, "Loving Them to Death."

4 http://www.escalante-cc.com/grand_staircase/grand_staircase.htm.

5 Aaron Bacon's journal, 3/1/1994, excerpted in Smith, Christopher, "'I Feel Like I'm Going to Die,' North Star Teen's Journal Charts His Own Demise," *Salt Lake Tribune*, 5/28/1995.

6 Essay by Aaron Bacon, 3/1/94, cited ibid.

7 Aaron Bacon's journal.

8 Aaron Bacon's journal, 3/5/1994.

9 Aaron Bacon's journal, 3/7/1994.

10 Letter from Aaron Bacon to his parents, 3/8/1994.

11 *State of Utah v. Fisher*, filed 12/24/1998, http://courtlink.utcourts.gov/opinions/appopin/fisher12_98.htm.

12 Aaron Bacon's journal, 3/1/1994, "'I Feel Like I'm Going to Die.'"

13 Letter from Aaron Bacon to his parents, 3/11/1994.

14 Aaron Bacon's journal, 3/12/1994.

15 Aaron Bacon's journal, 3/13/1994.

16 Aaron Bacon's journal, 3/17/1994.

17 Aaron Bacon's journal, 3/18/1994.

18 Aaron Bacon's journal, 3/19/1994.

19 Aaron Bacon's journal, 3/20/1994.

20 Ibid.

[21] Aaron Bacon's journal, 3/20/1994, cited from Krakauer, "Loving Them to Death."

[22] *State of Utah v. Fisher*, filed 12/24/1998, http:courtlink.utcourts.gov/opinions/appopin/fisher12_98.htm.

[23] Krakauer, "Loving Them to Death."

[24] Ibid.

[25] Morganstern, "A Death in the Desert."

[26] Krakauer, "Loving Them to Death."

[27] Ibid.

[28] Morganstern, "A Death in the Desert."

[29] Genuit, Thomas, et al., "Peritonitis and abdominal sepsis," *Emedicine*, updated 9/29/04, http://www.emedicine.com/med/topic2737.htm.

[30] Morganstern, Joe, "A Death in the Desert." Morganstern uses Mike Hill's account describing Costigan as saying, "Oh, shit."

[31] Krakauer, "Loving Them to Death."

[32] Ibid.

[33] Sherman, Lawrence W., Gottfredson, Denise C., MacKenzie, Doris L., Eck, John, Reuter, Peter, and Bushway, Shawn D., "Preventing Crime: What Works, What Doesn't, What's Promising," Department of Justice, July 1998, table 9-6.

[34] Krakauer, "Loving Them to Death."

[35] Adams, Brooke, "Outdoor Therapy Owes Start to BYU Instructor," 12/12/1999.

[36] Krakauer, "Loving Them to Death."

[37] Ibid.

[38] Ibid.

[39] Ibid.

[40] Additional sources for Chapter Three: Interviews: Cathy Sutton, Sally and Bob Bacon, Craig Barlow, Diana Parrish (née Hollis), others. Also, Aaron Bacon's journal; Smith, Christopher, "'I Feel Like I'm Going to Die,' North Star Teen's Journal Charts His Own Demise," *Salt Lake Tribune*, 5/28/1995.

CHAPTER FOUR

[1] CNN, "Earth Matters," 4/2/1995.

[2] Smith, Christopher, "A Divorce, A Daughter's Death and a Duel over Whose Grief Is Greater," *Salt Lake Tribune*, 3/12/1995.

3 Smith, Christopher, "Whose Grief Is More? Judge Decides Daughter's Death,"
   Salt Lake Tribune, 5/15/1995.

4 Krakauer, "Loving Them to Death."

5 Harrie, Dan, "Cartisano Wants to Work With Kids Again; Will Utah Let Him?"
   Salt Lake Tribune, 5/29/1992.

6 *Salt Lake Tribune*, 10/9/94, quoting attorney Charles Brofman on being
   "stiffed" by Cartisano.

7 Smith, Christopher, "Cartisano's Way: Tough-Love 'Em, Then Leave 'Em,"
   Salt Lake Tribune, 5/29/1994.

8 Smith, Christopher, "Justice Department Is Investigating Cartisano for Teen
   Treatment Camp," *Salt Lake Tribune*, 10/29/02.

9 Krakauer, "Loving Them to Death."

10 "WHO, Diet Nutrition and the Prevention of Chronic Diseases," report of a
   WHO study group, 1995 Tech Report Series #797, pp. 167–68.

11 Krakauer, "Loving Them to Death."

12 Harrie, Dan, "Cartisano Wants to Work with Kids Again."

13 Smith, Christopher, "'I Feel Like I'm Going to Die,'" *Salt Lake Tribune*, 5/28/95.

14 CNN, "Earth Matters," 4/2/1995.

15 Ibid.

16 Gregory, Gordon, "Deadly Discipline," *The Oregonian*, 2/12/00.

17 Krakauer, "Loving Them to Death."

18 National Vital Statistics Reports, Vol. 52, No. 9, November 7, 2003, p. 13.

19 Krakauer, "Loving Them to Death."

20 Donaldson, Amy, "Is Counselor Swapping Testimony for Immunity?" *Deseret
   News*, 5/5/1996; Anonymous, "North Star Witness Admits to Molesting Teen,"
   Deseret News, 10/10/1996.

21 Morganstern, "A Death in the Desert."

22 Smith, Christopher, "Trial to Burden Small County," *Salt Lake Tribune*, 5/29/
   1995.

23 Smith, Christopher, "North Star Hiker Looked Emaciated, Teens Testify," *Salt
   Lake Tribune*, 5/23/1995.

24 Smith, Christopher, "Mom Tells of Son's Bruises," *Salt Lake Tribune*, 5/24/95.

25 Ibid.

26 The quotes in this section are as reported by Smith, Christopher, "North Star
   Staff to Be Tried in Boy's Death," *Salt Lake Tribune*, 5/27/1995.

[27] Ibid.

[28] Krakauer, "Loving Them to Death."

[29] Smith, Christopher, "Prosecutors Ask to Move Trial in Death of Teen," *Salt Lake Tribune*, 7/25/1996.

[30] Ibid.

[31] Smith, Christopher, "Trial to Burden Small County," *Salt Lake Tribune*, 5/29/1995.

[32] Smith, Christopher, "North Star: Both Sides Win and Lose," *Salt Lake Tribune*, 1/22/1996.

[33] Smith, Christopher, "North Star Trial Begins for Dead Teen's Counselor," *Salt Lake Tribune*, 10/29/1996.

[34] Smith, Christopher, "North Star Employees Will Escape Jail Time," *Salt Lake Tribune*, 11/2/1996.

[35] Ibid.

[36] Smith, Christopher, "Counselor Ordered to Serve 1 Year for Boy's Death," *Salt Lake Tribune*, 12/20/1996.

[37] Smith, Christopher, "Former North Star Operator Warned for Violating Parole," *Salt Lake Tribune*, 10/18/1997.

[38] Smith, Christopher, "Court Upset After Convict in Teen's Death Leaves State," *Salt Lake Tribune*, 8/17/1997.

[39] Gregory, Gordon, "Deadly Discipline?" *The Oregonian*, 2/12/2000.

[40] Lynch, Jim, et al., "Wilderness Program: A Question of Restraint," *The Oregonian*, 10/22/2000.

[41] Ibid.

[42] Sinks, James, "Obsidian Trial Settles Wrongful Death Lawsuit," Bend (Oreg.) Bulletin, 1/31/02.

[43] Cart, Julie, "A Puzzling Death at Boys Ranch," *Los Angeles Times*, 6/13/1998.

[44] Szalavitz, Maia, "Camp Fear," *Redbook*, March 2002.

[45] Russell, K. C., and Hendee, J. C., "Definitions, common practice, expected outcomes, and a nationwide survey of programs," Outdoor behavioral healthcare: Technical Report 26, Idaho Forest, Wildlife, and Range Experiment Station, Moscow, Idaho. Available from the University of Idaho–Wilderness Research Center, 2000.

[46] http://www.kci.org/publication/bootcamp/prerelease.htm.

[47] Russell, K.C., "The theoretical basis, process, and reported outcomes of wilderness therapy as an intervention and treatment for problem behavior in adolescents." Unpublished doctoral dissertation, College of Natural Re-

sources, Moscow, Idaho, 83844-1144, 1999, p. 32, http://www.obhic.com/research/doctoral.pdf. Moore, T., and Russell, K. C., "Studies of the use of wilderness for personal growth, therapy, education and leadership development: An annotation and evaluation," 2002, p. 145, http://www.cnr.uidaho.edu/wrc/Pdf/indexupdate2002b.pdf.

[48] Gillis, H. L., and Thomsen, D., "A Research Update (1992–1995) of Adventure Therapy: Challenge Activities and Ropes Courses, Wilderness Expeditions, and Residential Camping Programs," Martinsville, Indiana: Bradford Woods, Indiana University: Coalition for Education in the Outdoors Symposium Proceedings, 1996, p. 2.

[49] Russell, K. C., "A Longitudinal Assessment of Treatment Outcomes in Outdoor Behavioral Healthcare," Technical Report 28, Idaho Forest, Wildlife, and Range Experiment Station, Moscow, Idaho. Available from the University of Idaho–Wilderness Research Center, 2002, http://www.cnr.uidaho.edu/wrc/Pdf/tech28postreview10-2.pdf.

[50] ABC News, "Wilderness Trek for Troubled Teens," *Primetime Thursday*, 8/15/2002.

[51] Marcus, David L., *What It Takes to Pull Me Through: Why Teenagers Get in Trouble and How Four of Them Got Out*, Houghton Mifflin, 2005, p. 28.

[52] Anonymous, "The Elan Report," *Bangor Daily News*, 9/10/2002.

[53] Gray, Kevin, "Bad Company: The Elan School," *Details*, 11/2001.

[54] Kastuck, Edwin P, "Basic School Approval Report Pertaining to the Elan School," State of Maine, Department of Education, 9/3/2002, http://www.state.me.us/education/Elan%20Report90302%20Final.htm.

[55] Gray, Kevin, "Bad Company."

[56] See http://www.geocities.com/shingle_expeditor/home.html and http://fornits.com/wwf/viewforum.php?forum=2.

[57] Additional sources for Chapter Four: interviews with Cathy Sutton, Craig Barlow, Sally and Bob Bacon, Diana Parrish (née Hollis), articles cited in previous chapter, interviews with former Elan students, and e-mailed manuscript of *Duck in a Raincoat: An Unauthorized Portrait of Joe Ricci*, by Maura Curley, Menukie Press (received 2001). Also, various news coverage of Skakel trial.

CHAPTER FIVE

[1] The Richardses did not agree to be interviewed for this book. However, they did provide copies of letters they'd written to other media about their life and

experience with Paul. Quotations from the Richardses are from these letters or, as cited, from interviews they gave to other journalists. The quotations in the preceding paragraphs are from a letter dated 7/15/1999 and another dated 10/14/1999.

2 From Paul's medical records, as provided by Laurie Berg.

3 Copy of list of expectations provided by Laurie Berg.

4 This comes from an account Paul gave in a police report from 3/9/1999, Snohomish County Sheriff's Office, report 97-11815.

5 CBS News, "Neighborhood Watch," *48 Hours*, 10/15/1998.

6 Kilzer, Lou, "Desperate Measures: 'Exit Plan' Shut Door on Teen," *Rocky Mountain News*, July 18, 19, and 20, 1999.

7 From a letter provided by the Richardses, 10/14/1999.

8 CBS News, "Neighborhood Watch," *48 Hours*, 10/15/1998.

9 Kilzer, "Desperate Measures" series.

10 From an unpublished account Paul wrote himself about his story.

11 Burton, Greg, "St. George Hospital Faces Scrutiny from State," *Salt Lake Tribune*, 3/10/1998; Burton, Greg, "St. George Youth Facility Shutting Down," *Salt Lake Tribune*, 3/12/1998. Also, documents from the State of Utah, especially memo from Craig Christopherson and Sharon McCombs to Deb Wynkoop-Green and Dave Eager, 2/19/1998, and Utah Department of Health Bureau of Licensing, Statement of Findings and Plan of Correction, 1/30/1998.

12 WHUTZ UP in Paradise Cove newsletter, 7/1997.

13 Letter from the Richardses, 2/21/2004.

14 Richards, Paul, "My Visit in Pago Pago," WWASP newsletter, "The Source," date unclear.

15 Cole, Wendy, "How to Save a Troubled Teen?" *Time*, 11/22/2004.

16 Lou Kilzer's "Desperate Measures" series notes the links between all of these programs and "Teen Help," which at the time he wrote his series was the referral arm of the organization. The connections between these programs and WWASP are acknowledged in numerous articles, including several in the *New York Times* by Tim Weiner, cited elsewhere here. The WWASP website, www.wwasp.com, accessed on 7/20/2005, lists Cross Creek, Majestic Ranch, Spring Creek Lodge, Academy at Ivy Ridge, Tranquility Bay, and Carolina Springs Academy.

17 See Burton, Greg, "St. George," and Kilzer, Lou, "Desperate Measures" series, and documents cited previously from the State of Utah regarding Brightway.

[18] Kilzer, "Desperate Measures" series.

[19] Stackhouse-Hite, Anita, "Officials Appeal Citation," *Porterville Recorder*, 5/19/2003.

[20] Kilzer, "Desperate Measures" series. Also, Kilzer, Lou, "Colorado Girl Pulled from Teen Help Compound; Conditions Deplorable at Mexico Camp Tied to Utah Group, Authorities Say," *Rocky Mountain News*, 12/22/2001.

[21] Weiner, Tim, "U.S. Youths Rebel at Harsh School in Costa Rica and Many Head for Home," *New York Times*, 5/27/2003.

[22] Kilzer, "Desperate Measures" series.

[23] *Milonas v. Williams*, U.S. Court of Appeals 10th Circuit, Sept. 13, 1982. See http://www.edjj.org/MilonasW.html.

[24] U.S. Supreme Court, *Parham v. J.R.*, 442 U.S. 584 (1979).

[25] A petition by a former participant demanding the closing of Provo Canyon was found online: http://www.beyondbusiness.net/index2.htm (accessed July 2005).

[26] Transcript of *WWASP v. PURE*, U.S. District Court for the District of Utah, Central Division, 8/2/2004, Judge Paul Cassell. Case Number 2:02-CV-0010.

[27] Adams, Brooke, "Founder's Passion Is Helping Youths," *Salt Lake Tribune*, 5/25/2003.

[28] Kilzer, "Desperate Measures" series.

[29] CBS News, "Second Thoughts," *48 Hours*, 10/15/1998.

[30] NBC News, "Lords of Discipline," *Dateline NBC*, 4/12/1999.

[31] Ibid.

[32] Kilzer, "Desperate Measures" series.

[33] Ibid.

[34] Registered Principal Search, conducted 7/2005, State of Utah. See also Kilzer, "Desperate Measures" series, and Weiner, "U.S. Youths Rebel," and Kellner, Tom, "Too-Tough Love?" *Forbes*, 3/22/1999.

[35] Weiner, "U.S. Youths Rebel."

[36] Leonard, Andrew, "Schools of Hard Knocks," *Salon*, 1/30/1998.

[37] Kilzer, "Desperate Measures" series.

[38] Letter from Bruce and Karen Richards, 11/20/1999.

[39] Watters, Ethan, *Spin* (title of article and date not known).

[40] Kilzer, "Desperate Measures" series.

[41] Kellner, "Too-Tough Love?"

[42] Kilzer, "Desperate Measures" series.

43 Ibid.

44 Ibid.

45 Lebor, Adam, "Czech School Shut Over Torture Charges," *The Scotsman*, 11/20/1998.

46 Bauerova, Ladka, "Torture Claims Shut 'School,'" *Prague Post*, 11/18/1998.

47 The disposition of these charges is not known.

48 Costanzo, Joe, "Suits Against Teen Help Now Popping Up in Utah," *Deseret News*, 11/21/1998.

49 Rocks, David, "Solitary Confinement or Time-out; Discipline: An American-run Academy in Czech Republic is Under Scrutiny for the Way It Punishes Students," *Baltimore Sun*, 11/14/1998. See also Bauerova, Ladka, "Morava Academy Heads Arrested Before," *Prague Post*, 12/9/1998.

50 Material from the State Department was released to Laurie Berg and Paul Richards under the Freedom of Information Act (FOIA). Date/Case ID: 16 May 2000, 199802296. Communiqué to Bill Warren 11/12/1997 64993.

51 Wooden, Kenneth, *The Children of Jonestown*, New York: McGraw-Hill, 1981.

52 Telegraph from American Embassy in Wellington to Secretary of State. March 1998, exact date unclear. Labeled "Wellin 00278."

53 Wooden, *The Children of Jonestown*.

54 Telegraph "Wellin 00278."

55 Letter to "Becky" from Paul Richards, exact date unclear, late 1997.

56 Ibid.

57 Communiqué from Secretary of State to Bill Warren and American Embassy in Wellington, 9/11/1998. FOIA Date/Case ID 24 Feb 1999, 199802296.

58 CBS News, "Neighborhood Watch," *48 Hours*, 10/15/1998.

59 Kreifels, Susan, "Laie Youth Reform Facility Subject of Controversy," *Honolulu Star Bulletin*, 9/29/1999.

60 "American, Canadian Teens Removed from Samoan Reform Camp Amid Abuse Allegations," *Nando Times*, 7/22/2001.

61 Letter from Paul Richards to Laurie and Michael Berg, 2/22/1999.

62 Kilzer, "Desperate Measures," series.

63 Kilzer, Lou, "Teen Overcomes Exit Plan," *Rocky Mountain News*, 7/2/2000.

64 Letter from the Richardses, 6/18/1999.

65 Letter from the Richardses, 5/3/1999.

66 Kilzer, Lou, "Lost Boy: Painful Journey Through Childhood Ends with Tragedy in Texas," *Rocky Mountain News*, 7/2/2000.

67 Kilzer, Lou, "Teenager Leaps to Her Death at Compound in Jamaica," *Rocky Mountain News*, 8/18/2001; PR Newswire, "Student Commits Suicide at Montana School," 10/8/2004.

68 Communiqué from Bill Warren to Secretary of State and American Embassies in Kingston, Jamaica; Tijuana, Mexico; and Prague, Czech Republic; June 11, 1999. UNCLAS WELL 00753. Released through FOIA 11/10/01, authorized by Margaret P. Grafeld.

69 Dibble, Sandra, "Scrutiny Increases on Centers for Teens; Four Compounds in Baja Closed in as Many Months," *San Diego Union-Tribune*, 1/10/2005.

70 Additional sources for Chapter Five: Interviews with Laurie Berg, Paul Richards, "S," other Paradise Cove participants and parents, other Tranquility Bay participants and parents, Judy Luck, Andy Sakamoto, Paul Michaels, additional FOIA documents, Gini Farmer Remines, and Craig Barlow.

CHAPTER SIX

1 Material from Karen Lile and Kendall Bean throughout this chapter comes from my interviews with them and from their written accounts. These accounts can be accessed in full at "Breaking the Vow of Secrecy" by Karen E. Lile, http:www.pianofinders.com/es/breakingthesecrecy.htm, and "Can I Trust Them?" by Kendall Ross Bean, http://www.pianofinders.com/es/canItrust them.htm.

2 Account by Kyrsten Bean, date unknown.

3 Aitkenhead, Decca, "The Last Resort," *Observer*, 6/29/2003.

4 California Department of Health Services, Complaint Visit #02-0011290.

5 Copy of contract, excerpt read on ABC News, "A Parent's Choice," *Primetime Live*, 1/21/1998.

6 ABC News, "A Parent's Choice."

7 Tranquility Bay parent manual.

8 "At Your Service, Forensic, Boundary Concerns," *Psychiatric News*, 38, no. 5, 3/7/2003.

9 NBC News, "Lords of Discipline," *Dateline NBC*, 4/12/1999.

10 Kilzer, "Desperate Measures" series.

11 Bob Lichfield's lack of a degree: Kilzer, Lou, "Desperate Measures" series. For

Karr Farnsworth's lack of a college degree, see *WWASP v. PURE* transcript. For Narvin Lichfield is a former used car salesman, see: Rogers, Tim, "Officials to Investigate 'Tough Love' Facility Here," *Tico Times*, 1/17/2003. Ken Kay is a former police officer: interview with Ken Kay. Jay Kay is a former gas station attendant: Cohen, Adam, "Is This a Camp or Jail?" *Time*, 2/26/1998.

12 Kilzer, Lou, "Whole-Family Healing: Architect of Teen Help Behavior Modification Says Parents Must Be Part of Solution," *Rocky Mountain News*, 11/20/1999.

13 Kilzer, "Desperate Measures" series.

14 Mathison, Dirk, "White Collar Cults, They Want Your Mind," *Self*, February 1993.

15 Kilzer, "Desperate Measures" series.

16 Info on legal cases against Lifespring from McAndrews, Anne, "I Lost My Husband to a Cult," *Redbook*, May 1994.

17 CBS News, *48 Hours*, 10/15/1998. Video shows a long line for psychiatric medication at Paradise Cove; director Viafanua says that "less than half" are on medications.

18 Kilzer, "Desperate Measures" series. Aitkenhead, "The Last Resort." For a story on a child admitted with bipolar disorder, see Cole, Wendy, "How to Save a Troubled Teen," *Time*, 11/22/2004. Interviews with numerous teens and parents confirmed accounts of admissions of teens diagnosed with attention deficit disorder, oppositional-defiant disorder, Asperger's syndrome, and many kinds of learning disorders.

19 Fisher, J., Silver, R., Chinsky, J., Goff, B., Klar, Y., and Zagieboylo, C., "Psychological effects of participation in a large group awareness training," *Journal of Consulting and Clinical Psychology*, 1989, 57, pp. 747–55. Lieberman, M. A., "Effects of large group awareness training on participants' psychiatric status," *Am J Psychiatry*, 1987 Apr;144(4): 460–64.

20 Hosford, Ray E., Moss, C. Scott, Cavior, Helen, and Kerish, Burton, "Research on Erhard Seminar Training in a correctional institution," American Psychological Association, *Catalog of Selected Documents in Psychology*, vol. 12(1), MS.2419, February 1982, pp. 8–9.

21 Lile, "Breaking the Vow."

22 Ibid.

23 Ibid.

24 Ibid.

25 Bean, "Can I Trust Them?"

26 Aitkenhead, "The Last Resort."

27 Haaken, J., and Adams, R., "Pathology as 'personal growth': a participant-observation study of lifespring training," *Psychiatry*, August 1983, 46(3): 270–80.

28 Lile, "Breaking the Vow."

29 Ibid.

30 Ibid.

31 Bean, "Can I Trust Them?"

32 Ibid.

33 Ibid.

34 Lile, "Breaking the Vow."

35 Ibid.

36 Ibid.

37 Bean, "Can I Trust Them?"

38 Bushman, B. J., Baumeister, R. F., and Stack, A. D., "Catharsis, aggression, and persuasive influence: self-fulfilling or self-defeating prophecies?" *J Pers Soc Psychol*, March 1999, 76(3): 367–76.

39 Kilzer, Lou, "Colorado Girl Pulled from Teen Help Compound; Conditions Deplorable at Mexico Camp Tied to Utah Group, Authorities Say," *Rocky Mountain News*, 12/22/2001.

40 CBS News, *48 Hours*, 10/15/1998.

41 Weiner, Tim, "Program to Help Youths Has Troubles of Its Own," *New York Times*, 11/6/2003.

42 Most of this section is based on interviews with Amberly Knight and on her letter to Costa Rican authorities regarding conditions at Dundee Ranch Academy.

43 SkyWest: http://www.skywest.com/about/j_atkin_bio.php, and affiliation with WWASP, Rogers, Tim, "Officials to Investigate 'Tough Love' Facility Here," *Tico Times*, 1/17/2003.

44 Varney, James, "Tough Love School Sent to Time-out," *Times-Picayune*, 6/25/2003.

45 Rogers, Tim, "More Questions about 'Tough Love' Program," *Tico Times*, 3/20/2003.

46 Letter from Amberly Knight to Costa Rican Minister of Child Welfare, 3/3/2003.

[47] Kilzer, "Colorado Girl Pulled from Teen Help Camp."

[48] Ibid.

[49] Ibid.

[50] Ibid.

[51] Knight, Amberly, letter to Costa Rican Minister.

[52] Rogers, Tim, "Officials to Investigate 'Tough Love' Facility Here," *Tico Times*, 1/17/2003.

[53] Zhang, Jane, "S. Utah–based Company Battles Abuse Claims," *The Spectrum*, 5/28/2003.

[54] Varney, "Tough Love School."

[55] Rogers, "Chaos Hits U.S. Reform Facility," *Tico Times*, 5/23/2003.

[56] Ibid.

[57] Weiner, "U.S. Youths Rebel."

[58] Ibid.

[59] Sullivan, Tim, "Dundee Ranch Students Head Back to U.S.," *Salt Lake Tribune*, 5/24/2003.

[60] Campbell, Duncan, "Costa Rican Authorities Raid U.S.-Run 'Boot Camp,'" *The Guardian*, 5/23/2003.

[61] Rogers, Tim, "Dundee's Future Uncertain," *Tico Times*, 5/30/2003.

[62] Rogers, Tim, "Students' Complaints Add to Academy's Woes," *Weekly Edition*, 9/5–9/11/2003.

[63] Kilzer, "Desperate Measures" series.

[64] Confirmed by Marilyn Matheus, South Carolina Department of Social Services.

[65] *Peterson's Guide to Secondary Schools*, www.petersons.com (accessed July 2005).

[66] Miller, W. R., and Sovereign, R. G., "The Checkup: A Model for Early Intervention in Addictive Behaviors," in Loberg, T., et al., eds., *Addictive Behaviors: Prevention and Early Intervention*, Amsterdam, Swets & Zeitlinger, 1989. For summary of research on confrontation (not one study found a positive effect): Miller, W., and Hester, R., *Handbook of Alcoholism Treatment Approaches: Effective Alternatives*, 3rd edition, Allyn and Bacon, 2003, pp. 34–35.

[67] Miller, W. R., Benefield, R. G., and Tonigan, J. S., "Enhancing motivation for change in problem drinking: a controlled comparison of two therapist styles," *J Consult Clin Psychol*, 1993 Jun; 61(3): 455–61.

[68] Additional sources for Chapter Six: Interviews with Kyrsten Bean, Acken*, Nina*, Doreen* and her mother, Ken Kay, two unnamed Cross Creek thera-

pists, Paradise Cove student and parent; teens from Dundee Ranch, Casa by the Sea, Tranquility Bay, Academy at Ivy Ridge, Spring Creek Lodge, Brightway Adolescent Hospital, Paradise Cove, Provo Canyon School; and parents of teens who attended all of the above except Provo Canyon.

CHAPTER SEVEN

[1] Rogers, Tim, "Parents to Sue Association," *Tico Times,* 6/26/2003.

[2] See Weiner, Tim, "Youths Rebel at Harsh School in Costa Rica and Many Head for Home," *New York Times,* 5/27/2003; Weiner, Tim, "Parents Divided Over Jamaica Disciplinary Academy," *New York Times,* 6/17/03; Weiner, Tim, "Parents, Shopping for Discipline, Turn to Harsh Programs Abroad," *New York Times,* 5/9/2003.

[3] Most of this chapter is based on my reporting from the trial itself and the trial transcript of *Lulu Corter v. KIDS of North Jersey,* Superior Court of New Jersey, Law Division, Civil Part Hudson County, Docket No. HUD-L-3548-00, as well as interviews with Lulu Corter and Phil Elberg. Attempts were made to contact Miller Newton through his attorney, but calls were not returned.

[4] Additional sources for Chapter Seven: Interviews with Britta, Ellen, Donald, and other former KIDS participants and parents, including Christine Johnson, Tom*, Marion*, and Kathryn Ottersten. Also interview with William Goldberg, MSW, a counselor who has treated former KIDS participants.

CHAPTER EIGHT

[1] Kennedy, George, "How Americans Got Their Right to Know," American Society of Newspaper Editors, 1996.

[2] CBS News, "Kids of America, Caring and Concern," *West 57th Street,* correspondent Meredith Vieira, 1/21/1989.

[3] Anonymous, "Drug Treatment Center Must Remain Closed, Judge Rules," *Orange County Register,* 8/4/1990.

[4] Additional sources for Chapter Eight: Interview with juror Carol Vozella.

CHAPTER NINE

[1] Currie, Elliott, *The Road to Whatever: Middle Class Culture and the Crisis of Adolescence,* Metropolitan Books, 2004, pp. 157, 161.

[2] Holbrook, T. L., Hoyt, D. B., et al., "Long-term posttraumatic stress disorder

persists after major trauma in adolescents: new data on risk factors and functional outcome, *J Trauma* 2005, 58(4): 769–71; Dohrenwend, B. P., "The role of adversity and stress in psychopathology: some evidence and its implications for theory and research," *J Health Soc Behav.*, 2000 Mar; 41(1): 1–19; Sieber, W. J., Rodin, J., et al., "Modulation of human natural killer cell activity by exposure to uncontrollable stress," *Brain Behav Immun.*, 1992 Jun; 6(2): 141–56; Restak, R. M., "The brain, depression, and the immune system," *J Clin Psychiatry*, 1989 May; 50 Suppl: 23–25; Volpicelli, Joseph, and Szalavitz, Maia, *Recovery Options: The Complete Guide: How You and Your Loved Ones Can Understand and Treat Alcohol and Other Drug Problems*, Wiley, 2000, p. 256.

3   Garifo, Chris, "State Agencies Probe Ivy Ridge: Alleged Abuse, Credentials Investigated," *Albany Times*, 2/16/2005.

4   Greenfield, S. F., Kolodziej, M.E., et al., "History of abuse and drinking outcomes following inpatient alcohol treatment: a prospective study," *Drug Alcohol Depend* 2002 Aug 1; 67(3): 227–34. See also Peele, Stanton, *The Meaning of Addiction*, Lexington Books, 1985, esp. pp. 104–05, and NIDA Household survey research.

5   Gregory, Gordon, "Deadly Discipline," *The Oregonian*, 2/12/2000.

6   Journey, Mark, "Ex-judge escapes long-term sentence," *St. Petersburg Times*, 8/30/1991.

7   Donaldson, Amy, "Is Counselor Swapping Testimony for Immunity," *Deseret News*, 5/5/1996; Anonymous, "North Star Witness Admits to Molesting Teen," *Deseret News*, 10/10/1996.

8   Dunnigan, Pat, "Straight Inc. Told to Close Virginia Treatment Center," *Tampa Tribune*, 3/13/1991; Aaronson, Trevor, "Suffering Together," *New Times Broward–Palm Beach*, 12/9/2004.

9   Hunt, Stephen, "Director of Troubled Youth Facility Resolves Remaining Charges," *Salt Lake Tribune*, 3/27/2003. Also, interview with prosecutor Craig Barlow.

10   Anonymous, "Workers at Drug Program Sentenced," *Bergen Record*, 12/24/1993.

11   Stewart, Kirsten, "Teen-Help School Hit with Abuse Allegations; Majestic Ranch: This isn't the first time complaints have been made, but charges are unlikely to be filed," *Salt Lake Tribune*, 2/16/2005.

12   The convictions in Aaron Bacon's death were for "abuse and neglect of a disabled child."

13 Weiner, "Program to Help Troubled Youth."

14 Melvin, Gayle Vassar, "Going Through Phases," *Contra Costa Times,* 2/9/
    1998.

15 Centers for Disease Control and Prevention, *Health, United States, 2003*
    (PHS), 2003-1232. GPO stock number: 017-022-01546-3, p. 45.

16 Bureau of Justice Statistics, cited in Butterfield, Fox, "Crime in schools fell
    sharply over the 10 years ended in '02," *New York Times,* 11/30/2004.

17 CDC, *Health, United States, 2003,* p. 46.

18 Johnston, L. D., O'Malley, P. M., Bachman, J. G., and Schulenberg, J. E., *Mon-*
    itoring the Future National Survey Results on Drug Use, 1975–2003: Volume I,
    Secondary School Students (NIH Publication No. 04-5507). Bethesda, MD:
    National Institute on Drug Abuse, 2003, Table 5-2. For 2004, Johnston, L. D.,
    O'Malley, P. M., Bachman, J. G., and Schulenberg, J. E., "Overall teen drug use
    continues gradual decline; but use of inhalants rises," Ann Arbor: University of
    Michigan News and Information Services, 2004. Available at: www.monitor-
    ingthefuture.org (accessed 02/09/2005).

19 CDC, Morbidity and Mortality Weekly Report, "Involvement by Young Driv-
    ers in Fatal Motor-Vehicle Crashes—United States, 1982, 2001," 12/6/2002,
    51 (48), 1089–1091.

20 CDC, National Center for Vital Statistic press release, 10/31/2003, on Re-
    vised Pregnancy Rates, 1990–97, and New Rates for 1998–99: United States.
    NVSR, Vol. 52, No. 7 (PHS), 2004-1120.

21 CDC, National Youth Risk Behavior Survey, 1991–2003, http://www.cdc
    .gov/Healthy/Youth/yrbs/pdfs/trends-sex.pdf.

22 CDC, National Center for Vital Statistic press release, 10/31/03, on Revised
    Pregnancy Rates, 1990–97, and New Rates for 1998–99: United States.
    NVSR, Vol. 52, No. 7 (PHS), 2004-1120.

23 CDC, *Health, United States, 2003,* p. 16.

24 Raeburn, Paul, *Acquainted with the Night: A Parent's Quest to Understand De-*
    pression and Bipolar Disorder in His Children, Broadway Books, 2004, p. 140.

25 U.S. House Committee on Government Reform, "Incarceration of Youth Who
    Are Waiting for Community Mental Health Services in the U.S.," July 2004,
    http://www.democrats.reform.house.gov/Documents/20040817121901-25170.pdf.

26 National Alliance for the Mentally Ill, *Families on the Brink, The Impact of Ig-*
    noring Children with Serious Mental Illness, 1999, www.nami.org.

27 See their websites, www.obhic.com and www.natsap.org.

[28] Butts, J. A., and Schwartz, I. M., "Access to insurance and length of psychiatric stay among adolescents and young adults discharged from general hospitals," *J Health Soc Policy*, 1991; 3(1): 91–116. Review.

[29] Labi, Nadya, "Want Your Kid to Disappear?" *Legal Affairs*, July/August 2004.

[30] Montel Williams, "Teen Rehab: An Investigative Report," *Montel Williams Show*, 1/18/2005.

[31] Transcript of WWASP v. PURE, U.S. District Court for the District of Utah, Central Division, 8/2/04, Judge Paul Cassell. Case Number 2:02-CV-0010.

[32] Press release from George Miller: http://www.house.gov/apps/list/press/ed31_democrats/rel42005.html. Also interviews.

[33] ABC News, "Wilderness Trek for Troubled Teens," *Primetime Thursday*, 8/15/2002.

[34] Nye County Sheriff's Office, Police Report 03-0102.

[35] Additional sources for Chapter Nine: Interviews with Cynthia Clark, Elliott Currie, Ph.D., Phil Elberg, Aaron White, Ph.D., John Weisz, Ph.D., who has proposed a "behavioral FDA." E-mail from Mark Sklarow, executive director, Independent Educational Consultants Association; interview with Jan Moss, executive director of NATSAP.

EPILOGUE

[1] Villano, "Money Man."

[2] State Department website: http://www.state.gov/r/pa/ei/biog/7043.htm (accessed July 2005).

[3] Harrie, Dan, and Gehrke, Robert, "Teen Help Operators Have Clout," *Salt Lake Tribune*, 9/19/2004.

[4] Ibid.

[5] Garifo, Chris, "Ivy Ridge Donating to GOP," *Watertown Daily Times*, 2/10/2005.

[6] Estrada, Sheila Mullane, "Church Question Moves Toward a New Ruling," *St. Petersburg Times*, 1/12/2005; Estrada, Sheila Mullane, Bankruptcy Case Zeroes In on Chapel," *St. Petersburg Times*, 4/3/2005.

APPENDIX

[1] Moffitt, T. E., "Developmental Course of Health Risking Behaviors, in Preventing Violence and Related Health-Risking Social Behaviors in Adolescents":

an NIH State-of-the-Science Conference, Program and Abstract Book, 2004, pp. 25–27, http://consensus.nih.gov/ta/023/youthviolencePandABookComplete.pdf.

2 Johnston, O'Malley, Bachman, and Schulenberg, *Monitoring the Future.*

3 Kessler, R. C., Chiu, W. T., et al., "Prevalence, severity, and comorbidity of 12-month DSM-IV disorders in the National Comorbidity Survey Replication," *Arch Gen Psychiatry*, 2005 June; 62(6): 617–27.

4 Sterling, S., and Weiser, C., Chemical dependency and psychiatric services for adolescents in private managed care: implications for outcomes," *Alcohol Clin Exp Res*, 2005 May; 29(5): 801–9. Armstrong, T. D., and Costello, E. J., "Community studies on adolescent substance use, abuse, or dependence and psychiatric comorbidity," *J Consult Clin Psychol*, 2002 Dec; 70(6): 1224–239. Review.

5 Faraone, S. V., and Wilens, T., "Does stimulant treatment lead to substance use disorders?" *J Clin Psychiatry*, 2003; 64 Suppl 11: 9–13.

6 Miller, W., and Hester, R., *Handbook of Alcoholism Treatment Approaches: Effective Alternatives*, 3rd edition, Allyn and Bacon: 2003. See also Miller, W. R., and Rollnick, S., *Motivational Interviewing: Preparing People to Change Addictive Behavior*, Guilford Press, 1991, and Riggs, P. D., and Whitmore, E. A., "Substance use disorders and disruptive behavior disorders," chapter 4 in R. Hendren (ed.), *Disruptive Behavior Disorders in Children and Adolescents*, American Psychiatric Association Annual Review Psychiatry Series, vol. 18, Washington, DC: APA Press.

7 Weisz, John R., and Kazdin, Alan E., eds., *Evidence-Based Psychotherapies for Children and Adolescents*, Guilford, 2003.

8 Riggs and Whitmore, "Substance use disorders."

9 Miller and Rollnick, *Motivational Interviewing.*

10 Miller and Hester, *Handbook of Alcoholism Treatment.*

11 Miller N. S., Ninonuevo, F. G., et al., "Integration of treatment and posttreatment variables in predicting results of abstinence-based outpatient treatment after one year," *J Psychoactive Drugs*, 1997 Jul–Sep; 29(3): 239–48; Harrison, P. A., and Asche, S. E., "Comparison of substance abuse treatment outcomes for inpatients and outpatients," *J Subst Abuse Treat.*, 1999 Oct; 17(3): 207–20. Also interview with Scott Henggeler.

12 March, J., Silva, S., Petrycki S., Curry, J., Wells, K., Fairbank, J., Burns, B., Domino, M., McNulty, S., Vitiello, B., and Severe, J.; treatment for adolescents

with depression study (TADS) team, "Fluoxetine, cognitive-behavioral therapy, and their combination for adolescents with depression: Treatment for Adolescents with Depression Study (TADS) randomized controlled trial," *JAMA*. 2004 Aug 18; 292(7): 807–20.

13 Gibbons, R. D., Hur, K., Bhaumik, D. K., Mann, J. J., "The relationship between antidepressant medication use and rate of suicide," *Arch Gen Psychiatry*, 2005 Feb; 62(2): 165–72.

14 Mihalic, Sharon, et al. "Blueprints for Violence Prevention," U.S. Department of Justice, Office of Justice Programs, Office of Juvenile Justice and Delinquency Prevention, July 2004, http://www.ncjrs.org/pdffiles1/ojjdp/204274.pdf.

15 Henggeler, S. W., Mihalic, S. F., Rone, L., Thomas, C., and Timmons-Mitchell, J., *Blueprints for Violence Prevention, Book Six: Multisystemic Therapy*, Boulder, Colo.: Center for the Study and Prevention of Violence, 1998.

16 Sexton, T. L., and Alexander, J. F., "Functional Family Therapy," U.S. Department of Justice, Office of Justice Programs, Office of Juvenile Justice and Delinquency Prevention, 12/2000. http://www.ncjrs.org/pdffiles1/ojjdp/184743.pdf.

17 Henggeler et al., *Multisytemic Therapy*.

18 Cynthia Clark, mother of Erica Harvey, reports, for example, that another girl died at the Catherine Freer program, of unknown causes.

4/06